T. Jensen Lacey

Amazing Alabama:

AMAZING STORIES, HISTORICAL ODDITIES AND FASCINATING TIDBITS FROM THE YELLOWHAMMER STATE

T. Jensen Lacey

T. Jensen Lacey

Copyright ©2019 T. Jensen Lacey

All Rights Reserved

No part of this book may be reproduced or utilized in any form by any means, electronic or mechanical, including photocopying and recording, or by any informational storage and retrieval system,, without permission in writing from the author. Please respect authors' rights.

ISBN: 978-0-9978344-4-4

Cover by Michael Ilaqua

www.Cyber-Theorist.com

AA-13

Printed in the United States

MOON HOWLER PUBLISHING, LLC
P. O. Box 1175
Fairhope, AL 36533

Acknowledgments

There is never a book that is written solely by the author. For this, the Bicentennial Edition of AMAZING ALABAMA, many "cooks" stirred the proverbial "pot," adding tidbits of history to spice up the final "dish" (I do love metaphors!).

First, I owe a huge debt of thanks to my family since I disappeared for a little more than a year while writing this book. I wish to especially thank my husband, Eric Lacey, for his patience, support and advice. For those many nights when I suffered self-doubts, I thank you for your encouragement and unrelenting faith in me.

A huge thanks goes to Governor Kay Ivey for writing the Foreword to AMAZING ALABAMA. Thanks also goes out to Daniel Sparkman in her office, who helped make this happen.

To my editor at Moon Howler Publishing, LLC, John O'Melveny Woods and his wife Judy Bishop Woods, thanks for your unwavering friendship, support, advice, and encouragement.

I wish to thank the following for their help, support, advice, photographs and information:

For those on their county's historical commissions, I could write a book just about how helpful you all have been! A special thanks goes out to the Alabama Historical Commission.

I owe a lot of folks at the Alabama Department of Archives and History a debt of gratitude, especially Ken Barr, Research Archivist.

For the information on the movie industry in Alabama, the Alabama Film Office was a great resource.

A big shout-out goes out to the Alabama Department of Tourism, and Lee Sentell, its Director, for your help. Thanks to all the staff members of the Welcome Centers in Alabama—what a great resource you all were!

Others include:

Donny Barrett, walking history encyclopedia and overseer of the Fairhope Museum of History; Sherry Johnston, Evergreen-Conecuh County Bicentennial Commission; Naomi Elliott, Russell County Historical Commission; Danny Crownover, President, Etowah Historical Society (Gadsden); Felisha Anderson, Director/County Archivist for the Baldwin County Historical Commission; Eleanor Drake, Perry County Librarian; Janice Williams, President of Friends of the Coon Dog Cemetery in Cherokee; Ben Raines, formerly with AL.com and now Executive Director of the Weeks Bay Foundation; Harriet Outlaw for her ghost stories and Alabama folklore; Robin Sterling for his Blount County tales; Woodrow Washington III of Archibald's Barbecue and the folks of Dreamland Barbecue; Alan Samry for sharing his knowledge of the "Clay City People"; Al.com columnists Leslie Anne Tarabella and Kelly Kazek for their oftentimes wacky and/or little-known tidbits of all things Alabama; Jim Evans, Sandi Jenkins and historian Ann Gay for their help with the story of the Simsites; Amy Rhudy, Director of the Blount County Memorial Museum, was a big help with the story on Myrtle Corbin; Dave McLellan, Beth Goodwin, Susan Carr and Bart Williams of Constitution Village for their help and hospitality; Brent Beall, Director of the Gulf Quest Maritime Museum for his hospitality.

Thanks to Steven Quinlivan and Marie Bidney of the Alabama Lighthouse Association for their help and information, "shedding some light" on history; Ove Jensen, Director of the Fort Toulouse-Fort Jackson Historic Site; Ralph Oalmann of Fort Gaines (for the blacksmithing presentation); Mark Ainslie and Pastor Dan Stone of the Flora-Bama Bar and Church; Rhonda Davis and Kristen Lee of the USS *Alabama* Battleship Memorial Park; James and Nancy Pinion, Managing Directors of the Jesse Owens Museum. Thanks to Kara Long, Director, and Jacqulyn Kirkland, Media Contact, both of Pond Spring Plantation, for their help. Jerry Barksdale, docent of the Veterans' Museum in Athens, a huge thanks goes to you.

Sharon Gaither of the Tallapoosee Historical Society, thanks for your many stories and information. Rebekah Davis of the Limestone County Archives, thanks for the time and help with the "Scottsboro Boys" story.

I also wish to acknowledge my Research Assistants who were so helpful and kept me organized: Holly Marie Wilson, Melia Marie Fiedler, Katlynn Elaine Wilson, Maggie Alyson Bailey, Brian Hunter Vaughn and Brandon Wilson.

Thanks to my proofreaders who helped me finalize this project: Donna and Charles Butler of New Hope; Donna Pittman Boswell of Robertsdale; Sarah Lacey Jones of Fairhope; Professor Emeritus of History, Dr. Robin Favela of Fairhope; and finally, my mom, Marian Bagwell Jensen of Huntsville, who is as ruthless with a pen as she is at the card table.

T. Jensen Lacey

SOME TIPS ABOUT HOW TO BEST ENJOY THIS BOOK

I love researching and writing history, and also, I enjoy telling folks where to see more about virtually any event (such as museums). Thus, at the end of the book you will find a section called "Virtual Alabama," which gives websites for places mentioned in each chapter. If you have an e-book, you can easily do a search for what you're interested in.

Thanks for reading my work! It was a true "labor of love."

T. Jensen Lacey

FOREWORD FROM THE GOVERNOR'S OFFICE

As Alabama celebrates her Bicentennial year in 2019, I am proud to represent the people of Alabama as their Governor. Alabama is a beautiful and welcoming state. From the mountains to the beaches and the plains to the black belt, Alabama's natural resources and people are unmatched.

I hope you will enjoy Lacey's stories about all Alabama has to offer in this "tour-able history" book. If you have never visited our beloved state, I join Lacey in encouraging you to come and experience the amazing sites and history our state has to offer. We welcome you with our trademark southern hospitality to our sweet home.

--Governor Kay Ivey

T. Jensen Lacey

AMAZING ALABAMA: AMAZING STORIES, HISTORICAL ODDITIES AND FASCINATING TIDBITS FROM THE YELLOWHAMMER STATE

THE BICENTENNIAL EDITION

CHAPTERS

1. Truly Bizarre Events and Notorious Alabamians – Page 3
2. Politics, Transportation and Military Tales – Page 21
3. Prehistoric Alabama – Page 71
4. Famous Alabamians in Education, Art, Science and Literature – Page 81
5. From Agriculture to Architecture = Page 117
6. Native American, Cowboy and Rodeo Tales = Page 131
7. Religion and Utopian Communities – Page 143
8. Sports, Recreation and Amusement Stories – Page 159
9. The Civil War and Alabama Page - 191
10. From Civil Wrongs to Civil Rights – Page 225
11. Wheelers and Dealers (Business and Entrepreneurs) – Page 243
12. Film, Music and Drama of Alabama – Page 259
13. Flora, Fauna and Natural Phenomena – Page 283
14. Food and Fascinating Cultural Tidbits – Page 303
15. Unusual Grave, Ghost and Burial-Site Stories – Page 321
16. Lighthouse and Coastal Stories – Page 339
17. Ghost Towns of Alabama – Page 349

    Bibliography – Page 357
    Virtual Alabama – Page 359
    General Alabama Websites – Page 360
    Chapter Notes – Page 361
    About the Author – Page 383

T. Jensen Lacey

Amazing Alabama:

AMAZING STORIES, HISTORICAL ODDITIES AND FASCINATING TIDBITS FROM THE YELLOWHAMMER STATE

T. Jensen Lacey

Chapter 1

TRULY BIZARRE EVENTS AND NOTORIOUS ALABAMIANS

"IT'S JUDGMENT DAY!" OR THE NIGHT THE "STARS FELL ON ALABAMA"

Many people love the song "Stars Fell on Alabama" that Jimmy Buffett sings. On the night of November 12, 1833, people living in Alabama then would have sworn it was a night of terror, not romance. David White of *The Birmingham News* wrote in 2009 that astronomers estimated that the Leonid meteor shower "bombarded the Earth's atmosphere with more than 30,000 meteors per hour." White quoted NASA astronomer Bill Cooke as saying, "The sky was literally filled with fireworks and people thought it was the end of the world."

The Leonid meteors were called that because they seemed to be falling from or near the constellation Leo. Cooke went on to say that the only people in Alabama who weren't terrified of this fireworks-falling-from-the-sky event were Native Americans, who perceived meteors as a sign of good luck. An article by John C. Hall in *Alabama Heritage Magazine* (2000) said that terror-filled people all over Alabama opened their "dust-covered Bibles" and burned their dice and cards.

Since that time, the heavenly event has inspired artists, musicians and poets. Dr. Carl Carmer, a University of Alabama English professor (who taught there in the 1920s) wrote a book about that fearful night. Titled *Stars Fell on Alabama*, Carmer recorded Alabamians' recollections of that meteoric event. Lyricist Mitchell Parish wrote the words to the now-famous song, "Stars Fell on Alabama," and Frank Perkins set the words to music. Since then, the song has been performed by such notable singers as Ella Fitzgerald, Billie Holiday, Frank Sinatra, Harry Connick, Jr., and, of course, Jimmy Buffett (as well as countless others).

HAVE YOU JUST SIGHTED SASQUATCH? THEN YOU NEED TO KNOW ABOUT THESE GUYS

The Yellowhammer State has its own Alabama Bigfoot Society. Located in Wadley, Alabama east of Alexander City (Randolph County), the society was founded in 1971 by a local man named Jim Smith. The society has posted many sightings on YouTube and they have their own channel on the website. Their website also asks for anyone who has observed other paranormal or unusual phenomenon, such as UFOs, to contact them. They pride themselves in never harassing a Bigfoot creature, referring to themselves as "A No-Kill Organization."

...AND WHEN THE STARS FELL IN OAK GROVE

Oak Grove has a historical marker commemorating the time when not one, but two, meteorites crashed in the area. Both happened on November 30, 1954, within a 24-hour period of each other. One meteorite came through the roof of a home owned by Elizabeth Ann Hodges, striking (but not killing) her. Hodges became an instant local celebrity.

The other meteorite crash was witnessed by a local farmer named Julius K. McKinney, who was in his mule-drawn wagon and came upon the 3 ½ pound rock. McKinney donated his meteorite to the Smithsonian (where it is displayed in the Hall of Meteorites) and Hodges gave hers to The University of Alabama's Museum of Natural History (Tuscaloosa).

In 2010, a historical marker was erected to commemorate both "stars," human and planetary. The marker is in Oak Grove on Old U.S. Highway 280 in Talladega County.

MYRTLE CORBIN, FAMOUS FOUR-LEGGED WOMAN OF BLOUNT COUNTY

Josephine Myrtle Corbin was the second child of a Confederate soldier (William) and his wife Nancy. She was unique in that she was born with not two, but four legs. As a matter of fact, everything on Myrtle's body was, from the waist down, double! The medical condition, although rare, is known as dipygus. Although the family originally hailed from Blount County, Myrtle was born in 1868 in Tennessee. There she was an immediate sensation; virtually every newspaper in Tennessee published an article about this unusual baby.

Myrtle Corbin in her heyday. Courtesy Alabama Department of Archives and History

In 1870 the family moved back to Blount County. Their father William was faced with an economic dilemma: all his three children were girls. So with no male help on the farm, he had to find another way to feed his family. He began to take Myrtle all over the country to fairs, museums and sideshows. When Myrtle was 14, she became part of P. T. Barnum's traveling show, for the princely sum of $250 a week.

After a few years of this, however, young Myrtle grew tired of this kind of attention and began to have thoughts of settling down with some deserving young man. She met and married James C. Bicknell in 1886 in Blount County, and the couple had seven children together.

After some years, Myrtle took her sideshow back on the road. She became part of the Ringling Brothers traveling circus and made appearances all over the country; her pay was now $450 a week.

In 1928 Myrtle developed an infection in one of her legs; the doctors couldn't treat the infection and she died. According to author Robin Sterling, who wrote *Tales of Old Blount County, Alabama*, "Myrtle was proof that even in the 19th century a woman with a severe handicap could have a successful career and be a wife and mother."

Today, you can see more about Blount County and more than one thousand of its families who have called this county their home at the Blount County Historical Museum in Oneonta. As of publication time, it is only open Tuesday through Thursday.

PROHIBITION, BOOTLEGGERS AND MOONSHINERS IN ALABAMA

During the Prohibition Era in Alabama (and the Yellowhammer State has been one of the "driest" states in the country), bootleggers and moonshiners became notorious for their making, concealing and selling their illegal liquor. When I say notorious, I mean to the extreme: for example, some moonshiners disguised their shoe prints by wearing fake cowprints on the soles of their shoes!

Two caves in Alabama were places where the selling, hiding and consumption of the illegal spirits was rampant. DeSoto Caverns in Childersburg was known as "The Bloody Bucket" because of so much violence that went on there (and in the walls visitors can still see bullet holes). It was closed in the 1920s but is now open for (non-alcoholic) tours.

Another such place was known as Bangor Cave (just slightly southeast of Cullman), which served as a place to entertain locals before a fire in 1915. Reopening in 1937, Bangor Cave was a "speakeasy," with a bar, gaming tables, a bandstand and a dance floor (the latter carved out of the rock). It was finally closed in 1939. Clay County, Alabama's last "dry" county, approved alcohol sales in March of 2016.

One famous moonshiner of this era was a man named Clyde May, who made up to 300 gallons a week in a still in the forests in Almeria (Bullock County). Although the making of spirits was initially made illegal in the 20th century, Clyde May's son (Kenny May) pushed to have it legalized, and it is now sold as Clyde May's Straight Bourbon Whiskey, which, ironically enough, by an act of legislation in 2004, is now the "official state whiskey" (or state spirit) of Alabama.

I wonder if Clyde would have approved?

"BLOODY BOB" SIMS: PROPHET TURNED MURDERER

Robert Bruce Sims was born in North Carolina in 1839. After marrying a woman named Eliza, the couple moved to Choctaw County, where they started a 240-acre farm. Sims served in the Confederate States of America Army in the 22nd Alabama Infantry but was injured, captured by Union forces and made a prisoner of war in Camp Morton, Indiana.

His experience as a prisoner of war apparently had a deleterious effect on the war veteran. Once back home in Choctaw County, although he had a good job as a surveyor for a time, Sims began to have run-ins with the local law. He also began to have increasingly divergent beliefs in opposition to his local Methodist church. Once he was in an argument so violent that he was thrown out of the church and charged with disturbing a church service (a crime at the time), for which he was fined $75.

Ultimately, Sims started his own church, where he preached to his followers (called "Simsites") to adhere to the Old Testament and, among other things, observe the Sabbath on Saturdays. He told his growing church members of more than 100 Simsites that civil authority was under the leadership of Satan, and it should be destroyed. In his ongoing rebellion against authority, Sims also began making moonshine.

This incited the anger of the law-abiding pastors around the county, so they filled their sermons with Scripture quotes against the consumption of alcohol. Things were bound to become violent, and in 1891 they did.

One of the most vocal pastors who preached against Sims was a Reverend Richard Bryant Carroll. One of Sims' followers professed himself to be in love with Carroll's daughter and came courting. The Reverend sent the young man away. Sometime that night, someone came after the pastor: he was found shot dead on his porch.

His was the first fatality of the so-called Sims War (Carroll lies interred in Harrison Cemetery). The townspeople were more alarmed than ever at this out-of-control sect. In Marion County, the newspaper *The Hamilton Times* began covering the many rebellious actions of the Simsites. Sims continued to distill alcohol, saying it was his God-given right and claiming he was suffering religious persecution from the law.

That summer, federal officials attempted to raid Sims' moonshine establishment but were always outnumbered. It was late summer when they were able to perform a successful raid, taking Sims into custody. While awaiting a steamboat to transport the prisoner to jail in Mobile, the arresting officers took lodging in a hotel in Bladon Springs. They put Sims in an outbuilding with a guard on watch.

Sims' followers and family weren't going to let him go without a fight. That night, his brothers Jim and Neal, along with Sims' son Bailey and three other Simsites, rode into town. In an attempt to break Sims out of custody, there was a gunfight. Bailey Sims was killed and Jim Sims was wounded and captured.

Afraid of revenge and tired of the illegal and bloody ways of Bob Sims and his followers, the townspeople organized, got Jim out of his cell, and hanged him two days after his capture. Unwilling to wait for the federal authorities to come with more men, some of the townspeople formed a posse and planned to round up Bob and Neal. But the two brothers had gone into hiding.

Bob Sims was drawn out when authorities announced they were auctioning his home to pay off his many legal fines.

It is said that a storeowner named McMillan turned Sims in to authorities and Sims was out for revenge.

Sims and his followers went to McMillan's house late in the night of December 23, 1891, and set it ablaze. As the occupants (including women and children) fled the house, the Sims gang shot them indiscriminately. By the end of the violent evening, one adult and three children were dead. The next day, angry and fed-up townspeople found and lynched John Sims and came to Bob Sims' home, now heavily fortified. The local sheriff began a parley with Sims, saying that Sims needed to protect the innocent people within his walls and promised safety and a fair trial if Sims would give himself up.

Sims finally did so. The sheriff took him and a handful of followers into custody. There were two wagons headed to the jail, one with women prisoners and the other with men. An angry mob chased the wagons, forced Bob and the other men out of the wagon, and hanged them all from nearby trees. The women were spared. The terror-raid of "Bloody Bob Sims" was over.

Today, you can visit the Sims family cemetery, located in Choctaw County east of Gilbertown, Alabama, behind the home of Mr. Powers Weeks. There are eight graves there, a melancholy reminder of how far the mighty can fall.

REUBEN HOUSTON BURROW: MOTHERED BY A WITCH

Born in Lamar County near the town of Sulligent, Reuben Burrow was one of ten children. His parents, Allen and Martha ("Dame") Burrow were probably eyed with suspicion among the people of Lamar County. It was rumored that Dame was a witch, and her pantry might hold items such as eye of newt and other things used for witch's spells.

Reuben's father Allen Burrow was a Confederate veteran and enhanced the family's income by the distillation of whiskey. When he was indicted in 1876, Allen left the country to avoid arrest. When he returned two years later, he'd made a deal with the federal government and lived a (supposedly) law-abiding life in Lamar County.

Rube, as he was called, seemed to be unable to resist the pull of living on the other side of the law. He moved to an uncle's ranch in Texas, where he met and married his first wife, Virginia Alvison. When she died of yellow fever, Rube took their two little children to relatives in Alabama and left his offspring in their care. He then married Adeline Hoover and tried again to make a go of farming in Texas, but his crops failed along with his marriage. That's when Rube turned to a career as a criminal.

He joined forces with his brother Jim, and they began to be known as the "Burrow brothers." In the years from 1886 to 1890, the brothers robbed trains in Louisiana, Texas, and Alabama, successfully staying just one step ahead of the law. Even the Pinkerton National Detective Agency was unsuccessful at catching the two brothers. In December of 1886, they joined forces with four other lawless criminal types. Their gang had a couple of unsuccessful train-robbery attempts, getting away with only a pocketful of money. They learned from these experiences, however, and in June 1887 took approximately $30,000 from a train they robbed in Ben Brooks, Texas.

Finally, Rube Burrow was placed on the Federal Wanted list. One of the men in the gang gave information to the Pinkerton detectives as to Rube's whereabouts at the time—he was back in Lamar County. Detectives pursued the brothers, caught wind that the two were on a train arriving near Birmingham, and police met them at the train.

Before they could be arrested, Rube shot a police officer and got away; Jim was arrested and sent to prison in Little Rock, Arkansas. In letters to his family, Jim wrote that he'd never get out of the jail alive. He was said to have died of tuberculosis in October of 1888 and it was recorded that he was buried in the prison cemetery.

Strangely enough, when the prison cemetery was being moved and caskets were being dug up—Jim's casket was found to be empty!

Meanwhile, Rube had joined forces with another criminal, Leonard Brock, who went under the alias Joe Jackson. Rube and Brock robbed a train in Mississippi, and during the robbery, Rube shot and killed a passenger. This was Rube's first murder and hardly the last. Upon returning to Lamar County, where the criminals stayed in hiding with relatives, all was quiet until Rube murdered the postmaster in a dispute over a suspicious-looking package. Since Postmaster Mose Graves was well liked in the area, the citizens of Lamar County turned against Rube and his gang. Rube and his thieving friends robbed two more trains that year, and probably would have robbed more, but they were tracked down by Pinkerton detectives and a posse of 40 men. In a shootout with the law near the Raccoon Mountains in Blount County, two deputy sheriffs were killed and a few more were wounded.

Rube and his gang managed to escape. He successfully eluded capture until 1890, when he was arrested in Marengo County. Once in jail in Linden, Alabama, Rube asked his jailers if they would hand him a sack of snacks he'd brought along, and they did. Inside the sack were not only snacks but also one of

Rube's pistols. He escaped the jail, but had a shootout with a merchant by the name of Jefferson Davis Carter. Carter was wounded, but he fatally shot Rube with a shot to the heart. The "King of the Outlaws" was dead.

Rube Burrow's body was put in a wooden casket and shipped to Lamar County to be positively identified by Allen Burrow. On the way there, the train carrying Rube's body made several stops to let the curious public view the body of the notorious outlaw. He was buried in the cemetery at Fellowship Baptist Church, in Vernon, Alabama.

An interesting postscript to the story about Rube Barrow, which was posted in Donna Causey's "Alabama Pioneers" online newsletter, was that his infamous ways led to a newspaper war. It was waged between the *Birmingham Age-Herald* and *The Atlanta Constitution*. It began when *Atlanta* reporter E. W. Barrett claimed that he had been granted an exclusive interview with the South's best-known outlaw of the time, and the *Atlanta* paper ran the story in 1889. The Birmingham paper said that the interview was a "bogus" one.

Finally, the truth got out: Barrett had traveled to Lamar County and interviewed a number of people, including Rube Barrow's father, but never the infamous outlaw himself. It also came out that, since Barrett had posted a $200 reward for anyone who could set up an interview between the journalist and the outlaw, some locals had arranged for Barrett to interview someone who resembled the infamous Burrow. When Barrett returned to Atlanta, he was convinced he had interviewed the real Rube Barrow.

The rivalry between the two papers, and the "scoop" the *Atlanta Constitution* claimed to have made, resulted in both papers selling out for quite some time.

THE INFAMOUS STORY OF "RAILROAD BILL"

The infamous African-American criminal "Railroad Bill," as he came to be known, went by many different names: Wild Bill McCoy and Morris Slater were two of his most commonly used aliases. Bill began his outlaw days when he was a worker in a turpentine camp in Escambia County, Florida, gathering pine-tree sap to make turpentine. It was in 1894 that, while visiting the camp, deputy sheriff Allen Brewton noticed that Bill always worked with a rifle tucked in his trousers. He told Bill to get a permit or he would confiscate Bill's weapon.

When Bill refused, a few days later Brewton returned with three more officers. They ended up in a shoot-out with Bill and although he was unhurt in this skirmish, he wounded one of the officers. He suddenly went from turpentine maker to outlaw.

Bill turned to robbing trains; it was said he stole other things besides money. He also stole goods and food, and sold them at a low price to the local poor in southern Alabama and northern Florida. Although he was despised by local law enforcement, he became something of a type of "Robin Hood" to the poor people that he helped.

As time went on and he became even more famous, the people nicknamed him "Railroad Bill." In late 1894, private detective agencies, railroad security officers and law enforcement were all on his trail. One detective, an African-American by the name of Mark Stinson, went undercover to try and earn Bill's trust and friendship, to capture him. Stinson was with Bill for several months, sending information about his movements and hideouts to authorities. Then the trail went cold. Stinson was never heard from again; authorities assumed Bill had figured out who Stinson really was and killed him.

In 1895, the city of Mobile posted a $500 reward for Railroad Bill for information leading to the capture or killing of the criminal. An informant sent word that Bill was hiding out near Bluff Springs (at the northwest Florida/southeast Alabama border), and Mobile's Sheriff McMillan rounded up a posse to capture or kill the murdering thief. In a shootout, Railroad Bill shot and killed McMillan. When the posse was unable to kill him, Railroad Bill's reputation began to have an air of the supernatural. Some people said the only thing that could kill Railroad Bill was a silver bullet.

The reward for information leading to Bill's capture or killing was more than doubled. Even the poor local people of northern Florida and southern Alabama began to see him for what he was: a bloodthirsty thief and murderer. The posse that finally took down Railroad Bill included bounty hunters from other states, Louisville & Nashville railroad company detectives, and members of the Pinkerton Detective Agency. Railroad Bill's end came via the rifle of posse member J. Leonard McGowan, who shot him from the window of a store in Atmore, Alabama.

Railroad Bill's body was put on display so everyone could see it to finally believe that the notorious criminal was dead. It was displayed from Atmore to Brewton and then taken to Montgomery. Finally, it was taken to Pensacola, Florida, and buried in an unmarked grave somewhere outside the city limits.

Despite Bill's body being displayed in so many places and photographs of his body published in nearly every Florida and Alabama newspaper, some people maintained their belief that Railroad Bill was still alive. Some people claimed he had been capable of shape-shifting and changed himself into something else, evading capture, and that it was someone else's body (who resembled the killer) that had been displayed. As a result of this, many other African-American men who were approximately the age of Railroad Bill were brought in for questioning; some were beaten and others, killed.

Since that time, Railroad Bill lives on in many ways. His name is mentioned on a state historical marker in Flomaton, and he has been the subject of blues songs, books, and even a New York City musical.

THE JAMES GANG IN ALABAMA

Frank and Jesse James have had many tales told about them and their infamous exploits, ranging from Missouri to Tennessee. For a time, they were with the so-called "Quantrill's Raiders," who harassed Union forces. But it was well after the war that they began to try their thieving ways in Alabama.

In 1881, a paymaster by the name of Alexander G. Smith was on horseback with more than $4,000 in cash, $500 in gold and more than $400 in silver (it was the payroll for men digging a canal in Muscle Shoals for the U.S. Army Corps of Engineers). Smith was accosted by the James brothers and robbed of the payroll.

Later, a man named Bill Ryan, who had taken part in the robbery, began bragging to a barkeeper in a tiny town outside Nashville, saying that he was an outlaw "against the ... United States Government." Ryan and the barkeeper argued; Ryan pulled his gun but in his intoxicated state was easily wrestled to the ground.

After being taken to jail in Nashville, a large amount of money and gold were found in Bill Ryan's possession. It didn't take long to get the story from the thief about the payroll robbery, including the role the James brothers played. When word got to Jesse James about Ryan's tale to the authorities, he fled back to Missouri. For added protection, he unwisely chose to stay with fellow criminals, friends Charley and Bob Ford, in St. Joseph, Missouri. Bob Ford shot and killed Jesse.

Bob Ford had hoped to get the $5,000 reward posted for the killing of Jesse James; instead, he was charged with murder. The Ford brothers were given a quick trial, sentenced to death, and then pardoned by Missouri Governor Thomas Crittenden.

Frank James left Alabama and went to Missouri, where he sought an audience with Governor Crittenden. Eventually, Frank James was brought back to Huntsville to be tried for his role in the payroll robbery. At the Calhoun House, which then served as a Federal Courthouse, on April 25, 1884, Frank James was tried and found not guilty by a jury.

During the time of Frank's incarceration in the Madison County jail in Huntsville (from March to the time of his trial), the legend of Frank and Jesse James had grown to such proportions that Frank had sudden celebrity status. People came to the jail just to see the outlaw. Local people in high society were allowed to sign Frank James out of jail for hours at a time. A local lawyer (William Hundley) signed Frank out of jail and took him on a quail hunt. By the time the trial actually started—April 17, 1884—Huntsville was overrun with journalists and the curious public. The trial itself received national attention.

Today, a trial comprised of a jury like the one sitting for Frank James' case would probably result in an objection by the prosecution. Frank James' jury was (mostly) made up of Civil War veterans. His defense lawyer was LeRoy Pope Walker, who had served as Secretary of War for the Confederate States of America. Walker capitalized on the jury's shared history, gaining sympathy for the jury's fellow Confederate brother-in-arms.

After receiving his acquittal, Frank James got back into some legal hot water for a crime he committed in Missouri. Governor Crittenden pardoned him, and Frank James lived out the rest of the 25 years of his life, quietly living within the law.

Today, you can see photographs and paintings of Frank James at the Huntsville Museum of Art. A play titled "The Trial of Frank James" has been written by playwright Jeff Robertson, who called it "Huntsville's Trial of the Century." There is a historical marker that stands at the site of the trial and acquittal of one of the most infamous criminals in U.S. history.

Q & A

Q. What notorious panic-inspiring disease gripped Mobile during the 1800s to such an extent that a group of people formed the "Can't Get Away Club," due to their being obliged to stay in the city?
A. Yellow fever; its symptoms were marked by fever, chills, back pain, vomiting, constipation and, finally, organ collapse.

Q. What Livingston officer of the law was so much of a criminal, he became known as "The Outlaw Sheriff," and in 1886, after being arrested for his many crimes, was taken out of his jail cell and lynched?

A. Steve Renfroe. Of his four wives, three died under mysterious circumstances, while still in their twenties.

Q. What former U.S. Vice President wound up being tried as a traitor (hint: he killed Alexander Hamilton in a duel)?

A. Aaron Burr. He was arrested at Fort Gaines in 1807. He was also acquitted due to lack of evidence of treason. There is a historical marker about the arrest, located on the grounds of Fort Gaines near the entrance.

Q. What infamous Spanish pirate is said to have left pirate treasure buried in several places in and around Mobile Bay?

A. Jose Gaspar, who became known as Gasparilla.

Q. What 18th century French pirate had his operations out of New Orleans but he, along with his brother, plundered the Gulf Coast, had a pirate colony at Galveston Island, Texas, and is said to have left a large part of their treasure buried at Bayou La Batre, Alabama?

A. Jean Lafitte.

Q. Legend has it that the notorious John Murrell and his outlaw gang once had headquarters in what county?

A. Dallas.

Q. What county in Alabama was birthplace of Lewis Powell, one of the co-conspirators to kill Abraham Lincoln and his Secretary of State, William H. Seward?

A. Randolph County.

Q. Who, in the late 1890s, was so murderous of an outlaw that his exploits had citizens referring to Bibb County as "Bloody Bibb"?

A. Bart Thrasher. After fifteen years of robbing and killing Bibb County's citizens and law enforcement officers, he was finally taken down by Deputy Sheriff Henry Cole and his posse in an ambush in 1896.

Q. In the aftermath of the Creek War, what murderer terrorized south Alabama?

A. John Haigue, also known as "Savannah Jack."

Q. What two outlaw brothers tortured, murdered and robbed travelers along the Natchez Trace between 1797 to 1804?

A. Wiley and Mica Harpe, also known as the "Terrible Harpes."

Q. What movie, starring Kathryn Grant and Richard Kiley, was about a young lawyer in a fight against racketeers over control of a historically lawless town in Alabama?

A. *The Phenix City Story*.

DID YOU KNOW?

The Houston Jail in Winston County is the oldest log jail in Alabama, and the second-oldest in the nation.

CHAPTER 2

POLITICS, TRANSPORTATION AND MILITARY TALES

KAY IVEY: FROM FARM GIRL TO GOVERNOR

I remember in the spring of 2018 seeing a campaign ad on TV in which Kay Ivey said, "Don't give me mountain oysters and tell me they're seafood." As long as I have been following her political career, Kay Ivey has always been thusly plainspoken. Born in Camden, Alabama, Ivey learned about hard work and its rewards from doing chores on her family farm. She went from lieutenant governor to governor when in 2017 Robert Bentley stepped down in disgrace from that role (enough said about that). Auburn graduate Kay Ivey, who had also been a high school teacher, bank officer, and (in 2003) State Treasurer, was suddenly thrust into the Yellowhammer State's limelight when she was sworn in to the

Governor Kay Ivey is hard at work for the people of Alabama. Photo courtesy of the governor's office.

office of governor on April 10, 2017.

Only the second woman to serve as governor for the state of Alabama (the first one being Lurleen Wallace), Ivey has handled this new role with efficiency, humor, and aplomb.

According to the official governor's website, Ivey's vision is to "bring conservative leadership with effective results to make this generation more productive and the next generation more prosperous."

Ivey has, indeed, opened many economic doors for the people of Alabama, breaking ground for new plants such as that for a Mazda-Toyota manufacturing facility (in Huntsville) in 2018 and bringing in other new companies from other states. Ivey ran again and won her re-election bid for governor in 2018. Hers is a legacy that continues to build upon itself.

"UP THERE WITH JULIA STRUDWICK TUTWILER AND HELEN KELLER"

Julia Ledlow Shores came from humble beginnings but showed promise in her quick and lively intellect. This Butler County native first became interested in the study of law when she was a legal secretary in Mobile. After attaining her B.A. degree from Samford University, she attended law school at The University of Alabama, completing her LLM at The University of Virginia.

She became the first woman to sit on the Alabama Supreme Court when she was elected to that position in 1974. President Bill Clinton considered her for the U.S. Supreme Court (he instead appointed Ruth Ginsburg). In Shores' unwavering and unbiased rulings, she had some detractors, but many admirers. Among them was U.S. Senator and fellow Alabamian Howell Heflin, who spoke at her retirement dinner in 1999. He said then, "In my judgment, the name Janie Ledlow Shores should be inscribed, along with Helen Keller and Julia Strudwick Tutwiler, at the top of the list of Alabama's greatest women."

Before she died in August of 2017, Shores penned her autobiography, *Just Call Me Janie: The Unlikely Story of the First Woman Elected to Alabama's Supreme Court* (Intellect Press, 2016). Now, the Alabama Law Foundation awards a scholarship in her honor to a promising female law student; the Litigation Council of America offers the Janie L. Shores Trailblazer Award.

As for Shores' admirer, Howell Heflin, he passed away in 2005. The Alabama School of Law in Tuscaloosa now has a conference room named in his honor (located in the Bounds Law Library). His childhood home of Tuscumbia has a street named after him; near Gainesville, one of the four lock and dam structures on the Tennessee-Tombigbee Waterway is named in his honor.

You can learn more about these amazing people at the Alabama Department of Archives and History in Montgomery.

THE BATTLE OF NEW ORLEANS HAS ITS ROOTS IN ALABAMA!

It was in 1814, just after the Creek Indian Wars, and Andrew Jackson and his soldiers were leaving Alabama to march to New Orleans to fight off the British invasion. This was at the end of the War of 1812, and although the Treaty of Ghent had already been signed, the news of the treaty hadn't reached the United States. The British soldiers were intent on taking over New Orleans and its port, which was the gateway to the west. For his part, Jackson, who had been a British prisoner of war during the Revolutionary War, was bent on vengeance (apparently he had not been treated well).

Jackson and his troops stopped on their march to New Orleans in what is now the town of Daphne. While there, he rounded up his troops, climbed on a low-hanging limb of a Live Oak tree, and exhorted them to rally behind him once again. Apparently, his speech had its intended effect, for British casualties at the Battle of New Orleans numbered more than 2,000; Jackson only lost approximately 100 of his men.

This mammoth oak tree is said to be the one Andrew Jackson climbed to rally his troops to victory before the Battle of New Orleans against the British. Photo by the author.

Today you can see a part of this "tourable history" in Daphne. The "Jackson Oak" is the highlight of the town's Village Point Preserve, a lovely 54-acre wooded area with a boardwalk through it. The tree, roughly sixty feet in diameter, has the boardwalk and a fence ringing around it for protection. It's quite a sight and well worth the short hike to see this part of living history.

HUGO BLACK: ONE MAN WHO HELPED FORM UNITED STATES LAW

Hugo Black was an enigmatic man, who was perhaps a living example of what it meant to be an Alabamian. Born in 1886 in Ashland in Clay County, Black didn't graduate high school, but went on to graduate from The University of Alabama's School of Law. He was a proponent for racial justice but at one time was a card-carrying member of the Ku Klux Klan.

As a later member of the Supreme Court, Black was a champion for individual rights and equality. He voted to end segregation in public schools, and also voted to allow African-American citizens the right to vote. He was also an avid proponent of Roosevelt's "New Deal." He stepped down from the Supreme Court a week before he died on September 25, 1971.

This paradoxical Alabamian is honored in a number of ways, the main one being the courthouse in Birmingham that is named after him. It's worth the trip to go there and look around. Also, you can see more about the man who shaped U.S. law at the Alabama Department of Archives and History in Montgomery.

ALABAMA'S CONSTITUTIONAL "CLAIM TO FAME"

Of Alabama's six constitutions, the last one not only is the longest constitution, but also is the longest constitution in the entire WORLD. It has been amended so many times that it is "forty times longer than the U.S. Constitution," in the words of my friend H. Randall Williams (*A Hundred Things You Need to Know about Alabama*). Every few years, reformers have sought to replace it with a more modern (and shorter) constitution—for example, the current constitution still declares the state must annually set aside a half-million dollars for the pensions of Confederate veterans (although the last such veteran died in the early 1930s). Hundreds of amendments to the constitution have altered such legislation, making the constitution even longer.

My mother-in-law, the late Jeanne Franklin Lacey, worked tirelessly for a new constitution (in her position as

President of the Alabama League of Women Voters) until her death in 2011. Perhaps I'll take up the torch in her honor!

If you want to read the original constitution, you can purchase a copy in Constitution Village (now known as Constitution Hall Park) in Huntsville's Twickenham Historic District. It's worth the visit!

STRANGE BUT TRUE: DRAFTING THE CONSTITUTION SO THEY COULD GO HAVE A DRAUGHT!

The delegates who decided to get together in 1819 and draft the first constitution for the newly formed State of Alabama had a definite objective in mind when they chose Huntsville as their meeting place: it was the only place in the Territory of Alabama that had a brewery, opened by brewers and brothers, James and William Badlun, who, conveniently enough, opened their brewery that same year.

CLEMENT COMER CLAY

In the early 1800s, an attorney by the name of Clement Comer Clay hung up his proverbial shingle, establishing his law offices in Huntsville. The building for his law office also served as a post office and a surveyor's office. Clay was a leader behind drafting the first Alabama Constitution. Besides going on to become Alabama's first Supreme Court Justice, he also served as Governor and Senator.

The building which housed his law practice is on the grounds of Constitution Village at the corners of Madison and Gates Streets in Huntsville.

DID YOU KNOW?

In Huntsville, the railroad depot was completed in 1860. It is the oldest railroad depot still in existence in Alabama and one of the oldest railroad depots in the entire United States. Today, you can tour it, since it's been made into a museum, and see all kinds of exhibits of artifacts relating to the rich history of the railroad in Alabama.

THE WOMAN WHO INVENTED WINDSHIELD WIPERS

Green County native Mary Anderson (1866-1953) invented windshield wipers for cars. Next time it rains and you're out on the road, send a mental thanks to her.

THE SPACE RACE AND ALABAMA'S ROLE IN IT

I remember in July of 1969 watching on live television when Neil Armstrong stepped out of his lunar-landing vehicle and spoke the iconic words, "That's one small step for a man, one giant leap for mankind." Had Alabama and its scientists not played such a pivotal role in the space race, another country's astronaut might have beaten the U.S. to the proverbial punch.

The first man on the moon was made possible because of the great scientific minds of Alabama. Photo courtesy of NASA.

Founded in 1958, the National Aeronautics and Space Administration, or NASA, has been an important part of Alabama history and space exploration. In 1960, NASA established the Marshall Space Flight Center, or MSFC, at Redstone Arsenal in Huntsville. The famous German researcher Wernher von Braun was at that time the head rocket engineer.

Marshall Space Flight Center not only was a major part of the moon launch and landing, but it also was involved with the Hubble Space Telescope's launching, the creation of the International Space Station, and more. There's a reason why, as travelers approach the Huntsville Welcome Center off I-65, there stands a real rocket. It's a Saturn 1B rocket, which the MSFC used in rocket-propulsion experiments in the 1970s and 1980s that welcomes visitors to Huntsville, which has become known as "Rocket City."

Something else that the U.S. Space and Rocket Center has done is created a Space Camp. Both for adults and young people, the Space Camp program has been a popular way for the space program to conduct outreach to civilians. Today, you can tour the Space and Rocket Center, which is the largest such space-exploration museum on the planet. The Space and Rocket Center is easy to find, as a replica of the Saturn V rocket is on the grounds and is the hallmark of "Rocket City's" skyline. Currently, the Center has an excellent Imax movie theater, a "Space Shot" ride which launches you up 140 feet in 2.5 seconds, and a "G-Force Accelerator" which allows you to feel what it's like to be under the influence of three times the force of gravity. The Center also has traveling exhibits.

THIS ALABAMIAN IS THE MAN TO CREDIT FOR OUR MODERN VETERANS DAY!

Armistice Day, which celebrates when World War I ended, was first commemorated in 1919. Afterward, World War II veteran and Birmingham native Raymond Weeks thought the U.S. should go beyond simply recognizing Armistice Day. He contacted then-Army Chief of Staff Dwight D. Eisenhower about making Armistice Day a day to celebrate and honor ALL veterans. In 1947, Weeks led a group of veterans to Washington, D.C., to help raise awareness of the importance of a day especially to celebrate those in uniform. In 1954, President Eisenhower signed it into law, making November 11 Veterans Day.

THE U.S., THE NEW DEAL, AND THE ROLE THAT ALABAMA PLAYED IN ITS SUCCESS

As anyone knows, the Great Depression had the nation in a stranglehold until the country's economy revived after the U.S. entered into World War II. President Franklin D. Roosevelt's economic plan to lift the country out of the Depression, called the "New Deal," had many native Alabamians to thank for its success. Some of the Alabama politicians who helped pass the New Deal legislation included Senators John H. Bankhead and Hugo Black. In the House of Representatives, William B. Bankhead, Lister Hill, John Sparkman and others were passionate proponents of the bill.

Other politicians helped Alabamians survive the hard economic times. One, Aubrey Williams from Springville, Alabama, served in FDR's administration. He helped form the Works Progress Administration, which saw more than 60,000 Alabamians find employment in building roads, buildings such as courthouses, infrastructure such as airports, and more. Another program, known as the Civilian Conservation Corps or CCC, helped Alabamians by giving them jobs in forest management and in the building of more than 16 state park construction projects (cabins, administration buildings and trails). It was during this era that, through the efforts of the aforementioned politicians, the Tennessee Valley Authority was created, which resulted in rural areas finally getting electricity.

ALABAMA: "SECOND IN FLIGHT" TO NORTH CAROLINA

After Orville and Wilbur Wright's successful first flight in Kill Devil Hills (historians say Kitty Hawk because that's where the news was sent out via telegraph), North Carolina, on December 17, 1903, the jubilant brothers from Dayton, Ohio began searching for a more optimal climate in which to fly their newly-patented Wright Flyer. In 1910, they found such a climate and decided on a cotton-growing plantation on the Alabama River just outside of downtown Montgomery, Alabama, on which the townspeople would build a hangar especially for this purpose.

The two Wright brothers opened the first-ever in the U.S. civil aviation school, moving their plane via rail from their factory in Dayton. On March 26, 1910, brother Orville made an initial test flight. They taught five students, and set records for both altitude and time spent in the air. Once Ohio warmed back up, however, the Wright brothers packed up and headed home.

Today, there are aviation-related displays all over the Yellowhammer State. For example, located on the grounds where the *USS Alabama* and the USS *Drum* are just outside Mobile, dozens of airplanes are on permanent display. One of my favorite aviation museums is in Birmingham at the Southern Museum of Flight, which is part of the Birmingham-Shuttlesworth International Airport. Here you can see, in the words of their website, "aviation artifacts spanning the 20th century and beyond." Among their artifacts is a night-landing light first used by Orville and Wilbur Wright at their Flying School in Montgomery.

Also in Montgomery, there is a Wright Brothers Park, located on the Alabama River approximately a mile from where the flying school once stood (that property is now part of

Maxwell Air Force Base). Here in this park is a stainless-steel sculpted likeness of the Wright Model AB aircraft, appearing to soar high above the Alabama River.

"MARION MADE": MARION MILITARY INSTITUTE

Marion Military Institute (MMI), located in Marion, Alabama (slightly northwest of Selma), has earned international fame for its "Marion Made" graduates. As of publication time, MMI has produced more than 210 admirals and generals for the United States military. Of only four military junior colleges in the U.S., it is the oldest of the four, founded in 1842. Marion welcomes visitors.

THE REVOLUTIONARY WAR IN ALABAMA

Did you know that, way before it became a state in 1819, citizens of what became Alabama took part in the Revolutionary War? Exactly 22 Alabama counties are named in honor of patriots of the American Revolution.

There are a number of places where you can go and learn more about Alabama's role in the American Revolution, and have fun doing it! Fort Conde (formerly Fort Charlotte, but also called Fort Carlota by the Spanish) in Mobile was the site of one of two battles of the American Revolution fought in Alabama. Both battles were fought in Mobile; one in 1780, and another in 1781 (and, interestingly enough, Mobile was actually part of West Florida at the time).

In 1780, Fort Charlotte was under British control, and Spain had entered the war in 1779 in support of the colonies. In 1780, Spanish general Bernardo de Galvez attacked Fort Charlotte, desiring control of not only the fort but also the Port of Mobile. According to the website ExploreHistory.com, three days after the Spanish attacked, the British gave up control of the port. In 1781, British forces tried to re-take the fort, but were again defeated. Now known as Fort Conde, it is the site of the Welcome Center for the City of Mobile and is open for tours.

Founded in 1995, the American Village in Montevallo is something to see. Many visitors say it's like stepping back into the 1700s. Some of the more interesting things to see here include Washington Hall (which was inspired by George Washington's Mount Vernon), a colonial courthouse, a colonial chapel (which was inspired by one of the oldest churches in the U.S., Bruton Parish Church in Williamsburg), a replica of the interior of today's Oval Office, the National Veterans Shrine and Register of Honor, and even a replica of the Liberty Bell (the original of which is in Philadelphia), complete with a crack in its side.

Historic, dramatic re-creations happen on important days such as Memorial Day, Veterans Day and Independence Day, but tours are offered daily if you can't manage to be in Montevallo during those events.

One museum that houses items that Mount Vernon didn't want is the Karl C. Harrison Museum of George Washington. It seems that many of George Washington's descendants settled in Shelby County near Chelsea and Jemison, so history buff and Columbiana resident Karl C. Harrison wanted to have a museum honoring "The Father of Our Country."

Open since 1982, this museum is about all things George Washington. It contains art and artifacts from the colonial period through 1865, including letters, furniture, porcelain, jewelry, paintings and more. Two of the things I found most interesting were writing instruments and survey tools from George Washington's survey case. Since this museum is not too far from the American Village, you could probably tour both in one day (but I suggest taking two).

Finally, American Revolution monuments are sprinkled throughout Alabama. Here's a partial list: Dale County, Fayette County, Jefferson County, Fort Conde and Spanish Fort), Baldwin County, Pike County, Clarke County, and Tuscaloosa County. Last, more than 800 American Revolution soldiers are buried in Alabama, which includes Martha Jefferson's cousin, Frances Eppes Harris, who's buried in Harris Hill Cemetery in Madison County; Colonel John Owen of the North Carolina Militia, who is buried in Tuscaloosa's Greenwood Cemetery; and Jim Capers, of the 4th South Carolina Regiment and a "Free Man of Color," buried at Bethlehem Missionary Baptist Church (Pike County).

GEORGE WALLACE: AN ENIGMA

Most people think of Clio, Alabama-born George Wallace as a racist or white supremacist when they think of his infamous stand in the doorway of a building at The University of Alabama, preventing African-American students from entering. But he had many different faces.

In her book, *George Wallace: An Enigma*, author Mary Palmer wrote about this multi-faceted governor of Alabama. She wrote, "George loved the limelight," and perhaps she was right. Even when he was no longer eligible to serve as Alabama's governor, he asked his wife, Lurleen, who was terminally ill at the time, to run for the office.

Meeting him in person as I did, he came off as the proverbial "boy next door." If he met you once, he never forgot a name. He was affable with everyone he met. In his early years, he excelled in boxing (and was inducted into the Alabama Sports Hall of Hall in 1975).

Although he is well-known for saying, "Segregation now, segregation tomorrow and segregation forever," he said afterward that he meant to say "States' rights" all three times. After his infamous stance in the doorway at The University of Alabama, he said that he meant to eventually have integration in every public place but did not want it imposed by a mandate from the Federal government.

While running for office of President of the United States in 1972, Wallace was shot by a would-be assassin. After he was wheelchair-bound following this, he seemed to pursue a softer image. He reached out to the African-American community, even attending their church worship services. After his death in 1998, he was interred next to his wife, Lurleen, in Greenwood Cemetery in Montgomery, Alabama. Incidentally, his blood-stained clothes he was wearing at the time of the assassination attempt are in the possession of the Alabama Department of Archives and History (ADAH).

LURLEEN WALLACE: ALABAMA'S OWN "STEEL MAGNOLIA"

When I think of the 1989 movie, *Steel Magnolias*, starring Sally Field, Dolly Parton, Olympia Dukakis, Julia Roberts and Daryl Hannah, I also think of Lurleen Wallace. Born in 1926 in Tuscaloosa, she would rise to fame when she became the 46th Governor of Alabama in 1967. She was Alabama's first woman governor (seconded only by Governor Kay Ivey, who became governor in 2017). She was inducted into the Alabama Women's Hall of Fame in 1973.

In 2015, her portrait, and the portrait of Governor George C. Wallace, her husband, were both moved from their places at the Capitol Rotunda to the building's main entrance, a move that infuriated some politicians, among them Alabama State Auditor Jim Ziegler. Ziegler said that, in light of the movie,

"Selma," and the 50th anniversary of "Bloody Sunday," the move was a form of "historical revisionism." This was denied by the Alabama Historical Commission.

Lurleen Wallace's major contributions to the state of Alabama included working for improved conditions for those living in mental institutions and taking steps to better education for all. She was a lady in every sense of the word, except, according to some journalists, when she was crossed. As one journalist wrote, "She had a small foot—until she put it down."

Loved by many people in Alabama, so much so that when she died of cancer in 1968, the entire state mourned their own "steel magnolia." She is remembered in many ways throughout the state. There is an exhibit of her in the Women's Hall of Fame; many cities have streets named after her; and The University of Alabama in Birmingham (UAB)'s Cancer Treatment Center is named for her.

And unless they moved her portrait back to its original spot at the Capitol Rotunda, you can still see it at the building's main entrance. Maybe, if you look closely enough at her portrait, you will see the glimmer of "steel" in her eyes.

ALABAMA'S OWN SUPERWOMAN

Condoleezza Rice could well have stories, experiences and accomplishments that could put information about her in almost every chapter in this book.

Born in Birmingham in 1954 to a PE teacher dad (John Wesley Rice) and a science-teacher mom (Angelena Rice), young Rice at first led a somewhat sheltered existence. Her parents homeschooled her as a young child; thus, she was likely protected from the harsh realities of the segregation issues of the early 1960s.

Rice's father went on to become pastor of Westminster Presbyterian Church, and it may have been at this point that he met the Reverend Fred Shuttlesworth (see the chapter on "From Civil Wrongs to Civil Rights" for more on him). Rice's first exposure to the Civil Rights violence was when segregationists bombed the 16th Street Baptist Church in Birmingham (one of her playmates named Denise McNair was one of the four girls killed in that bombing).

In 1966 the Rice family moved to Tuscaloosa, where Rice's father became dean of students at Stillman College; two years later they moved to Denver. Rice attended the University of Denver, where she became interested in international relations. After being awarded a bachelor's degree, she went on to Notre Dame, where she earned her Master's in International Relations. Back at the University of Denver, Rice studied Soviet and International Relations, and earned her PhD in 1981. After this, she was offered a fellowship at Palo Alto's (California) Stanford University where she taught from 1981 until 1993. It was there that she was named Senior Fellow at not one, but two Stanford institutions: the Hoover Institution and the Institute for International Studies. It was around this time that she began leaning more towards politically conservative views.

From 1989 to 1991 Rice served President George H. W. Bush as advisor on his National Security Council. After a stint at Stanford, where Rice served as provost, then-Texas Governor George W. Bush approached her and asked her to be a part of his staff, providing him with foreign policy advice. Once Bush was elected U.S. President, Rice served as National Security

Advisor beginning in 2001. During this time she was, in the words of the *Encyclopedia of Alabama*, "one of the president's closest confidantes."

Rice received criticism for failure to take heed of warnings related to the attacks of 9-11-2001, and after this, she took on the role of dealing with the media. In 2004, after Bush was re-elected President, he named Rice as his Secretary of State, replacing Colin Powell (Rice was the first female African-American to be in this position). In 2011 Rice published her memoir, *No Higher Honor: A Memoir of My Years in Washington*.

Condoleezza Rice continues to inspire; we have yet to see what else she contributes to history and the political landscape of not only Alabama but the entire country.

DID YOU KNOW? THE PARTY THAT <u>REALLY</u> WENT OVER-BUDGET!

The Marquis de Lafayette was a big help to "the colonies" in gaining independence from England. When the Marquis traveled through Alabama in 1825, Governor Israel Pickens threw him a huge and very lavish ball and banquet. How huge was it? According to the *Encyclopedia of Alabama*, it cost a bit more than $15,000—a fortune in those days! You can see more about this time period and these people at The Museum of Alabama in Montgomery and Constitution Village in Huntsville. See "Virtual Alabama" for websites.

WOMEN IN UNIFORM DURING WORLD WARS I AND II: TWO STORIES

THE AMAZING SNOOK MILITIA

"Shoot the ashes off my cigar." This is what an anonymous woman who once served in the so-called "Snook Militia" told me John Snook said to her when they were having target practice during World War II. But these women weren't soldiers in actuality: they were telephone switchboard operators who worked at the Snook Telephone Company. Owner John Snook, who ran his company out of Foley, Alabama, wanted his all-female employees to be ready in case the Germans attacked the coast. He armed the workers with machine guns and trained them in how to use the weapons; many of them became skilled sharpshooters.

Snook also carved out a series of underground tunnels in Foley; this secret passageway was a mystery to most people, and few have ever seen it. Snook began to receive all kinds of notoriety for both his so-called "Snook Militia" and his tunnel-making. He was written about in *Life Magazine, The Foley Onlooker, The Perdido Pelican* and other publications.

John Snook's widow, Marjorie Younce Snook, owns the Hotel Magnolia in Foley (once called the Magnolia Hotel but sometimes also referred to as Magnolia Inn). In 2013, she was interviewed by a Mobile-based news journalist Darwin Singleton. In a televised meeting, she told him about the building of the tunnel, which connected John Snook's telephone company to the hotel. In addition to the tunnel being useful for moving about during inclement weather such as hurricanes, she said John Snook also wanted the tunnel to be a kind of bomb shelter.

When John Snook was building the tunnel, Mrs. Snook said he found an old cannon ball from the Civil War. The cannon ball is under glass and on display in the parlor of the Hotel Magnolia. Today, the tunnels still exist in Foley, but they currently aren't open for tours. Things might change any time, however! You can see photos of Snook and his all-female militia at the Foley Library Archives or in Montgomery at the Alabama Department of Archives and History.

THE MONTGOMERY MOTOR CORPS

Comprised entirely of women, the Montgomery Motor Corps was under the auspices of the National League for Women's Service. The corps was established during World War I to have a ready body of auto drivers to respond to emergency calls during this time when national security and readiness was a constant need. The corps was divided into six teams of women, each group serving on a different day of the week. A seventh group of women served under the command of the Red Cross, to make medical calls. The corps was established at Camp Sheridan, at that time located three miles from the city of Montgomery.

In addition to being prepared for emergencies, the corps of women gave wounded soldiers rides home in order to convalesce there; they also gave rides to the hospital for the family members of wounded soldiers. In addition, they delivered flowers, gathered gifts for soldiers for Christmas, and made holiday items for those soldiers recovering in the hospital. They provided assistance to the U.S. Public Health Service during its health campaigns (anti-malaria, anti-typhoid and baby clinics). Finally, these women provided education to the soldiers in Camp Sheridan. They helped more than 2,000 young soldiers to read and write. During this effort, the corps gave rides to more than 3,200 teachers to bring them to the camp for lessons.

While the corps was disbanded during the 1920s, the women who volunteered for this special mission were every bit as patriotic as the men who volunteered for the battlefield.

Today, you can read more about this remarkable group of unsung heroes through exhibits and pictures at the Alabama Department of Archives and History.

DID YOU KNOW?

According to Monique Laney, who wrote an article titled "Von Braun's Team in Huntsville" for *Alabama Heritage Magazine* (2017), the center of all space and rocket propulsion projects originated in Huntsville. The Space and Rocket Center established there by German native Wernher Von Braun is one of the main reasons Americans led the "Space Race" of the 1960s.

FOUNDING THE VISION: BEFORE THERE WAS A CONSTITUTION

It was in July of 1819 that 45 delegates from 23 counties met in Huntsville to discuss the Territory of Alabama's possible statehood and form the state's first constitution. Now, the site is known as Constitution Village. Located on Gates Avenue in southeast Huntsville, Constitution Village is an open-air living history museum. It's part of a trinity of museums known as the "EarlyWorks Family of Museums," which includes Constitution Village, the Huntsville Depot and EarlyWorks Museum. They're all three quite accessible and within about a half-mile of each other. When I was doing the research for this book, Constitution Village itself was closed for renovations so they could open for the Bicentennial in 2019, but they did give me a personal tour. It's worth seeing for yourself!

THE YEOMAN FARMERS, THE PLANTATION ELITE, AND ALABAMA'S FIRST POLITICAL BATTLE

When Alabama became a state in 1819, the state's cotton growers witnessed a worldwide drop in the price of their so-called "white gold." The yeoman (small-time) farmers found themselves in dire straits, while the plantation-dwelling elite owned the richest land and would recover from this cotton-induced depression. The plantation elite, most of whom had come from Georgia to buy the richest cotton-growing land, were also the political machine behind the first two Alabama governors, brothers William and Thomas Bibb. They were part of a political machine known as the "Georgia faction."

The yeoman farmers looked to a former North Carolina farmer to help them fight against the elite cotton-growing plantation owners. Israel Pickens had come from the Tar Heel State, where he had first served as a state senator, then in the U.S. House of Representatives. Afterward, he was appointed land registrar for the St. Stephens Office in the Alabama Territory. In 1819, at the State Constitutional Convention, he represented Washington County.

The "Georgia faction" controlled the state's first (and biggest) bank, Planters and Merchants of Huntsville. Pickens, leading the race as head of the "North Carolina faction," came to serve as president of the Tombeckbe Bank (Alabama's first chartered bank) and the Bank of Mobile, and was declared as "the spokesman for the have-nots."

In the gubernatorial race of 1821, the yeoman farmers put their political clout behind Israel Pickens, who ultimately became the third governor of Alabama. The "Georgia faction" was broken, and the common man's interests were finally being served. This movement would be a sign of things to come when Andrew Jackson was elected President of the United States in 1828.

Today, you can see more about Israel Pickens and his life through the website of the Alabama Department of Archives and History; you can also see artifacts in the "Alabama Voices" exhibit in the Museum of Alabama in Montgomery. One thing there of special interest to me is a shoe mold, made for Pickens' workers to make his shoes.

ANOTHER VISIONARY SHAPING ALABAMA'S HISTORY

Governor David Bibb Graves, who twice served Alabama as governor, hailed from Hope Hull, Montgomery County. Born in 1873, he would become known as a progressive and one of Alabama's most important governors. By the time he first ran as a gubernatorial candidate, his name was already well-known throughout the Yellowhammer State. He also was cousin to Alabama's first two governors, William Wyatt Bibb and Thomas Bibb. After studying first in Texas and then at Yale University, Graves settled in Montgomery, where he married his first cousin, Dixie Bibb, and began to practice law. He served in the Alabama House of Representatives in 1899 and again in 1900.

He also served Alabama as adjutant general of the Alabama National Guard (1907-1911) and organized the First Alabama Cavalry Regiment, defending the American border where it met Mexico due to cross-border raids organized by Mexican revolutionaries. When World War I broke out, Graves served honorably in France with the 117th Field Artillery.

After the war, Graves formed the American Legion in Alabama and served as its chairman. Despite his being a part of the KKK (from which he resigned and renounced), he successfully ran for governor in 1926, backed at the time by women in the Suffrage Movement and by Prohibitionists (the latter for his leanings toward temperance). Under his administration, Alabama saw the beginning of a welfare system, improvements in education, and a plethora of new roads. He also founded the Alabama Department of Labor that supported organized labor, cracked down on child labor and ended the convict-lease system. In addition, he made strides for improving care for the mentally ill and for those at the Alabama Institute for the Deaf and Blind (located in Talladega).

He ran again for the governor's office in 1934 after a stint in legal practice (the Alabama Constitution prohibited two back-to-back terms) and won. After the Great Depression, he was an avid supporter of Franklin D. Roosevelt's "New Deal." Before he could run for an unprecedented third term for governor, Graves died unexpectedly in 1942.

Today, you can see more about this era of Graves' heyday in Alabama history at the Alabama Department of Archives and History in Montgomery. A portrait of Graves hangs in the Governor's office at the Capitol Building. You might have to pull some strings to see that!

AMERICA'S EARLIEST HIGHWAY ... IN ALABAMA?

In 1805, a group of Creek delegates were summoned to Washington, D.C. by President Thomas Jefferson. America had just doubled in geographic size due to the Louisiana Purchase and needed a better land route not only for postal service, but to allow people to move with their animals and goods. The best route had been determined to be southward from Washington down to Georgia, then to Mobile, Alabama, via Creek territory. The president needed Creek approval to do this to avoid tensions between the Creeks and white settlers. The delegates reached an agreement with Jefferson, although there was much grumbling from many Creeks who said that their desires weren't being represented. They also said that this would cause an even greater influx of land-greedy white settlers.

But the deal went through as planned, and road construction began in 1806. It was at first a rather crude and somewhat narrow path (about four feet wide), and many early travelers complained that it was the worst road ever. This new highway, known as the "Federal Road," made the traveling distance from Washington to New Orleans 300 miles shorter.

And the Creeks who said that this new road would bring in more land-hungry settlers were right: there were suddenly more white settlers entering Creek lands. Soon, tensions began to mount, which ultimately led to the Creek War of 1813-14. Today, you can drive on interstates that run through Alabama from Georgia to Louisiana and know that once this was part of the Federal Road. There are a number of historical markers on roadways, telling the story of the Federal Road. You can also see drawings of taverns and inns that sprang up along the way and other artifacts relating to the Federal Road, at The Museum of Alabama in Montgomery. See "Virtual Alabama" for websites relating to this.

DID YOU KNOW? "ACCESSIBLE ALABAMA"
The newest edition of the Official Alabama State Highway Map also has a listing of all tourist sites accessible for people in wheelchairs or who are deaf or blind. Virtually every tourist site I checked out is accessible for such visitors who have special needs. For example, with advance notice, the Museum of Alabama in Montgomery will even obtain a deaf-interpreter for those who are hearing-impaired!

THE PHENONENA KNOWN AS "ALABAMA FEVER" and THE INFLUENCE OF "KING COTTON"

After the Creek War and then the infamous Trail of Tears, land was suddenly open for the taking. The Mississippi Territory, of which Alabama was a part, had rich, fertile soil. Settlers were suddenly assured of their safety with the put-down of the Creeks; and the whole world wanted one thing--cotton.

In other southern states such as the Carolinas and Georgia, many farmers' lands were depleted of nutrients needed to grow cotton. But Alabama had plenty of fertile land, much of it flat, especially in what came to be called the Black Belt area of Alabama. This, combined with the invention of the cotton gin (which removed the seeds from the cotton bolls—try THIS time-consuming task yourself) and the development of the steam engine, meant cotton could be grown, ginned, and transported more easily and on a more massive scale than ever before.

Between the years 1820 to 1860, "King Cotton" so dominated Alabama culture that Hiram Fuller, who visited Alabama from England, is often quoted as offering this observation: "They buy cotton, sell cotton, think cotton, eat cotton, drink cotton, and dream cotton." Indeed, during those years when "King Cotton" reigned over many aspects of Alabama life, the Yellowhammer State was (during this time) one of the top ten wealthiest states in the U.S.

The end of slavery brought an end to this reign. The cotton grown now in Alabama is, like everywhere else in the country, planted and harvested with the use of machinery. Cotton is still so plentiful in the state that many tourists like to park beside a field full of cotton and have a picture taken of what some Alabamians call "Alabama snow." Virtually every museum in Alabama, but especially those in the fertile area of the Black Belt, has some kind of display relating to the time when "cotton was king."

THE FRENCH "PELICAN GIRLS"

In 1704, the land that would later become Alabama was primitive, with harsh, demanding conditions. Furthermore, male settlers greatly outnumbered female settlers, especially single ones. The Mobile colony's founder, Jean-Baptiste Le Moyne de Bienville, had written to King Louis XIV telling him of the unstable social conditions and asking for help in providing the colony with a good selection of immigrant women. Bienville also wanted to discourage his French settlers from pursuing Native American women. The king responded to Bienville's request, saying in a letter, "His majesty sends ... 20 girls to be married to the Canadians and others who have begun habitations at Mobile in order that this colony can firmly establish itself."

The French girls, who had been orphaned, were hand-picked by the Catholic Church and the Bishop of Quebec. These girls were chosen for their demeanor and character and their ability to work to be suitable brides for the single settlers. Their ship was *The Pelican* (or *Le Pelican,* as you would spell it in French), and people still refer to them as "Pelican Girls." They were also referred to as "casquette" or "casket" girls for coming with their boxes (or "casquette") of necessities.

The girls arrived with Father Henry La Vente, along with three other priests and four nuns. La Vente had been instructed by King Louis XIV to marry the girls to Frenchmen "as quickly as possible."

Today, there is a wonderful animated exhibit about the "Pelican Girls" at the GulfQuest National Maritime Museum of the Gulf of Mexico in Mobile.

GUESS WHO INFLUENCED THE LIKES OF FAULKNER AND TWAIN?

Alabama's early newspapers (the first one was the *Centinel*, published in Mobile in 1811) included the writings of humorists who wrote about life and the people of the "Alabama frontier." Their folksy style often poked fun at politics of the time similar to TV comedy shows today. One of these humorists was Johnson J. Hooper, who equally lampooned legislators and the general population. It was writings such as his that influenced authors Samuel Clemens, whom you know better as Mark Twain, and William Faulkner. You can see a painting of Hooper in the Alabama Department of Archives and History in Montgomery.

THE BRAVE AND VISIONARY TUSKEGEE AIRMEN

The year was 1941 and the U.S. was on the brink of World War II. Before this time, African-American pilots were not allowed to fly for any branch of the U.S. military. But, in 1941, this changed. The Army Air Corps began to train African-Americans to maintain and fly combat aircraft. The Tuskegee Airmen consisted not only of pilots, but also included instructors, support staff, navigators and other personnel to help keep the combat aircraft flying.

Tuskegee was chosen because it had facilities and technical and engineering instructors as well as a nearly year-'round climate conducive to flight training. The site of newly-constructed Moton Field was where this program would take place. Named after Robert Russa Moton, the second president of Tuskegee Institute, the Institute would provide flight training for the cadets, via a contract with the U.S. Department of Defense. The Army Air Corps chose officers to supervise training for the cadets, and the flight students were provided clothes, parachutes, and textbooks. The aspiring airmen were put under the command of Captain Benjamin O. Davis, Jr., who then was the first black general in the U.S. Air Force.

After the cadets' preliminary training was complete, they transferred to Tuskegee Army Air Field to finish their aviation education with the Army Air Force. Although still segregated, the air field was a full-scale military base. In the years from 1941 to 1945, Tuskegee Institute trained more than 1,000 African-American aviators. The program received a boost in media attention when First Lady Eleanor Roosevelt visited in March 1941 and took a short flight with pilot instructor C. Alfred "Chief" Anderson.

The young aviation students most commonly flew a North American P-51 Mustang. When the pilots painted their airplanes' tails red, the moniker "Red Tails" was given to them and the nickname stuck. The "Red Tails" flew missions in Africa, Italy, Austria, Germany, Poland, Hungary, Czechoslovakia, France, Anzio and others. The 99th Fighter Squadron earned three Distinguished Unit Citations, and the 332nd Fighter Group earned one (for their aerial combat over Berlin). Pilots of the 332nd Fighter Group received 96 Distinguished Flying Crosses.

These brave and visionary men faced all kinds of adversities during their training period, working to overcome prejudice and segregation and succeed despite many saying they could never be as well trained as their Caucasian counterparts. They proved to the world that they could not only be as good as their Caucasian pilots: they could be better. Over time they became known as one of the most highly trained and respected aerial fighting groups of World War II.

Flash forward to 1998. President Bill Clinton signed into law a bill that established the **Tuskegee Airmen National Site at Moton Field** to, in the words of the National Park Service website (www.nps.gov), "commemorate and interpret the heroic actions of the Tuskegee Airmen during World War II." In 2007, the Tuskegee Airmen were collectively awarded a Congressional Medal of Honor by President George W. Bush. That medal is currently on display at the Smithsonian Institution in Washington, D.C.

Although Willie Rogers, the last of the Tuskegee Airmen, died in 2016, the legacy these men left behind lives on in many ways. In 2006, a commemorative postage stamp was created, honoring their achievement. The surviving members of the Tuskegee Airmen were invited to Barack Obama's first Presidential Inauguration (in 2008). Highways in several states around the country are named in honor of the Tuskegee Airmen; an airfield in South Carolina has a memorial on display in their memory; and in 2012, movie producer George Lucas came out with his film, "Red Tails," about the aviation cadets' experiences. They have been featured in many other artistic renderings as well as documentaries, movie shorts, and full-length films.

Today, you can visit the Tuskegee Airmen National Historic Site (under the auspices of the U.S. National Park Service). Hangar #1 and Hangar #2 museums are open Monday through Saturday except for most major holidays. Visit—and let your inspiration "take wing"!

A GOVERNMENTAL RENAISSANCE MAN

Theophilus Lindsey Toulmin had an illustrious political career in the early days of Alabama. He served in the Civil War as a general but also served Mobile County between the years 1831 and 1865, first as a state legislator, then county sheriff, and finally state senator. While looking to see where some of his artifacts might be, I happened to track down one of his distant descendants, Charles Torrey, who works as a Research Historian at the History Museum of Mobile. Torrey told me more about Toulmin and some other significant family members.

"Theophilus Lindsey Toulmin's father was Judge Harry Toulmin," he said, "the first judge in the Alabama Territory. As the first judge, he wrote *Toulmin's Digest,* the first compilation of laws for the first Mississippi Territory, then Alabama Territory. His great-grandson, Harry T. Toulmin, wrote *People and Places of Toulminville*, which is about an early settlement (also called Oakland Farms) near St. Stephens Road in Mobile."

He also told me that Theophilus Lindsey Toulmin's home has been moved from the old settlement and is now at the University of South Alabama, serving as the Alumni Affairs building. It is open for tours. You can find Theophilus Lindsey Toulmin's grave in Mobile's Springhill Cemetery.

AN OLD TOWN RIVALRY

This story was first published in *The Tuscaloosa News* in 1939. Tuscaloosa at the time had a major rival town called Newtown, and one of its founders began raising funds for a deaf institution. Newtown was for a short time the county seat until Tuscaloosa became the new county seat; then, a tornado hit Newtown, destroying the courthouse. Newtown was absorbed into Tuscaloosa and is now known as West End. There is a historical marker on Martin Luther King, Jr. Boulevard to mark this history.

HOW SCHOOLCHILDREN BROUGHT A BATTLESHIP TO ALABAMA

It was a hot, tense day at the Panama Canal. Reporters and other interested and curious people watched as the huge (45,000-ton) battleship, the USS *Alabama*, squeezed its way through the locks. Suspense grew as onlookers saw the tiny clearance the massive ship had: only 11 inches on each side.

The USS *Alabama* had been built in 1940 as part of a fleet of battleships known as the South Dakota class. The ship and its crew of 2,500 served their time admirably in the war effort in both the North Atlantic and South Pacific and led the victorious way into Tokyo Bay in September of 1945 for the Japanese surrender. The ship they called the "Mighty A" earned 9 battle stars for her service as the "Heroine of the Pacific."

Flash forward to May, 1962: the U.S. government announced that the Navy was sending the fleet of South Dakota class battleships, including the USS *Alabama*, to the scrap-yard. Seeing this announcement in the newspaper, Mobile Chamber of Commerce member Jimmie Morris became alarmed. That very day, he organized a committee of concerned Alabamians to try and not only save the USS *Alabama* but to bring it home to the Port of Mobile. In September of 1963, the Alabama Senate gave their approval for the project, and Governor George C. Wallace proclaimed, "Let's bring our ship home!"

The problem was, there was no budget for the project. There was a solution to this problem: get the state's schoolchildren on board. With the fundraising slogan of "Let's Bring Our Ship Home!" students organized across the state, donating nickels, dimes, pennies and, occasionally, quarters.

Some businesses added to the fund, and restaurants in Birmingham donated what they took in from their patrons one day. The first school system to meet their fundraising goal was that of the city of Opp. By 1964, the schoolchildren and other fundraisers had donated enough money to pay for the ship's journey to the Port of Mobile.

The USS Alabama near dusk. Photo courtesy of Larissa Goodrich Photography.

It was an arduous journey for a 45,000-ton ship to be towed 5,600 miles from Bremerton, Washington, to Mobile, Alabama. It still holds the record for the longest non-military dead-weight tow in the history of the U.S. Navy. The trip took two months, starting in July 1964. In a fitting tribute to the original crew of the battleship, Navy sailors who had called the ship home during World War II were part of the homecoming hands. The USS *Alabama* came into the Port of Mobile on September 14, 1964, and after some refurbishing, it opened to the public in January of 1965.

The USS *Alabama* has been declared a National Historic Landmark and is located at USS *Alabama* Battleship Memorial Park in Mobile. She has been restored to reflect how she looked during her glory days of World War II. There are five World War II historical re-enactments held at the park each year, and to date nearly 17 million visitors have stepped aboard. In addition, school groups and others, such as the Boy Scouts, often have campouts on the ship.

There was an addition to the park in 1969, when the USS *Drum*, a 311 foot WWII submarine, was also donated. It opened for tours on July 4, 1969. Now, according to their website, the USS *Alabama* is "easily the most recognizable symbol of the State of Alabama."

As far as the school children go, they received something in return for their donations: they were each awarded a USS *Alabama* Charter Member Card, which allows them to tour their battleship at no charge—with no expiration date. Furthermore, some of those school children have become famous in their own way. Former student at Murphy High School Don Siegelman would go on to become governor. Terry Ankerson, then the student body campaign chair at the former McGill Institute (today called McGill-Toolen High School), now serves on the Battleship Commission. Another McGill Institute student who donated funds would later become known to the world as musician and author Jimmy Buffett (singer of such hits as "Margaritaville" and "Cheeseburger in Paradise"). One of my proofreaders, retired English teacher Donna Boswell, was most excited about this story for this book: "I was one of those schoolchildren!" she exclaimed.

With websites today such as GoFundMe.com, this feat of raising money to move a huge vessel thousands of miles would not be remarkable; but before the internet, social media and other instant ways to get the word out, what the school children of Alabama did in the 1960s was something of a miracle.

FROM TRAILS TO RAILS: ALABAMA'S FIRST RAILROAD

Other than crude highways such as the Federal Road, before 1830 the people of Alabama were reliant primarily on the steamboat for transportation. River traffic was often the only way to get goods and people from various places in the young state to the ports on the coast. Alabama's first railroad was a two-mile-long, horse-drawn one, Tuscumbia Railway in Franklin County, which was put in place to bypass the rapids of the Tennessee River in Muscle Shoals. This rail service soon acquired the state's first steam locomotive, the *Fulton*, so it could expand.

Eventually all of Alabama was connected by rail lines— at least, before the Civil War, when Union soldiers destroyed much of them. Today, you can see the history of Alabama's railroads by going to The Heart of Dixie Railroad Museum. Located in Calera just south of Birmingham, it is the official railroad museum of the state of Alabama. This fascinating place has outdoor exhibits featuring trains (both narrow-gauge and standard) and two completely restored depots. Indoors, they have all kinds of artifacts relating to the heyday of Alabama's railroads, including cabooses, locomotives and railroad cars.

For those of you who want to experience what a train ride was like "back in the day," you can: The Calera and Shelby Rail Line runs on a part of the 1891 L&N Alabama Mineral Railroad. The ride in vintage cars, with engineers dressed in period costume, will take you back more than a hundred years. And for those who have kids (or are themselves a kid at heart), you can buy a ticket to ride with the brakeman (in the caboose) or the engineer (in the locomotive).

For adults, the museum offers a train ride to a nearby vineyard (Ozan Vineyard and Winery), which includes a walk through the vineyard, lunch and wine tastings.

TOWN NAMES, NOW AND THEN

Many towns in Alabama have had more than one name over the course of their diverse history. Decatur, for example, was originally called Rhodes Ferry. The town of Utopia was renamed Ariton, then even later, renamed Bethel. Dean Station was renamed Charlton. Old Richmond was also known as Wiggins Springs. Scott's Mill was renamed Scottsboro and Ozark was first known as Woodshop. Athens was first known as Athenson when it was founded in 1816. The town of Troy, however, may have all other towns beat as far as other names it's had: it has been known as Deer Stand, Zebulon and Centreville. When the town of Linden was first settled in 1823 by French immigrants, they called it "Hohenlinden." The first black municipality in Alabama, Hobson City, was originally called Moree Quarter. When it was founded in 1813, the town now known as Crawford was Crockettsville, to honor Davy Crockett. The lovely town of Montevallo was originally called Wilson's Hill, and Camden was first known as Barboursville. The charming town of Alpine was originally known as Welch's Depot.

There's more! When Alabama was still only a territory, the town of Courtland was called Ebenezer. Until 1861, Uniontown was known as Woodville. Eufaula was known as Irwinton until 1843. The town of Bluffton became Lanette in 1893. Dothan was first known as Poplar Head and New Site was the name first given to the Covington County town of

Andalusia. The original name for Goodwater was Adkins Gap. The town of Northport was first named Canetuck, due to a dense canebrake in the area. Big Spring was what Tuscumbia used to be called. The Cullman County town of Hanceville was originally called Gilmer. Dauphin Island, first discovered by French explorer Iberville in 1699, was named Massacre Island because of a mysterious mass grave he discovered on the island. Huntsville was originally known as Hunt's Spring, then later Twickenham. The town of Wilburn still sometimes goes by its former name, Bug Tussle.

Finally, the last two are probably the most amusing. When it was first incorporated in 1820, Greenville was known as Buttsville. The mountain community of Sauta Bottom had citizens who were so uncivilized that it was first called "Hell's Half Acre."

HORACE KING, SLAVE TURNED LEGISLATOR—"BRIDGING RACIAL DIVIDES"

Born as a slave in 1808 in South Carolina, Horace King was taught to read and write. At an early age, he also learned carpentry, and by the time he was a teenager, he was proficient in the craft. In 1824, he also began to learn the art and craft of bridge building, when a bridge architect by the name of Ithiel Town came into the area to build a bridge over the Pee Dee River (in Cheraw, S.C.). Town's hallmark lattice truss design would be instilled in King's future works.

In 1830, when King was 23, his owner died; King was then sold to a contractor named John Godwin. Godwin and King began working on many bridge and house-building projects. For the next ten years, Godwin and King worked together on projects throughout the South. They must have been close, for they shared the income they earned from the projects, and

Godwin even sent King to college (Oberlin College in Ohio, the first in the U.S. to admit African-Americans). The two went on to build bridges and courthouses. In Alabama, they built the courthouse in Russell County. They also continued to build bridges throughout Georgia, Alabama, and Ohio.

King eventually was given permission to marry. He married a free woman of color named Frances Gould Thomas (this was unusual during this time period, because the law then stated that if a free woman married a slave man, their children would also be free). King rose to prominence as his reputation for excellence in architecture grew and even outstripped that of Godwin. King worked on his own on bridges in Mississippi and Alabama (mainly Florence, Wetumpka and Eufaula). In 1846, he used some of his earnings to purchase his freedom (although the *Encyclopedia of Alabama* states that he may have been given his freedom by the Alabama Legislature). By whatever means, King obtained his freedom.

Horace King bridged racial divides. Photo courtesy Alabama Department of Archives and History.

Prior to becoming free, King had made friends with a senator by the name of Robert Jemison, Jr. At this point in history, the law stated that a slave had to leave Alabama within one year after being emancipated. Jemison arranged a waiver with the state legislature, so King and his family could stay in Alabama. The two were friends for the rest of their lives. As for Godwin, when he died in 1859, King had a monument put over his grave.

In 1849, the Alabama State Capitol building burned; King was hired to build a new one, complete with twin spiral staircases. There is a postscript to the story about the spiral staircases, so stay with me.

When the Civil War broke out, King opposed secession and was a staunch Unionist; he was obliged, however, to take on construction jobs to aid the Confederacy, such as building obstructions on the Apalachicola River to prevent a Union naval attack on the city of Columbus, Georgia. He also constructed defenses on the Alabama River. During the course of the Civil War, many of King's bridges were destroyed by Union forces. Then, in 1864, King's wife died. He was left a widower with five children. In the Reconstruction Era, King's reputation led to new opportunities for him. He built bridges and warehouses in Alabama and Georgia and built a courthouse in Lee County, Alabama.

King then began to develop an interest in politics. He became a registrar for new voters in Russell County and successfully ran for a seat in the Alabama House of Representatives in 1868 as a Republican. When his term was up, however, King did not seek re-election. He left the Alabama Legislature in 1872 and continued building bridges. When in 1885 King passed away, major newspapers across Alabama and Georgia ran obituaries lauding his accomplishments— something rare in that time period for anyone of African-

American descent. He was also posthumously inducted into the Alabama Engineers Hall of Fame at The University of Alabama in Tuscaloosa.

Now for the rest of the story about the spiral staircases. In February 2017, the Alabama state government unveiled a portrait of King in the State Capitol that he helped build. It is, as the *Montgomery Advertiser* stated, "the first portrait of an African-American to hang in the seat of the Alabama government." It hangs, appropriately enough, at the foot of the spiral staircases. The Capitol is open for tours; see their website in Virtual Alabama for more.

FORKLAND, HOME TO … WHAT THE HAY???
Just outside Forkland, Alabama, you will find an unusual kind of outdoor folk-art exhibit. Self-proclaimed "hay artist," Jim Bird, loves to see the look of surprise when passersby see his work. Bird has created whimsical works of art using bales of hay. His artwork includes a windmill, an accurate rendition of Big Bird, and a replica of the Tin Man from "Wizard of Oz" fame. The Tin Man should be called "Mr. Tin Man." It stands at 32 feet tall, made from bath tubs and fuel drums, and the replica is complete with a heart and an axe.

THE "ENVIRONMENTAL DISASTER" THAT RESULTED IN A BOON IN WILDLIFE
Back in 1979, the U.S. Army Corps of Engineers decided they needed to create a deeper ship channel for larger ships (with deeper drafts) to be able to enter the Port of Mobile. They were trying to decide exactly how to do the dredging and were debating about what to do with the dredged material. A Mobile dentist by the name of Dr. M. Wilson Gaillard approached the Corps with an idea. Dr. Gaillard was also a conservationist and had a vision for something that would not only help the Port of

Mobile expand but also attract wildlife (especially seabirds) to the area. He proposed this idea: dredge the ship channel, transport the dredged material by barge to a part of Mobile Bay, and dump it there, creating a man-made island.

Environmentalists were concerned. Many said that this would be an "environmental disaster" for the bay, ultimately harming or killing sea life, polluting the bay, and endangering the tourism industry, which was largely dependent on the loveliness and environmental health of Mobile Bay. After some debate, the Corps of Engineers agreed to Dr. Gaillard's plan. They put a total of 31 MILLION cubic yards of dredged material on this island and put the material into a special shape (triangular) to protect the island from erosion caused by wave action. They also planted marsh plants along its shore to help keep the island intact.

When the island was finished in 1981, people such as scientists and biologists began to take note of the seabirds nesting there. They were especially excited to see the endangered Brown Pelicans beginning to roost and lay their eggs on the island (in the early 1900s, Brown Pelicans' numbers were in great decline, first because of the demand for their feathers to decorate ladies' hats and then the widespread use of the pesticide DDT). Thanks to Gaillard and his vision for the bay, the Brown Pelican is now off both the Alabama and Federal Endangered Species lists.

Gaillard Island, called by many locals Pelican Island, is now home to thousands of species of sea birds, including the White and Brown Pelicans, Herons, Terns, Egrets and many others. Humans have also found it a delightful place to visit. The fishing is incredibly good in the vicinity of the island, and if you go near it in the spring, the cacophony of thousands of birds calling to their young is deafening!

No one is allowed on the island as it is a protected site, but you can get close enough (with a boat and binoculars) to view the birds for yourself. Also, on occasion, the Mobile Bay Audubon Society conducts excursions to the island. See "Virtual Alabama" for their website.

Incidentally, Dr. Gaillard's nephew, Frye Gaillard (read about him in Chapter 4 on Famous Alabamians in Literature), met with me in the spring of 2018 and told me that, years ago, his uncle Dr. Gaillard had written a book about this experience. The title of it is *Moving the Earth for a Song*, and it is still in print.

THE INFAMOUS ARCHIVES WAR OF 1901

Prior to 1900, the city of Daphne had been the county seat for Baldwin County. In 1900, the county seat was designated to be Bay Minette by an act of the Alabama Legislation. The people of Daphne did not take kindly to this piece of legislation. They resisted it, sometimes violently. Things all came to a head one night in October of 1901.

A posse of men from Bay Minette sent word to Daphne and informed the sheriff and his deputy there that there had been a murder, and the killer was on the loose. The Daphne sheriff and his deputy left to go track down the fictitious killer, and with the law out of town, the posse of men pounced. They traveled the 30 miles to the city of Daphne, stole the county records, and delivered them to the city of Bay Minette.

The people of Daphne were outraged and horrified, but the damage had been irrevocably done. With the county records and archives at their newly official home, there was nothing more they could do. Legend also has it that the group of men from Bay Minette also stole the courthouse bell, which the townspeople of Daphne used to call the volunteer firefighters to put out fires and such. But with the passing of time, no one is alive to verify or deny this legend.

A WORLD WAR II HERO

Son of "Spider" and Mary Gaston, Ernest "Barney" Gaston signed up for the war effort along with millions of other men after the unprecedented attack on Pearl Harbor. As a World War II pilot, Barney Gaston flew many successful missions. The most important contribution he made to the war effort was the act which resulted in his death: he was flying around the area of Sivry-Courtry in France, when he noticed a German train down below. He could tell it was filled with munitions and was going to Sivry with the goal of destroying the town.

Barney bombed the German train and successfully kept it from making it to its destination in Sivry, but in doing so, one of his plane's wings clipped a tree. Barney's plane crashed and he was killed instantly.

His heroism did, however, save the entire city of Sivry. Now, there is a memorial in the shape of an airplane propeller at the site where Barney's plane crashed. Every year, this city in France honors his sacrifice. His body was returned to Alabama and he lies interred in Colony Cemetery (Fairhope) next to his parents. When you're in the area, go by and pay your respects. On occasion, cemetery tours are held with re-enactors who portray people interred in Colony Cemetery. See "Virtual Alabama" for websites.

SYDNEY E. MANNING: ONE OF GENERAL PERSHING'S "IMMORTAL TEN"

Sydney Earnest Manning was born in Flomaton, Alabama, in 1892. When World War I was declared, he signed up for duty at the Armed Services Registration office in Flomaton. He rose up through the ranks, eventually attaining the rank of Corporal in the U.S. Army.

He was in a battle fighting for control of a strongly fortified place in France overlooking the Ourcq River when both his platoon commander and sergeant became early casualties. He took command of the platoon, leading 35 of the remaining platoon members to gain a foothold on the enemy's position. By the end of this siege, with only seven men remaining, he fought on.

He kept his last seven men safe, holding off a large body of the enemy, shooting at them with his automatic rifle at a distance of only 50 yards. He refused to take cover until his men were consolidated with the platoon at the front. Once they were safe, he finally dragged himself to shelter. He had received a total of nine wounds through this battle.

For his bravery, he was awarded the Congressional Medal of Honor, a Purple Heart, a World War I Victory Medal, the Croix de Guerre and Medaille Militaire (both from the French Republic), the Croce al Merito di Guerra (from Italy) and the Medal for Military Bravery (from the Kingdom of Montenegro).

After the war, Manning, whom General Pershing referred to as one of his "Immortal Ten," returned to Flomaton. When he died in 1960 at the age of 68, he was buried in Little Escambia Cemetery in Flomaton. Also in Flomaton is a historical marker telling more about Manning's bravery.

When you go to Flomaton, go by the cemetery and pay your respects to one of Pershing's "Immortal Ten."

THE STORY ABOUT THE "BAGWELL BRIGADE"

In North Alabama there once lived an unusually patriotic family which was dubbed "The Bagwell Brigade" by a local newspaper (*The Arab Tribune*, 2004). Of the 12 children of Leo and Simmie Bagwell, all eight sons and two of the four daughters were in the military. (Leo himself served in World War I). Four of the oldest sons joined the Army or Navy shortly after the Japanese bombed Pearl Harbor. Others served during the Korean and Vietnam wars.

You can see more about brave young men and women like these who honorably wore American uniforms from pre-Revolutionary War days to today's conflicts at a wonderful, relatively new museum. Located in the old L&N Freight Depot on West Pryor Street in Athens, the Alabama Veterans Museum and Archives is a wonderful way for you and your family to spend a day. If you're as lucky as I was, you can have your tour enhanced by volunteer docent Jerry Barksdale, who himself is a walking encyclopedia.

Oh—and how do I know about the Bagwells and their children? My mom, Marian Bagwell Jensen, is one of those who were in the so-called "Bagwell Brigade." DID YOU KNOW?

THIS TOWN IS WHERE "WHAT IS YOUR EMERGENCY?" FIRST ORIGINATED

Since 1958, the U.S. government had been discussing how, with whom and in what way to implement a nationwide emergency-calling system. It was finally decided in 1968 to have it in place; it was first set up in Haleyville, Alabama. The FCC along with President of AT&T, B. W. Gallagher, had the first call to go into Haleyville, since it had the best equipment to take such 9-1-1 calls. Alabama Speaker of the House Rankin Fite made the fall from a candy-apple red rotary-dial phone in the police station; Congressman Tom Bevill answered with only "hello." The town celebrates this achievement every June with bands, food, a parade and other entertainment. The phone itself is located at the National Law Enforcement Museum in Washington, D.C.

...AND ANOTHER FAMILY OF SOLDIERS

Another family whose offspring showed dedication to defending their country was the Crommelin brothers. Born in Wetumpka, the five brothers—John, Henry, Richard, Charles, and Quentin—all graduated from the U.S. Naval Academy and fought in the Pacific in World War II. Two of the brothers, Charles and Richard, died in conflicts. Two others—John and Henry—rose to the rank of admiral and retired. Quentin retired as captain. The U.S. Navy had a new missile frigate it launched in 1981, named USS *Crommelin*, in honor of the patriotic brothers. You can see more about such patriotic brothers-in-arms at the aforementioned Alabama Veterans Museum and Archives in Athens.

DID YOU KNOW?

According to the Congressional Medal of Honor website (see back of the book), the number of Alabama military who have received the Congressional Medal of Honor for their bravery and valor in wartime currently stands at 33. This includes the Civil War through current conflicts.

Q. & A

Q. What Mobile native and World War II veteran penned the famous war book, which the *Encyclopedia of Alabama* proclaimed as "a graphic portrayal of combat," titled *With the Old Breed: At Peleliu and Okinawa*?

A. Author and veteran Eugene B. Sledge.

Q. What were the first two steamboats to ply the waters of Alabama rivers?

A. *The Alabama* and the *Harriett*. Today, *Harriett II* offers tours of the Alabama River, from a launch in downtown Montgomery.

Q. What U.S. senator in the late 1800s was known as the "father of the federal road system"?

A. Senator John H. Bankhead. U.S. route 78, which runs from Washington to San Diego and comes through Alabama in Birmingham, was named in his honor.

Q. What type of aircraft is on display at the U.S. Army Aviation Museum in Fort Rucker—the largest collection of its kind anywhere in the world?

A. Helicopters. Incidentally, the museum has been in constant operation since its founding in 1956.

Q. The Women's Army Corps Museum is in what town?

A. Anniston.

Q. What aviator from Birmingham taught Charles Lindbergh to fly?

A. Glenn Messer.

Q. Often on the days before Mother's Day, what town's post office receives many requests for postmarks for stamps bearing the reproduction of "Portrait of the Artist's Mother"?

A. The town of Whistler.

Q. What state senator hailing from Mobile saw the state's first child labor law through the legislature in 1887?

A. Daniel Smith.

Q. What was the first modern highway to be constructed in Alabama?

A. Also known as the "Bee Line Highway," officially it was U.S. Highway 31.

Q. What man, a graduate from Tuskegee University, became the first African-American four-star general in U.S. history?

A. General Daniel "Chappie" James.

Q. What Alabama senator began the movement that led to Congressional approval for the completion of the Panama Canal?

A. Senator John T. Morgan.

Q. To whom did France relinquish lands that would later become Alabama in the 1763 Treaty of Paris?

A. England.

Q. Who was the inspiring and energetic military leader from Tennessee who won decisive battles at both

Talladega and Horseshoe Bend against the Creek Indians in 1814?

A. Andrew Jackson.

Q. What did Andrew Jackson stand upon to give an inspiring speech to his troops just before fighting in the Battle of New Orleans in 1815?

A. The Jackson Oak. It still stands and is now the center of a park and hiking trail, Village Point Preserve, in Daphne, Alabama.

Q. Who was the Territory of Alabama's first delegate to Congress?

A. Jim Crowell.

Q. What type of early transportation companies were the Telegraph Line, People's Line and the Mail Line?

A. Early stagecoach lines.

Q. During the Spanish-American War, what native Alabamian sank the ironclad Merrimac in an attempt to trap the Spanish fleet in Santiago Bay?

A. Lieutenant Richard Pearson Hobson.

Q. What two men were the first U.S. Senators to represent Alabama?

A. John W. Walker and William Rufus King.

Q. The airplane of what famous general is on display at the Army Aviation Museum at Fort Rucker?

A. General Douglas MacArthur.

Q. What president appointed William Wyatt Bibb as the first governor of the Territory of Alabama in 1817?

A. President James Monroe.

Q. Why did Thomas Bibb succeed his brother as governor of the state of Alabama in 1820?

A. William was killed in a horseback-riding accident; Thomas was serving as president of the state senate and was next in line for the office.

Q. What is the geographic center of the state of Alabama?

A. The town of Chilton, 12 miles southwest of Clanton.

Q. What is unique about the Boy Scouts of America Troop Number 47?

A. It is the oldest continually-operating troop in the state of Alabama.

Q. List the five towns that served as Alabama's state capitals.

A. St. Stephens was the capital of the Alabama Territory, but the five that served as state capitals are Cahawba, Selma, Tuscaloosa,

This is the capital building in Montgomery, Alabama. Photo courtesy of Governor Kay Ivey's staff

Huntsville and finally, Montgomery.

Q. How many counties are there in Alabama?

A. Sixty-seven.

Q. What city was the first county seat of Escambia County?

A. Pollard.

Q. What nickname for Alabama refers to its geographical location?

A. "The Heart of Dixie."

Q. What is the state motto?

A. "We dare defend our rights."

Q. What is the highest covered bridge over water in the U.S.?

A. Horton Mill Bridge, near Oneonta (Blount County), with the highest point being 70 feet above the Black Warrior River. Blount County itself has three covered bridges within its boundaries, and they have Covered Bridge Art and Music Festival every October in Oneonta.

Q. How many covered bridges are in the state of Alabama?

A. Currently, eleven.

Q. What is the largest underwater vehicular tunnel in Alabama?

A. Bankhead Tunnel, in Mobile, at more than 3,100 feet in length.

CHAPTER 3
PREHISTORIC ALABAMA

DID YOU KNOW? THERE ARE PETROGLYPHS IN ALABAMA

Long before any explorers came to what is now Alabama, Paleo Indians, who came to this area more than 12,000 years ago, lived and thrived here. Archeologists have found several places bearing evidence (such as stone tools and projectile points) of prehistoric people living in several places in Alabama. The Paleo Indians were followed by the Archaic Indians. These were followed by the Woodland Indians and then the Mississippian Indians.

Researchers determined that there were three main places where these indigenous people lived. One is Russell Cave in the northeastern corner of Alabama. Russell Cave is said to have been used as a shelter by all these indigenous groups due to a freshwater source inside the cave, and an abundance of materials (to make tools and weapons with) in the surrounding forests. Russell Cave itself has been designated a National Monument; it is under the auspices of the U.S. National Park Service and open virtually every day for tours.

Another cave called Dust Cave can be found in the northwest corner of the state. Yet another cave in Colbert County (Tuscumbia) is not truly a cave per se but more of a bluff shelter. It was in this bluff shelter that several boulders were discovered with prehistoric carvings called petroglyphs on them. Found on property owned by Robert B. Martin, Jr. and

Donnie Martin, they became increasingly concerned in 1990 when they discovered that the petroglyphs were being vandalized by trespassers. The "Martin Petroglyphs" were eventually moved with care and donated to have a permanent home at the Tennessee Valley Museum of Art in Tuscumbia, Alabama.

Some boulders have carvings of snakes and human footprints; others have holes thought to be utilized in the processing of food, such as in the grinding of nuts. The exhibit, located within two rooms of the Museum of Art, replicates the bluff shelter as it might have appeared in what is now Tuscumbia. The space replicates the bluff shelter, complete with other simulated rocks, panoramic murals, painted foliage and nature sounds, to immerse the visitor in the feel of what life might have been like in the Paleo era for the people who came before us. Just seeing this exhibit is worth the visit! It's open every day but Saturday, and admission is free on Sunday.

THE BOTTLE CREEK INDIAN MOUNDS STORY

Second in importance only to Moundville (outside Tuscaloosa), Bottle Creek Indian Mounds on Mound Island in Baldwin County is one of the most important Native Americans sites in Alabama, dating back to prehistoric times. It's a bit tricky to visit—you should take a shallow-draught boat since it's located in the very center of the Mobile-Tensaw Delta.

Bottle Creek was occupied by early Native Americans around 1250 AD and was a major site for religious and political gatherings. The Mobilian Indians occupied the island, and according to the Alabama Historical Commission, French explorer and founder of Mobile, Jean-Baptiste Le Moyne de Bienville visited here in 1702.

There are more than 18 mounds on the island, with the tallest one rising up as far as 52 feet above the swamp. In the summertime, most of the mounds are difficult to discern due to the abundance of dense foliage. There are guided tours in colder months, however, when you can make out the mounds more easily. Private, self-guided tours are discouraged due to a danger of predators, poisonous snakes, and the sensitive nature of the protected site. It's worth going on one of the guided tours, however. Bottle Creek is under the protection and auspices of the Alabama Historical Commission.

ALABAMA'S GOT ITS OWN T-REX!

It was in 1982 in southeastern Montgomery that a man named Dr. David King and his wife Janet Abbott-King were out fossil hunting. What they found that day turned out to be the fossilized remains of a sub-species of Tyrannosaurus Rex. The finding of this sub-species, identified as *Appalachiosaurus Montgomeryiensis* (pronounced APA-lay-CHEE-o-SAW-rus, which means "Appalachian Lizard"), excited archeologists and paleontologists from all over the world. The Kings only found 40 percent of the skeleton, but it's the most complete skeleton of its kind in the world. The rest of the skeleton was created out of artificial materials.

Alabama has its share of dinosaur fossils like this one. Photo courtesy Michael Ilacqua.

This enormous fossil is now part of a larger exhibit called "Dinosaurs of Alabama" and is on permanent display at the McWane Science Center in Birmingham. It is the first *Appalachiosaurus* to be exhibited anywhere in the world!

DID YOU KNOW? ALABAMA HAS ITS OWN STONEHENGE AND JURASSIC PARK!

In the coastal town of Elberta, you can find a replica of England's Stonehenge—locals call it "Bamahenge." It's near Barbour Marina, and it's in the woods. Located in the same area, you can see replicas of dinosaurs, and they look quite lifelike, there in the forest. The dinosaur replicas were featured in a Mercedez-Benz commercial in 2018. You can see the dinosaurs and Bamahenge for free!

THIS IS ONE MAJOR STAR THAT FELL ON ALABAMA!

The story of when the stars fell on Alabama can be found in Chapter 1, but long before that meteor shower—approximately 81.5 million years prior—the place that is now the city of Wetumpka was the site of one large meteor that crashed to earth. I caught up with Merilee Tankersley, President of the Wetumpka Crater Commission, to get the story.

Tankersley told me that the people of Wetumpka knew the asteroid had struck Earth back in prehistoric days but didn't know for certain how long ago that had happened until Dr. David King, Jr., a geologist at Auburn University, took a core sample. "That was back in 1998," she said, "and there was so much iridium in the core sample that it proved the crater was made by a meteor." She explained that iridium is commonly found in meteors but is rare in Earth samples. She said the core sample also told how long ago the meteor made impact: 81.5 million years ago.

The website: www.wetumpkaimpactcratercommission.org, has on its homepage this statement: "Scientists estimate that the energy released by the Wetumpka impact was over 175,000 times the

This is a view of the Wetumpka Impact Crater. Photo courtesy of Barry Chrietzberg, Chrietzberg Photography

energy of the nuclear bomb detonated at Hiroshima, Japan, in 1945."

The eight-member Impact Crater Commission gives tours of the crater site (which, Tankersley said, is five miles in diameter). The site is on private property—approximately 3,000 people live in the area—but the tours are offered during one weekend in either January, February or March. "People can see signs we just put up in 2018, directing them to sites within the crater," she said, "but during the rest of the year, it's too difficult, due to dense foliage, for them to really make out what they're seeing." Thus, the winter-weekend tours. "The commission people do give regular school tours," Tankersley added.

In addition, the city of Wetumpka has a room at the Wetumpka Administration Building especially dedicated to the impact event. The room holds a display of photographs by local celebrity photographer Barry Chietzberg and artwork by Kelly Fitzpatrick (in the Kelly Fitzpatrick Memorial Gallery) which tells the story of the meteor. The crater can be found just off Highway 231 outside Wetumpka itself. You can also access Dr. King's writings, both technical and non-technical, about the crater and the geology in and around the area by going to www.Auburn.edu.

FORT TOULOUSE: ANOTHER WETUMPKA EXPERIENCE

Fort Toulouse is an old fort located in what is now the city of Wetumpka; the fort was first established by the French in 1717. This lovely 180-acre park is actually home to not one but two forts: Fort Toulouse and Fort Jackson. This historically- and archeologically-significant park was added to the National Register of Historic Places in 1966 and was acquired by the Alabama Historical Commission in the 1980s. But there's more to see here than just forts: here you will find a 39-site RV campground which borders the Coosa River. You can also bird-watch (it's a big place for "birders"), and check out the Mississippian Indian Mound.

It seems there's nearly always some event either being planned or carried out here. Every November, beginning the first Wednesday of that month, the Alabama Historical Commission and the "Friends of the Forts" host "Alabama Frontier Days," which is their largest event of the year (they have nearly 200 re-enactors!). Re-enactors range from soldiers in period uniform to Creek re-enactors and dancers, to bag-pipe players, to weavers, blacksmiths and more. Archeologist Dr. Craig Sheldon, who is also a re-enactor, told me that this event is the largest re-enacting event in the entire Southeastern United States.

Site Director Ove Jensen added, "Frontier Days is the largest education-based historical event in the state, hosting more than 10,000 visitors over a four-day period."

DID YOU KNOW?

The state of Alabama has its very own official state fossil. Its scientific name is *Basilosaurus cetoides,* a specimen of which currently hangs in the atrium of The University of Alabama's Museum of Natural History in Tuscaloosa.

MOUNDVILLE ARCHEOLOGICAL PARK

Located in Moundville (just outside of Tuscaloosa), Moundville Archeological Park is one fascinating place to spend a day (or more). It is one of the two most significant sites of Mississippian-era indigenous culture in the U.S. (the other is in Illinois). This is an expansive park of 26 mounds surrounding a large plaza. If you go inside to the park's Jones Archeological Museum, you can see all kinds of artifacts and exhibits relating to these rather sophisticated and organized people and discover how they lived during the Mississippian era (roughly between 1000 to 1520). There is also an exhibit about the Moundville people in the Alabama Department of Archives and History in Montgomery.

T. Jensen Lacey

Q. & A.

Q. What now-famous archeological park welcomes summer campers to dig for fossils and other items of historical interest?

A. Old Cahawba. The camp is held in June of every year, and there are other archeologically related events as well.

Amazing Alabama

DID YOU KNOW

In Marion County you can visit Natural Bridge, which is said to have been used for Native American people of more than 10,000 years ago for shelter. It's the longest natural bridge east of the Rocky Mountains.

Natural Bridge was used for a shelter during prehistoric times. Photo courtesy of Jim and Barbara Denton, owners, Natural Bridge Park.

T. Jensen Lacey

CHAPTER 4

FAMOUS ALABAMIANS IN EDUCATION, ART, SCIENCE AND LITERATURE

ALABAMA'S MOST PROLIFIC NOVELIST

Shortly following the Korean War, a former military correspondent moved to Ozark and then Fairhope, Alabama, and began writing, in his words, "anything that could be published and sold." Convinced that he had to "just keep writing," William E. Butterworth III first produced (under his name as well as a dozen pen names), books on everything from grand prix racing, to tank driving, juvenile delinquents, and even a few romance novels.

Over the years he has enjoyed tremendous success, writing the popular M*A*S*H series and, under the pen name of W.E.B. Griffin, more than 55 *New York Times* bestsellers.

An afternoon with the two Butterworth authors: Bill Butterworth III (in the middle) and son Billy Butterworth IV (to his left). Photo by Eric Lacey.

His WWII military genre fiction series kept him in the top range of the *New York Times* bestseller list for decades.

Lately, his Cold War spy novels have brought new generations of fans to his succinct style and compelling dialogues. Since 2007, the 20 bestsellers he has co-authored with his son (William E. Butterworth IV), who was born in Dothan and raised on Mobile Bay, have carried on this literary tradition. These include thrillers about World War II and Cold War spies, present-day counterintelligence in the worldwide fight against terrorism, and gritty, behind-the-scenes tales of the Philadelphia Police Department.

For perhaps four decades, my friend Bill Butterworth has encouraged me as an author to pursue my literary ambitions. In December of 2018, I asked him how many books he has published. "Well over 200," he said. William E. Butterworth III and son William E. Butterworth IV are Alabama's most prolific novelists!

HELEN KELLER: AN ENLIGHTENED LIFE

Little Helen Adams Keller, born in Tuscumbia in 1880, was a joy to her parents, Captain Arthur and Kate Keller. Even as an infant, Helen was vivacious and precocious and said her first words at an early age. At the age of 19 months, however, tragedy struck: baby Helen came down with a high fever (some historians say it was caused by scarlet fever, others, meningitis). When the fever finally subsided, Helen was left deaf and blind.

The Kellers were grief-stricken by their child's sudden inability to communicate, and found a teacher for her. This teacher was Annie Sullivan, a former student at the Perkins Institute for the Blind in South Boston. Sullivan herself had, by her own admission, "nowhere else to go," and took the position within the Keller household. At this time, Helen was just shy of her seventh birthday.

Annie Sullivan at first was frustrated at every turn in her efforts to get Helen to understand that Sullivan's finger-motions in Helen's palm meant something. Also, Helen possessed a quick and fierce temper. Sullivan realized that part of her struggles with Helen had to do with the fact that they were under the same roof as Helen's parents, and that as long as this situation continued Sullivan would not make any progress with Helen.

Sullivan asked the Kellers if she and Helen could stay in a little cottage at the edge of the property, and after some misgivings, they agreed. Sullivan spent two weeks, spelling words into Helen's open palm. Helen would spell the finger-spellings back to her teacher, but she still didn't understand that the word meant the thing.

After the two weeks were up, Annie Sullivan and Helen returned to Ivy Green, and Helen, to her tempestuous ways. At dinner that night, she threw a tantrum, and dashed a pitcher of water on her teacher. Having a temper herself, Sullivan took Helen from the table to make Helen refill the water-pitcher.

Once at the water pump outside, Sullivan did what she had always done, spelling "w-a-t-e-r" into Helen's open palm. As the water poured over her hand, Sullivan kept spelling the word. Suddenly, Helen understood: she became transfixed as the realization of the word's meaning struck her. Immediately, she began running around the yard, touching the ground, a tree and other objects, imperiously asking for the word for each. By the end of the day, Helen had learned 30 new words. More importantly, she knew what the words meant—that everything had a name.

Helen's world suddenly opened up. With Annie Sullivan at her side, Helen first attended the Perkins Institute for the Blind, and finally graduated with honors from Radcliffe College. As time passed and her reputation grew, she met many famous people, including Mark Twain, Alexander Graham Bell, and Presidents Grover Cleveland, John F. Kennedy and Lyndon B. Johnson. A resolute spokeswoman for the disabled, Keller's life was in part what inspired the Americans with Disabilities Act's passage. She wrote 12 books and several articles for newspapers and magazines. She was awarded the Presidential Medal of Freedom in 1964 (under Lyndon B. Johnson) and was elected to the National Women's Hall of Fame in 1965. She died in 1968, and was buried at the National Cathedral in Washington, D.C. (Annie Sullivan preceded her in death in 1936).

Today, you can visit the Helen Keller Museum in Tuscumbia, where the water pump drama is acted out every year. You can also see displays about her life and achievements in other places: at the Alabama Women's Hall of Fame (in Bean Hall, Judson College, in Marion) into which she was posthumously inducted in 1971, and the Alabama Writers Hall of Fame (in Tuscaloosa), which inducted her in 2015. Playwright William Gibson wrote a play, *The Miracle Worker*, which was made into two movies (one which came out in 1962, and one released by Disney in 2000). In 2018, the play was enacted as part of The Shakespeare Festival in Montgomery, Alabama.

You can tour Helen Keller's birthplace, Ivy Green, in Tuscumbia. The town hosts the Helen Keller Festival every June. The hospital in Tuscumbia is named after Helen Keller in honor of her achievements. There are also two statues in honor of Helen Keller: one in the Rotunda in Washington, D.C., and one in the Capitol Visitor Center in Montgomery.

F. SCOTT AND ZELDA FITZGERALD: THE AFFAIR BEHIND *GATSBY* AND *TENDER IS THE NIGHT*

F. Scott Fitzgerald is perhaps best known for his novel, *The Great Gatsby*, and his other and almost as popular *Tender is the Night*. A recent book, written by Kendall Taylor, titled *The Gatsby Affair: Scott, Zelda and the Betrayal that Shaped an American Classic*, points to an affair that the author says was behind the inspiration for both works.

F. Scott Fitzgerald first met Montgomery socialite Zelda Sayre when he was stationed in nearby Camp Sheridan at the outbreak of World War I. It was well after the war was over in the summer of 1924, when Scott was feverishly writing his *Gatsby* novel. He, Zelda (whom he married in 1920) and their little daughter "Scottie" (Frances Scott) were living in a villa in France on the French Riviera, where Scott devoted every minute of the day to working on the novel. Meanwhile, Zelda, left to her own devices, and with a nanny to care for their little girl, was alone and probably lonely. In her book, Taylor describes the appearance of a handsome, 25-year-old French lieutenant named Edouard Jozan, who came into Zelda's life at this point. Taylor writes about their affair, which may have been the affair described in the *Gatsby* novel between Jay Gatsby (as Jozan) and Daisy (as Zelda).

Although their affair was a brief one, it did serve to fuel fodder for the *Gatsby* novel. Taylor writes that Zelda did ask Scott for a divorce, but Jozan didn't have a serious relationship in mind and ended the affair. The result was that Zelda attempted suicide by taking an overdose of sleeping pills. For approximately 20 years afterward, she was in mental institutions. F. Scott Fitzgerald died at the age of 44 of heart failure; Zelda would outlive him by four more years, dying in a fire in the mental institution in North Carolina. Scott didn't live long enough to see his works rise to popularity, with *Gatsby* posthumously being hailed as one of the greatest American novels of the 20th century.

Today, you can see more about their lives at the F. Scott and Zelda Fitzgerald Museum in Montgomery (on Felder Avenue). There are exhibits relating to Zelda's writing as well as her husband's, and you can see how a 1920s-era home would have been furnished. You can even stay overnight at the home that used to be known as the residence of, in Taylor's words, "the golden couple of the Jazz Age."

DID YOU KNOW?

Besides being author of the poem, "Alabama," which became the state song, Julia Tutwiler was also known for being an advocate for prisoners' rights and women's education. Born Julia Strudwick Tutwiler in 1841, she received a classical education before teaching in Tuscaloosa and Hale counties. Her tireless efforts to promote equal educational rights for women led to The University of Alabama admitting female students in 1892. The universities of Montevallo and West Alabama stemmed from her pro-education efforts.

Her efforts to improve prison conditions throughout the state earned her the moniker, "Angel of the Stockade," resulted in a new position created for State Prison Inspector, and helped build the Tutwiler Prison for Women in Wetumpka. She currently has two exhibits about her life and accomplishments: one in the Alabama Hall of Fame and another in the Alabama Women's Hall of Fame. At Livingston University, there is a building named after her: the Julia Tutwiler Hall is part of the State Teachers' College there.

GUESS WHO?

This Birmingham native wrote the novel *Addie Pray* (1971), which became the hit movie "Paper Moon," starring Ryan O'Neal and his daughter Tatum O'Neal. His previous novel, *Stars in My Crown*, written in 1947, was inspired by an 1897 hymn of the same name. Both of these novels reflected the author's years of growing up in Alabama in the 1920s and 1930s. His early jobs included working for the Birmingham *Post* and the Dothan *Eagle*, before signing up to serve in the Army Air Corps during World War II.

After returning from the war, this author began writing a series of short stories about, in the words of Alabama Heritage writer Bert Hitchcock, "a Bible-tapping, two-pistol-toting Methodist minister named Josiah David Gray." Given the same name as the hymn, the anthology *Stars in My Crown* was published in 1847 (William Morrow and Company), and Metro-Goldwyn Mayer released a film version in 1950. The film, set in the fictitious town of Walesburg, was not said to be set in Alabama per se, but references to such places as Jones Valley and the Black Warrior River made it an unmistakably Alabama story. Actor Joel McCrea starred in the role of Parson Gray, and the movie was an instant hit.

After this success, this writer lived the life of a celebrity before writing for the New York *Daily News*. Then in the years 1949 to 1957 he served as a foreign correspondent for *Time* and *Life*. During these years he traveled to India, France, England and the U.S.S.R. It was in the late 1960s that the author penned the novel *Addie Pray*. In 1974, he was awarded the Alabama Author Award for novel. He died in 1976. Who is he? Joe David Brown.

KATHRYN TUCKER WINDHAM, AN INTERLOPER AND A STORY OF AN OLD PINE CASKET

Many people plan for their eventual demise, but for brilliant storyteller and author Kathryn Tucker Windham, she was a bit ahead of the proverbial curve. Selma native Kathryn Tucker was born in 1918 and, growing up in a large family in Thomasville, was often entertained by her banker-father, James Wilson Tucker, who was fond of making up and telling stories. At the tender age of 12, Tucker began writing movie reviews for the newspaper, *The Thomasville Times*, which her cousin (Earl Tucker) owned. In addition to writing, Tucker realized, also at a young age, that she loved photography. Both talents would come to serve her well during her lifetime.

After graduating (valedictorian) from Thomasville High School and then Huntingdon College in Montgomery, Tucker began writing for *The Alabama Journal* in Montgomery in 1940, when she replaced a male writer who was going into the military. A couple of years later, Tucker moved to Birmingham, where she edited articles for the *Birmingham News* and also served as a photojournalist.

She met and married Amasa Benjamin Windham, a World War II veteran, as well as fellow journalist and editor. They had three children together. When the Windham family moved back to Selma, the woman now known as Kathryn Tucker Windham wrote for *Progressive Farmer* magazine as well as a variety of Alabama-based newspapers.

Windham wrote a column, "Around Our House," from 1950 to 1966, which was locally syndicated. When in 1956 her husband Amasa died, Windham worked as a staff writer for *The Selma Times-Journal* until 1973. It was during these years in Selma that Windham began writing and publishing her many books. The first, *Treasured Alabama Recipes*, was a staple in many Alabama kitchens from the beginning. She also began writing a series of books on ghosts (my favorite is *Thirteen Alabama Ghosts and Jeffrey*) and a book on Alabama folklore, *Alabama: One Big Front Porch*. Windham also wrote about the Gee's Bend quilters (see more about them in Chapter 11), and wrote extensively about the quilters, their culture and their craft.

In the early 1970s, Windham began to also make a name for herself as a storyteller and was featured many times in the National Storytelling Festival in Jonesborough, Tennessee (now it has grown to such proportions that it's become the International Storytelling Festival). Listeners of all ages would sit, entranced, as Windham wove her tales.

Windham's work became more in demand as time went on. In 1998, a publication of her photographs and stories, titled *Encounters: Kathryn Tucker Windham*, was released.

And now for the story about the "interloper" and the old pine casket. As Windham entered the "golden years," she began to write about someone who had been taking up residence in her house. This "interloper" Windham referred to simply as "She." "She" would misplace things, leave work undone, and other things. For the next year or two, Windham wrote her thoughts about this "She" person, who was really Windham in her waning years. It's a bittersweet, sometimes funny, but always poignant book titled *She: The Old Woman Who Took Over My Life* (2018: New South Books, Montgomery).

Windham had a friend who had built a pine casket for her. For years, the casket sat in a shed in her backyard; she filled it with china and crystal (as extra storage) until the time came that she herself would need it. When she died in 2011, she was buried in that casket, and now lies interred in the Live Oak Cemetery in Selma.

Today, you can learn more about this great storyteller, photographer and author. One place is the Alabama Southern Community College in her childhood home of Thomasville, which is home to the Kathryn Tucker Windham Museum. There is more to learn about her and her achievements at the Alabama Women's Hall of Fame, into which Windham was posthumously inducted in 2015. Her journalistic achievements resulted in her induction (in 2015) into the Alabama Newspaper Hall of Honor, located at Auburn University.

AT THE HEART OF THE MATTER!

Did you know that the very first open-heart surgery was performed in Alabama in 1901 by Dr. Luther Leonidas Hill (1862-1946)? Dr. Hill made medical history when, in Montgomery, he performed surgery on a 13-year-old boy who was the victim of a stabbing. While the boy's heart was still beating, Dr. Hill opened the patient up, stitched the wound in the heart's left ventricle, and closed the incision. The boy returned to health and Dr. Hill to instant and international fame.

You can see a portrait of Dr. Hill hanging in the Alabama Department of Archives and History (ADAH) in Montgomery.

... AND, ON A RELATED NOTE, ONE OF THE STRANGEST MUSEUMS IN ALABAMA

One of the best medical museums I've ever visited is in the lovely coastal town of Foley. Holmes Medical Museum, at one time the first and only working hospital in Baldwin County, today still looks much like it did when it was in operation in the late 1930s. Dr. Sibley Holmes and his son, Dr. W. C. Holmes, operated the hospital for many years until in 1958 the son turned the key in the lock and retired.

Inside, you can tour the surgical room, an x-ray room, a newborn incubator and patient wings. It's virtually a step back in time. Except for maintenance and structural improvements, the hospital is much like it was in the 1930s and 40s. Many physicians find it especially fascinating to see what was then considered state-of-the-art medical tools and instruments. This is one of the strangest and most fascinating museums in all of Alabama! Docent Zana Price (seventh-generation Alabamian) told me that it is listed in Atlas Obscura as one of the top 15 strangest museums in the Yellowhammer State. I hope you'll be lucky enough, as I was, to have a knowledgeable and friendly docent such as Mr. Bill Swanson give you a tour. The museum, located at the corner of McKenzie Street and Highway 59, is open Monday through Saturday. Tours are free but donations are cheerfully accepted.

AN ACCIDENT LEADS TO AN INVENTION

Born in what is now Tennessee around 1760, George Guess (or George Gist) was the child of Wurteh, a prominent Cherokee woman, and Nathaniel Gist, a white hunter and soldier. While George was still a youngster, his father left the family, and he and his mother moved to Willstown, Alabama in what is now DeKalb County. One day, while young George was out hunting, he had an accident and was forced into a period of inactivity. During this time, he became fascinated with the marks white people made on paper. He called the paper "talking leaves" because he realized it was a way people could communicate with each other—that it was written speech.

George decided he would develop an alphabet for his Cherokee people. It took him twelve years to create the first

Native American people's alphabet, or syllabary. It consisted of 85 letters in all. According to *The Encyclopedia of Alabama* online, while George was working on the alphabet, his wife (Sally Benge, whom he married in 1815) became so angry because her husband was wrapped up in his new alphabet and therefore wasn't helping her, that she took his work-in-progress and burned it. Undeterred, he began his work again, completing it in 1821. He successfully demonstrated the effective communication of the alphabet in the Cherokee National Council gathering at Sauta (near what is Jackson County today), and within a matter of months most of the Cherokee people were literate.

George Gist, whom you now know as Sequoyah, achieved other important things in his lifetime. He fought against the Red Sticks in the Creek War of 1813-14, and after fighting in the Battle of Horseshoe Bend, was honorably discharged. He served as a delegate for the western band of Cherokees to Washington, DC. in 1827, and was one of the signers of the Act of Union that united the Eastern and Western Bands of the Cherokee Nation.

He voluntarily removed to Oklahoma during the great Indian Removal known as the "Trail of Tears." After settling in Oklahoma, he continued to teach Cherokee people their written language. In 1828, the "Eastern Band" of Cherokee (those who refused to remove to Oklahoma) were printing their own newspaper, *The Cherokee Phoenix*, which people could read in both Cherokee and English.

In addition to Sequoia National Park in California, the alphabet inventor has been honored in a number of ways. His statue is on display in Statuary Hall at the U.S. Capitol. In Alabama, a redwood tree was planted in 1961 in Sequoyah's honor at the campus of The University of Alabama in Huntsville. In 1980, the U.S. Post Office issued a postage stamp honoring the brilliant linguistic inventor. In Valley Head, Alabama, there are some privately-owned caves named Sequoyah Caverns. An artist, Charles Bird King, painted Sequoyah's portrait during his Washington trip in 1827; that painting now hangs in the Smithsonian's National Portrait Gallery in Washington, D.C.

Because of an accident which offered Sequoyah a huge block of time in which to be creative, an entire culture and language was preserved.

DID YOU KNOW?

According to an *Alabama Heritage* article in 2017 by Haley E. Aaron titled "Alabama Nightingales: World War I Nurses at Home and Abroad," the first nursing academy established in Alabama was at St. Vincent's Hospital in Birmingham in 1898. The first nursing training program for African-American women was founded at Tuskegee University in 1892. African-American nurses from Alabama proved to have an integral role in fighting the influenza epidemic that swept across the U.S. in the fall of 1918.

GEORGE WASHINGTON CARVER: DON'T EVEN THINK PEANUT BUTTER!

Until I began doing research for this book, I, like most people, was under the assumption that George Washington Carver invented peanut butter. Although he didn't invent it, he devised more than one hundred different uses for the legume!

Born into slavery in Missouri in 1864, Carver had a natural and vivacious curiosity about all things, especially anything that was plant related. His "owners" were Moses and Susan Carver. Only a week after his birth, baby George, along with his sister and mother, were kidnapped by marauders from Arkansas. Only George was ever found and returned to the Carvers. After his return to them, and then when the Civil War was over in 1865, the Carvers decided to keep George and his brother James. They taught the boys to read and write, since there was no local school that would educate African-Americans at that time.

When George was a young man, he left home and traveled to a school ten miles away that would teach African-Americans. Later he was accepted to Highland College in Kansas, that turned him down upon learning of George's race. Undaunted, he began conducting biological experiments. Finally, in 1890, Carver was accepted into Simpson College in Iowa, where he took up painting and drawing. He also began drawing sketches of plants that interested him. Eventually he enrolled at the Iowa State Agricultural College to study botany there. He was the first African-American ever to be admitted!

He not only received his Bachelor of Science degree in Iowa but also went on to get his Master's Degree, and as a graduate student, did intensive experiments in plant pathology. This passion he had developed would determine the course of the rest of his life.

In 1896, Booker T. Washington hired Carver to administer the Agricultural Department at what was then called the African-American Tuskegee Institute (Washington was president at the time). In this role, Carver developed crop rotation and diversification methods which helped farmers improve their production and ensure fertility of their soil. This especially helped those who were struggling financially, such as sharecroppers.

Bringing his lessons to farmers, Carver developed a mobile classroom called a "Jessup wagon," named after New York financier and Tuskegee donor Morris Ketchum Jessup. Carver made a huge name for himself in Alabama, and was internationally recognized for his achievements. In 1916 he was inducted as a member of the British Royal Society of the Arts. He advised Mahatma Gandhi on nutrition and agricultural matters in India. He toured the U.S., giving scientific talks and promoting agricultural innovation.

Carver became one of the most famous African-Americans of his lifetime. He also spoke out on racial inequality, speaking to white colleges in the South between 1923 and 1933. Carver's life's work improved the quality of life for many farming families not only in Alabama but in the entire U.S.

He died in 1943 and lies buried next to Booker T. Washington on the grounds of Tuskegee University. Alabama and the world continue to remember him and honor his memory in a variety of ways and places. In Austin, Texas, you will find the George Washington Carver Museum and Cultural Center. In Diamond, Missouri, you can see a monument to Carver's life and achievements—ironically, it's not only the first monument in the U.S. to honor an African-American, but it lies near the old plantation grounds where Carver had been a slave. The monument is part of a 210-acre complex and includes a cemetery, museum and nature trail.

Many schools and naval vessels bear Carver's name. Two U.S. postage stamps bearing his likeness appeared (the first one in 1948 and the second in 1998), and a 50-cent piece was made in the mid-1950s in his commemoration. In St. Louis, Missouri, you can tour the George Washington Carver Garden and statue. The garden opened in 2005.

Closer to home, in Tuskegee, you can see his and Booker T. Washington's gravesites. On Carver's tombstone is this inscription: "He could have added fortune to fame, but caring for neither, he found happiness and honor in being helpful to the world."

... AND ABOUT BOOKER T. WASHINGTON

I currently teach high school English, so when my students ask me if one person can change the world, I think of many great people who did just that, and had their roots in Alabama. Booker T. Washington was one of those people.

Born circa 1856 as Booker Taliaferro Washington in Virginia, the little baby was born into slavery. After being freed, his mother Jane took her son to join her husband, Washington Ferguson, in West Virginia. The ever-curious young boy taught himself to read and write.

Booker was educated at the Hampton Normal and Agricultural Institute, which is now known as Hampton University, and earned his degree at Wayland Seminary (which is now known as Virginia Union University).

Washington was named as the first president of the newly established Tuskegee Institute in 1881 (Tuskegee, Alabama), which was founded with the goal of higher education for African-Americans. As you know from the previous story, one of his hires was George Washington Carver.

In this role as university president, Washington became the spokesman for many who could not or were afraid to speak for themselves—African-Americans who were struggling with poverty, inequality, racism and a lack of education.

In 1895, he offered his famous Atlanta Address, and gained the support of people in black communities in the South as well as philanthropists, and educational and political leaders in the U.S.

Washington raised funds to build thousands of schools across the rural south to help young African-American people raise themselves out of poverty through education. Although he had critics who called his work the "Tuskegee machine," Washington believed that cooperation with white people who supported his cause, instead of confronting them with force, was the only way to erase racism.

He challenged laws that he thought were unfair to African-Americans and was an informal advisor to U.S. Presidents Teddy Roosevelt and William Howard Taft. He was also a prolific writer; many people were inspired by his book, *Up From Slavery*. His life's work served to help millions of people, especially disenfranchised African-Americans, to overcome many obstacles so they could achieve a level of education and success in their lives.

Today, you can tour Booker T. Washington's house at Tuskegee University; on the grounds you can also see his tombstone, which, as mentioned in the previous story, is next to George Washington Carver's grave.

Can one person change the world? I'm sure by now, you know what I think.

THE INIMITABLE HARPER LEE

"You never really understand a person until you consider things from his point of view." These immortal words come from the fictitious novel written by Harper Lee, *To Kill a Mockingbird*.

Another of her quotes is one of my personal favorites: "Real courage is when you know you're licked before you begin, but you begin anyway and see it through no matter what." Writers, especially, can relate to that one.

Born Nelle Harper Lee in Monroeville, Alabama, on April 28, 1926, she probably grew up not even aspiring to be a novelist, much less a writer who would win a Pulitzer Prize for her *Mockingbird* novel, which she wrote in 1959. Much like the character of Scout in the novel, Lee grew up as the youngest of four children, living the life of a carefree tomboy in a small town (like fictitious Maycomb, the setting of the novel). Her father was a lawyer, who was likely the model for the novel's lawyer, Atticus Finch. Many scenes from *Mockingbird* might have been reminiscent of Lee's own childhood. For example, one of her childhood friends was Truman Capote (originally known as Truman Persons). In the novel, Scout defends her younger brother Jem; in actuality, as a child, Lee defended the young Truman from being bullied, and local residents say that the character Dill is based upon that of Capote.

After graduating high school, Lee attended the all-female Huntingdon College in Montgomery. When she transferred to The University of Alabama in Tuscaloosa, Lee served for a time as editor of the school's newspaper, *The Rammer Jammer*. While still a junior in college, Lee was accepted into The University of Alabama's law school, which obliged her to step down from her editorial position so she would have time to devote to her studies.

After a while, Lee began to realize her true calling was not the law, but literature. She dropped out of law school after the first semester and moved to New York City. It was in the "city that never sleeps" she reconnected with Truman Capote, who was fast becoming the celebrity of the literary salons. She also became friends with a Broadway composer, Michael

Martin Brown, along with his wife, Joy. This friendship would have an impact on the rest of Lee's life.

In Christmas of 1956, the Browns offered Harper Lee a great gift: enough money to allow her to quit her day job and write full time. The Browns also helped Lee secure an agent and publisher (the latter being the J. B. Lippincott Company). *To Kill a Mockingbird* was published in 1960, an immediate and smashing success. It was in 1960 that Lee won the coveted Pulitzer Prize for Literature for her novel.

It was some time after she finished the novel that she helped Capote write an article for *The New Yorker magazine*. This article would come to be developed into Capote's nonfiction masterpiece, *In Cold Blood*.

In 2007, President George Bush awarded Lee the Presidential Medal of Freedom. Many Monroeville residents have told me that, in her twilight years, Lee became more reticent. However, she wasn't finished with being in the limelight. In 2015, her second novel, *Go Set a Watchman*, was released.

Although Harper Lee died in 2016, she lives on through her immortal *Mockingbird*, and today, you can go see performances of the play based on Lee's novel. It is performed every April and May in Monroeville. The play is performed in two parts: one part is in the iconic Monroeville Courthouse, and the first act is in the open-air amphitheater behind the courthouse itself.

You can also pay your respects where Lee lies interred in the family plot at the First United Methodist Church in Monroeville. When you walk around the town, you can see the red brick building where Harper Lee's father practiced law.

Throughout Monroeville, you can see birdhouses that are part of the so-called "Birdhouse Trail." Each of these wooden birdhouses, handmade by locals, depicts scenes from *Mockingbird*.

At the Old Courthouse Museum, you can see many exhibits and photographs of Harper Lee with Truman Capote. Outside the museum, you and your family can have your pictures taken next to a sculpture depicting Scout, Dill and Jem (the sculpture was created by Birmingham artist Branko Medenica and installed in 2014). In 1997, the Alabama Bar Association erected a statue of the character Atticus Finch with an inscription that reads in part, "The legal profession has in Atticus Finch, a lawyer-hero who knows how to use power and advantage for moral purposes, and who is willing to stand alone as the conscience of the community."

Lee's work has inspired other people to do their own re-creations of *Mockingbird*. The dramatic adaptation of Lee's work, written by Horton Foote, was made into a movie starring Gregory Peck as Atticus Finch. In 2018, *Mockingbird* came to Broadway, with a dramatized version of the novel written by Aaron Sorkin.

The state of Alabama has published the pamphlet, "Alabama's Civil Rights Trail," which states, "The most famous fictional town in the Civil Rights Movement was probably Maycomb."

In 2017, Alabama author and brilliant historian Wayne Flynt wrote a tribute to Lee. Titled "Mockingbird Songs: My Friendship with Harper Lee," it covers years of the exchange of letters between the two writers. Another Monroeville native, Marja Mills, wrote a book, *The Mockingbird Next Door: Life with*

Harper Lee. Lee's work continues to resonate with people from all over the world.

"LIKE A TURTLE ON ITS BACK": THE LIFE OF TRUMAN CAPOTE

I remember being a student at The University of Alabama in the early 1980s when Truman Capote came to speak. He held the large audience captive with his flamboyant form of dress and unusual personality. His early years were troubled by his parents' divorce, his mother's desertion, and his many moves. Although he was born in New Orleans, he was sent to live with relatives in Monroeville when he was only four. He told one interviewer, "When I was young, I felt out of place … like a turtle on its back."

But all these experiences gave him fodder for some of his best writing. The short story "A Christmas Memory" is a tale told of his holiday experiences while living with an older cousin (Nanny Rumbley Faulk, whom he nicknamed "Sook"), along with a handful of other relatives. Around 1935, he wrote a short story, "Old Mrs. Busybody," for a children's writing contest sponsored by the newspaper *The Mobile Press-Register*. This short story earned him recognition from The Scholastic Art and Writing Awards in 1936.

He moved with his mother and her new husband, Joseph Capote, to New York. Truman's new stepfather adopted him and renamed him Truman Garcia Capote. Not too long after this, Truman's stepfather was convicted of embezzlement, and the young budding writer once again was moved from place to place.

One of his first jobs after graduating high school was serving as a copy boy for *The New Yorker*. When he angered poet Robert Frost, Capote was fired; he once again moved back to Alabama. One of his earliest stories was "Miriam," which he published in 1945; it caught the attention of an editor at Random House Publishing. Four years later, he wrote the novel *Other Voices, Other Rooms* under contract with the publishing giant. *Voices* made *The New York Times* bestseller list, selling more than 26,000 copies in nine weeks.

He was published widely in some major magazines of the time, including *The Atlantic* and *Mademoiselle*. In the 1950s, Capote took on plays and films, and even toured the Soviet Union with the cast of "Porgy and Bess." In 1958, his fame continued with *Breakfast at Tiffany's*; playwright Norman Mailer hailed Capote as "the most perfect writer of my generation."

What really got America's attention was the "nonfiction novel" (his term) *In Cold Blood*, which was about his journalistic investigation into the murders of a Kansas farm family in their home (perhaps because of his investigation, the two killers were caught some months after the murders, and executed several years later). Working alongside his good friend Harper Lee, Capote took four years to finish that book. He spent the next few years appearing on television talk shows. Some other investigative journalists criticized Capote's "nonfiction novel," saying there were quite a few deviations from the truth of what happened. In any case, *In Cold Blood* was Capote's last major work.

In the 1960s, Capote became the darling of the social elite; the high point of this hobnobbing was in 1966, when he hosted an elaborate masked ball in the Plaza Hotel's Grand Ballroom in New York City in honor of *Washington Post* publisher Katharine Graham. He snubbed some Southern authors such as Carson McCullers, instead inviting the upper echelons of New York society.

Capote had had a long-standing relationship with partner Jack Dunphy since the 1950s; they became estranged as Capote's drinking bouts became more frequent and intense. In 1973, Capote befriended John O'Shea, a banker from Long Island. The two developed a romantic and business relationship, with O'Shea managing Capote's interests. Friends were concerned when they learned that O'Shea seemed to be taking control of Capote's fortunes. Capote began writing a tell-all novel about his jet-setting experiences. This further estranged his elitist friends, as they worried that Capote would publish sordid details about them. The backlash Capote received after publishing the work seemed to drive him further into drinking and drug use.

Capote did publish a few more short pieces, including one about his friendship with artist Andy Warhol, but by this time he had made many enemies. When he died in 1984 of liver disease and multiple drug intoxication, his nemesis Gore Vidal called it "a wise career move."

Today, you can see more about Capote's life at the Old Courthouse Museum in Monroeville, which has a permanent exhibit covering his life with his relatives in this small Alabama town, with photos, letters and memorabilia. One of my favorite items there is Capote's baby blanket, that his relative nicknamed "Sook" made for him, and which he was rarely without, even as an adult. As you walk the town of Monroeville, you can read a historical marker about the author near his old home-place on South Alabama Avenue (the home burned some years back).

MONROEVILLE WRITERS' TRAIL

The town of Monroeville is so thick with writers for such a small town, that AL.com writer Kelly Kazek ran a column all about "Monroeville Writers' Trail." She wrote that Monroeville is "correctly billed as the Literary Capital of Alabama." Besides Truman Capote and the one locals called "Miss Nelle," Nelle Harper Lee, my friend and fellow author Mark Childress (best known for his novel, *Crazy in Alabama*, which was made into a moving starring Melanie Griffith), also hails from Monroeville (one of Mark's books, *V for Victor*, was chosen to be part of the Alabama Bicentennial reading list). Pulitzer Prize-winning columnist Cynthia Tucker is another Monroeville native, as is Rheta Grimsley Johnson, who has been a syndicated columnist and author of *Enchanted Evening and the Second Coming* (among other works).

FORREST GUMP: A CULTURAL ICON

It was in 1994 that I first met fellow author Winston Groom at a writers' conference; I was impressed with his humility and approachability. Groom's book, *Forrest Gump*, was initially not a hit. What made it a cultural icon was the screenwriter. The phrases "Stupid is as stupid does" and "Life's like a box of chocolates" were not in the text, and the movie was very loosely based on the book as far as plot and character (for example, Gump himself was much more innocent and naïve in the movie).

When the movie was released, though, it sparked an interest in the book, and Groom's novel sold nearly two million copies shortly afterward. Groom capitalized on the popularity of *Forrest Gump*, with other related works (such as two cookbooks), but to me his best writing has been in the realm of historical nonfiction. His first such project, *Shrouds of Glory: From Atlanta to Nashville; The Last Great Campaign of the Civil War*, was released in 1994 (and is among my favorite of his). His latest historical fiction came out in 2015. Titled *The*

Aviators: Eddie Rickenbacker, Jimmy Doolittle, Charles Lindbergh, and the Epic Age of Flight, had a 4 ½ star rating on Amazon.

In 2011 Groom was recipient of the Harper Lee Award for Alabama's Distinguished Writer of the Year. He was inducted into the Alabama Writers' Hall of Fame in 2018 (about time, I say). A long-time Mobile resident, he currently lives in Point Clear.

"FATHER GOOSE" OF ALABAMA

It was approximately 30 years ago that I first met author Charles Ghigna at a poetry workshop. In 2017, Ghigna penned a book especially for the children of Alabama. Titled *Alabama: My Home Sweet Home*, it was chosen by the Alabama Chapter of the American Academy of Pediatrics for its 2019 "Reach Out and Read" program for children.

All pediatricians in the Academy are giving their young patients a free copy of Ghigna's book during the Bicentennial year of 2019.

I caught up with Charles Ghigna in May of 2018, while doing research for this bicentennial book. He very graciously agreed to be interviewed about his unique book, and explained what led him to write it.

"This book represented Alabama at The National Book Festival in Washington, D.C., Sept 21, 2018," he explained. "It was commissioned by the Alabama Bicentennial Commission for me to write, and it took about 6 months for me to finish. Alabama artist Michelle Hazelwood Hyde did the illustrations."

He also told me that the Alabama Literacy Association chose his book for the first Annual Statewide Read Alabama Event, held on November 15, 2018.

Make sure to get a copy of this very important and commemorative children's book! Check with your local bookstore—or ask your pediatrician.

ARGH! HE'S ALL ABOUT PIRATES!

My dear friend, author and entrepreneur John O'Melveny Woods has long had a fascination for all things related to pirates and pirate treasure. For example, one of his books, *Return to Treasure Island*, is a sequel to Robert Louis Stevenson's novel, *Treasure Island*. His sequel won the Silver Medal Book of the Year from the Independent Book Publishers' Association. Another (nonfiction) book of his, *The Jesse James Secret: Codes, Cover-ups and Hidden Treasure*, was made into a show which first aired on The History Channel.

This California native came to his senses some years back, moved to Fairhope, Alabama and married his long-time sweetheart (Judy Bishop Woods). He continues to write, create and be in films and documentaries. You never know what's next for this extraordinary author.

HARRIET OUTLAW: STORYTELLER EXTRAORDINAIRE

Perhaps one of the best contemporary storytellers in Alabama would be my friend and fellow author Harriet Outlaw. Her best stories (in my opinion) are her ghost stories (my story of "The Girl with the Pearl Necklace" in chapter 15 was inspired by hers). She has been a columnist of all things Alabama, especially Baldwin County, and her (so far) most popular book is *Haunted Baldwin County*.

JOE FORMICHELLA AND SUZANNE HUDSON: ONE DYNAMIC DUO

I first met Joe Formichella when he was signing copies of his nonfiction book, *Here's to You, Jackie Robinson*, some years ago. Although most of what he has written is nonfiction, his two novels, *Waffle House Rules* and *The Wreck of the Twilight Limited* have become inimitable Southern classics. He writes from his coastal home on Waterhole Branch, which he shares with wife Suzanne Hudson, who is herself an author.

AN AWARD-WINNING NOVELIST

Alabama author Judith Richards currently has not one but two novels, *Summer Lightning* and *Too Blue to Fly*, both of which earned her the Alabama Library Association Award. She was married to the late author C. Terry Cline, author of *Damon* (which was made into the hit occult movie, "The Omen") and other works. Cline died in May of 2013.

ANDY ANDREWS: CHANGING LIVES ONE BOOK AT A TIME

Andy Andrews is a New York Times Bestselling author, motivational speaker, and an inspiration to tens of thousands of devoted fans. You only have to hear this energetic and insightful man speak one time to "get it." He had me hooked when I read his inspiring novel, *The Traveler's Gift*. When he slows down enough to "light," the ubiquitous Andrews makes his home in the coastal town of Orange Beach.

HE WAS WHAT ALL THE "BUZZ" WAS ABOUT: DR. WILLIAM C. GORGAS

It was in the late 1800s when Toulminville-born visionary physician William Crawford Gorgas contracted a deadly disease: the dreaded yellow fever. A highly contagious disease, it is carried by mosquitoes, something no one knew back then. The illness is characterized by sudden onset and renders its victims prostrate, with high fever, headache, jaundice, and sometimes hemorrhaging. Most of its victims died.

But Dr. Gorgas didn't die. He was early in his army career, young and quite healthy. After his recovery, he began to study the disease that had almost killed him. He conducted experiments on how mosquitoes might transmit yellow fever to humans. He also began researching ways to prevent the contraction of the disease. He conducted his research and experiments when he was sent to Fort Brown, Texas, after being appointed to the U.S. Army Medical Corps in 1880. When Dr. Walter Reed announced his discovery that yellow fever was, indeed, transmitted by disease-carrying mosquitoes, Dr. Gorgas knew that his suspicions were correct. In 1898 he was sent to U.S.-occupied Cuba to begin sanitation measures to eradicate yellow fever there.

He set to work, getting rid of mosquito-breeding spots at the camp in Havana (Siboney) and was so successful in eradicating the disease from that city that he was suddenly famous in international medical circles. In 1904, when construction began on the Panama Canal, Dr. Gorgas was sent there to head up sanitation and malaria prevention measures. History will forever record him as making completion of the Panama Canal possible by keeping the workers healthy and able. He later achieved similar results in Ecuador. He was named U.S. Surgeon General in 1914.

Today, you can tour Gorgas House, named for the Gorgas family who occupied the dwelling from 1879-1953. It was constructed on The University of Alabama campus in Tuscaloosa. It is the oldest structure built on The University of Alabama campus when it was built in 1829. The house, which was added to the National Register of Historic Places in 1971, is open for tours and events.

In 2014, the Panama Canal celebrated its centennial anniversary of its opening. In Tuscaloosa, The Gorgas House Museum celebrated the research and work of Dr. William Crawford Gorgas with a special exhibit during that year. Today, when you visit Gorgas House, you can see many memorabilia and artifacts of his and other family members.

And now you know the irony of it all: had it not been for this doctor becoming deathly ill with a mosquito-borne disease, we might never have seen the eradication of yellow fever and malaria—and the Panama Canal might never have existed!

DID YOU KNOW?

In addition to Dr. Gorgas's contribution toward eradicating malaria and yellow fever so the Panama Canal could be constructed, another Alabama native had a huge hand in its construction. General William L. Sibert, a native of Gadsden, was in charge of supervising the building of some of the locks of the canal (called Gatun Locks because of their location). Later, as chief engineer for the Alabama State Docks Commission, he planned the Port of Mobile's construction.

DON'T MONKEY AROUND! THE STORY ABOUT "MISS BAKER"

The U.S. Space and Rocket Center in Huntsville has on its grounds a rather unusual memorial. It's a monument commemorating one of the first (of two) animals launched into space and recovered alive. Miss Baker, a squirrel monkey, was born in 1957. She and a rhesus monkey named Able took their experimental flight in 1959. After the successful mission, Miss Baker was treated as a celebrity, and thousands of visitors came to see her (Able was not so fortunate—four days after the flight, she died of complications from surgery to remove some electrodes scientists had implanted).

Miss Baker went on to live a long life enjoying celebrity status in Huntsville. She died of kidney failure in 1984. Today, you can pay your respects by visiting her memorial monument, which is at the entrance to the Space and Rocket Center. Many visitors, including Space Camp attendees, often leave a banana or two as a token of their esteem.

Q & A

Q. Bellingrath Gardens and Home possesses the world's largest display of porcelain sculptures created by what sculptor?

A. Edward Marshall Boehm.

Q. The Gulf States Paper Corporation in Tuscaloosa is home to what collection of American art?

A. The Jack Warner collection. It's open to the public and is one astounding collection.

Q. What community is named in honor of a novel by Augusta Evans Wilson?

A. Saint Elmo.

Q. In what present-day town was the first recorded school built in 1799?

A. Tensaw.

Q. The great educator Dr. Clarence William Daugette, who for 43 years was president of Jacksonville State University, was born in what community?

A. Bell's Landing, in Monroe County.

Q. What informal concerts are held every July by Montgomery's Alabama Shakespeare Festival?

A. Coffee Concerts.

Q. What museum in Alabama features bronzes by painter and sculptor Frederic Remington?

A. Birmingham Museum of Art.

Q. What Alabama performing arts center is home to one of the five major Shakespeare troupes in the United States?

A. It's in Montgomery, called The Carolyn Blount Theatre and Wynton M. Blount Cultural Park.

Q. What Tuskegee author and student became famous for his novel *The Invisible Man*?

A. Ralph Waldo Ellison.

Q. In what town sits the house that is the focal point of the novel, *Locust Hill*?

A. Tuscumbia.

Q. Where is a large, 120-foot by 6-foot mural which depicts a Coosa Indian Chief greeting Spanish conquistador Hernando de Soto?

A. Childersburg.

Q. Similar to Thoreau's experiences he recounted in his work *On Walden Pond*, a poet named Sidney Lanier came from Georgia and lived in a tent for nearly a year. Near what community did this visionary poet live this way?

A. Verbena.

Q. What museum highlights the artwork of Zelda Fitzgerald?

A. Montgomery's Museum of Fine Arts.

Q. The Kennedy-Douglas Center for the Arts serves what city in Alabama?

A. Florence.

Q. Andre Penigaut is credited with being Alabama's first what?

A. First literary figure. He wrote vivid accounts of the explorations of today's Mississippi Gulf Coast, present-day Mobile, and Louisiana.

Q. With what French brothers did Penigaut explore this area?

A. Pierre Le Moyne, Sieur d'Iberville and Jean Baptiste Le Moyne d'Bienville. Bienville Square in Mobile is named after the latter brother.

Q. What prominent historian wrote the four-volume *History of Alabama* and *Dictionary of Alabama Biography* in 1921?

A. Thomas McAdory Owen. He also founded the Alabama Department of Archives and History, in 1901.

Q. Who wrote the lyrics to the Alabama state song?

A. Julia S. Tutwiler initially wrote "Alabama" as a poem.

Q. What was the name of Alabama's first newspaper?

A. *The Mobile Centinel*.

Q. Who was the first African-American to earn literary recognition in Alabama?

A. Booker T. Washington.

Q. Who was the first Alabama author to receive international recognition as a literary figure, and as such, was appointed by Alabama governor John Winston as the state's commissioner to the Paris Exposition in 1855?

A. Mobile native Octavia Walton LeVert.

Q. Birmingham's Gail Godwin penned what collection of short stories published in 1976?

A. *Dream Children*.

Q. Established in 1930, what is the oldest museum of fine arts in Alabama?

A. The Montgomery Museum of Fine Arts.

Q. What Italian immigrant rose to become Alabama's first noted sculptor?

A. Guiseppi Moretti. He sculpted the statue of Vulcan, in Birmingham.

Q. What is unique about the Alabama School of Fine Arts, located in Birmingham?

A. It is the only state-supported school of fine arts for grades 7 through 12 in the entire United States.

Q. Who was the first Poet Laureate of Alabama (given this honor in 1931)?

A. Samuel Minturn Peck.

Q. What was the name of the famous educator in Fairhope, who taught at the School of Organic Education during this utopian colony's early days?

A. Marietta Johnson. The School of Organic Education is still in operation, and you can tour the SOE Museum located on the campus of Coastal Alabama Community College in downtown Fairhope.

Q. Who wrote the novel *Rocket Boys*, about a young man living in coal country who meets Wernher von Braun and gets invited to come to Huntsville?

A. Homer Hickham.

Q. What Troy native played football at Auburn before creating character Nick Travers and a novel series about people living on the fringes of society?

A. Ace Atkins.

Q. What Birmingham-based author received the National Book Award in the years 1962 (for *The Moviegoer*) and in 1982 (for *The Second Coming*)?

A. Walker Percy.

Q. What other Birmingham native whose specialties are horror fiction and historical fiction, wrote *Boy's Life*, about a young man who discovers a murder victim?

A. Robert McCammon.

Q. What Auburn graduate wrote a novel, *Heartbreak Hotel*, about a socialite Southern girl who grows up during the Civil Rights era?

A. Anne Rivers Siddons.

Q. What Fairhope resident and artist created nine murals celebrating Alabama's Bicentennial?

A. Dean Mosher. Many of his works are also on display in the Smithsonian in Washington, D.C.

Here's a picture of one of nine murals created by Fairhope artist Dean Mosher. Created for the Bicentennial celebration, the murals will be a traveling exhibit in 2019. Photo of "The Wright Brothers Flying School" by the author.

CHAPTER 5
FROM AGRICULTURE TO ARCHITECTURE

DID YOU KNOW? ALABAMA HAS AN OFFICIAL STATE AGRICULTURAL MUSEUM!

In Dothan you can enjoy a tour of Landmark Park, which is a one-hundred-acre living-history museum. This park contains exhibits and offers activities that relate to the nature, heritage and culture of the part of the state known as the "Wiregrass" region. In 1992, the Alabama Legislature named

You can learn more about cotton-growing at Dothan's Agriculture Museum.

Landmark Park as the official State Agricultural Museum. The park has events and activities throughout the year, including birding workshops, seed swaps, quilting retreats, astronomy workshops (at night, of course), guided hikes through their nature trails, and a summer camp for kids. It's open 7 days a week!

WHERE AGRICULTURE MEETS TOURISM

Many states now offer a venue for tourists to learn more about agriculture, and Alabama is no exception. Throughout the state, farms, orchards and cattle ranches offer people a way to delve into what it's like to live and work there. Called "Agritourism," the state of Alabama's Department of Agriculture's website has many such farms that offer this interesting twist to tourists. For example, in the fall, farms throughout the state offer pumpkin patch tours, hayrides, and mazes for visitors to explore. See "Virtual Alabama" for websites.

PLACES WHERE YOU CAN SEE MORE ABOUT HOW EARLY SETTLERS LIVED

Alabama offers many places where you can learn more about what life was like to be an early settler and farmer. The places I've most enjoyed visiting are the Pioneer Museum of Alabama (in Troy), Baldwin County Heritage Museum (in Elberta), and Burritt on the Mountain (in Huntsville). All three take visitors back in time to see what life was like in early (and even territorial) Alabama, and all are unique. For example, the Baldwin County Heritage Museum has a working windmill, and the Pioneer Museum has a carriage-drawn jail paddock. In addition, all three offer unique events, with live demonstrations such as blacksmithing and quilting and are open for special events such as group tours and weddings. See this chapter's "Virtual Alabama" for websites.

IT WILL "BUG" YOU IF YOU DON'T SEE THIS IN ENTERPRISE, ALABAMA: THE STORY BEHIND THE BOLL WEEVIL STATUE

In the small but friendly town of Enterprise, there is a statue unique in all the world: The Boll Weevil Monument sits in the hands of a 13-foot tall statue of a female dressed in Grecian robes. People might wonder: Why would anyone, especially the people of a town that nearly died because of the economic downturn brought on by such a destructive pest, honor it in a monumental token of appreciation?

The humble boll weevil originally came to the United States from Mexico. It got its name because the female boll weevil makes her nest in the seed-capsule, or boll, of young cotton. The destructive pest first arrived in Texas around the mid-1800s, but it didn't take long for the boll weevil to find its way to the luxurious and plentiful cotton fields of Alabama. By the early 1900s, the boll weevil was striking fear in the hearts of cotton farmers all over Alabama. By 1915, it was found in the cotton fields of Enterprise, and more than half of the farmers' cotton crops were destroyed by the tiny yet voracious insect. Farmers tried various kinds of pesticides, but the boll weevil quickly developed an immunity to just about any insecticide the farmers tried. Suddenly, the entire cotton-growing South in general, and Alabama in particular, was in dire economic straits.

The people of Enterprise began to heed the writings of George Washington Carver, who extolled the virtues of the humble peanut as a crop that the boll weevil would never eat or nest in. They also took note that nearby Dothan, the "Peanut Capital of the World," seemed to be doing better than other towns, economically speaking. So, the farmers began planting and harvesting peanuts instead of cotton. By 1917, Coffee County was the top producer of peanuts in the entire U.S. In spite of the boll weevil and the Great Depression, Enterprise began to thrive once again.

Enterprise and Coffee County had the tiny boll weevil to thank for their innovation and resulting economic survival. So on December 11, 1919, in an unveiling ceremony, the city of Enterprise revealed their newest statue, which was at that time just the Grecian-looking woman with her hands upraised over her head. The boll weevil monument was placed atop her hands in 1949.

Over the years, the boll weevil and sometimes the statue of the Grecian woman, too, have been stolen or vandalized (and Alabama author Rick Bragg wrote a piece on this titled, "A Town Once Menaced By a Bug Wants it Back" in one of his columns in the *New York Times* in 1998). According to *Smithsonian Magazine*, the statue was damaged beyond repair in 1998. Another statue, a replica of the previous one, was made and now stands where the former one did.

You can see the original statue inside the Pea River Historical and Genealogical Society History Museum in downtown Enterprise. It will "bug" you forever if you don't travel to Enterprise and see the only monument in the entire world honoring an insect!

... AND THE OFFICIAL STATE AGRICULTURAL INSECT

The Queen Honey bee was given this honor by the Alabama State Legislature in 2015. This tiny honey bee is responsible in large part for the success of Alabama's agriculture (last I checked, it was a 70 BILLION DOLLAR industry).

THE CATFISH CAPITAL OF ALABAMA

In the 1980s, many farms in what is called the "Black Belt" region of Alabama (so-called because of its rich soil) were in financial trouble. Farmers were faced with rising costs and low commodity prices, so they had to come up with another way to remain farmers and stay economically viable.

Enter the humble catfish. Farmers in the Black Belt region knew that their area, with its climate and soil, would be the perfect place to raise catfish, and suddenly a new type of agriculture emerged in Alabama. Current President of Catfish Farmers of America, Greensboro-based Townsend Kyser, said that today Alabama ranks second in the nation for catfish production (surpassed only by Mississippi). Alabama produces 33 percent of all catfish consumed in the United States. Some of the catfish farms offer visitors tours. If you go, you'll have information "up to the gills" about all things catfish.

"PLANTING THE SEEDS" FOR AGRICULTURAL SUCCESS: REUBEN F. KOLB, SR.

Reuben Kolb does not have his portrait hanging with the rest of the previous Alabama governors—it is said the elections of 1892 and 1894 were stolen from him—but he ranks high in the annals of those who worked to promote agriculture in the state of Alabama. Born to a prominent planter family in Eufaula in 1839, when the Civil War broke out he was in command of Confederate artillery. After the war, he went back to the family farm, where he began to be more interested in the diversification of crops and looked at agriculture from a scientific point of view.

In 1883, he helped to form the Alabama Department of Agriculture and Industries (and later became its commissioner).

Following this, he became trustee of what became Auburn University and served as president to the National Farmers' Congress. He worked tirelessly to promote the needs of farmers throughout the state and was active in the Alabama Farmers' Alliance. Because of his efforts, the economic needs of farmers in Alabama are at the forefront of politics today. You can see more about him in the Alabama Department of Archives and History (ADAH).

ARE WE IN ITALY? NO, WE'RE IN EUFAULA

A mansion in Eufaula (Barbour County) is one of the Yellowhammer State's most outstanding examples of Italianate architecture. Known as Fendall Hall, it is a lovely place to tour, and tells the story of Eufaula's citizens and the town's role in shipping and trading "back in the day." To me, the interior is the most striking, with murals throughout several rooms, and an elaborately decorated foyer. Under the auspices of the Alabama Historical Commission, Fendall Hall is open for events such as weddings and receptions, and is decorated for seasons such as Christmas. You will be totally enchanted with this place, that makes you feel as though you are in Italy, not Alabama!

"HOOF IT" TO THIS UNUSAL MUSEUM!!

In the city of Montgomery on South Bainbridge Street, you can learn all about the cattle industry in Alabama. In this venue, which is called The MOOseum, there is something for everyone. An animated mannequin dressed as a cowboy is the MOOseum's "greeter." He starts your tour by showing a short film about Alabama's cattle industry. Then you can explore the "Hoof Prints through History," which is a timeline on their floor-to-ceiling exhibit which goes back to 1494. Your children will love going to "Slim's Kitchen," where they can dress up as chefs and cook their own hamburgers.

The MOOseum also has a Cowboy Play area, a Cowboy Arena with a barrel that was used in real rodeos, a Cow Pen with Coco the Cow (a real cow that was stuffed by a taxidermist) and a well-stocked General Store with plenty of merchandise for mementos. Operated under the auspices of the Alabama Cattlemen's Association, The MOOseum and its activities are currently coordinated by Kara Harden.

THE "ECONOMIC MOSES OF THE SOUTH"

Born in 1857 in Florence, Alabama, this woman rose to prominence as a successful farmer who dedicated herself to agriculturally-sound practices, both for the state of Alabama and the entire U.S. She was an early proponent of crop rotation and crop diversification. So successful was she in leading the state toward improved agricultural techniques, that she was called the "Economic Moses of the South" (Times-Picayune, May 12, 1918) for helping the state become more economically independent. A 1917 issue of *American Magazine* declared her as being "worth $20 million dollars to the state of Alabama." Who was she? She was Ida Elizabeth Brandon Mathis, who was inducted into the Alabama Women's Hall of Fame in 1993.

ALABAMA'S AMAZING ARCHITECTURE

Just about anywhere you travel in Alabama you're bound to find some examples of architectural brilliance. Here is just a sampling, and stories in this chapter go more in-depth about some other places:

1. In Montgomery, the Alabama State Capitol Building.

2. Birmingham's Quinlan Castle (in Southside).

3. In Guntersville, the Guntersville Museum & Cultural Center.

4. Sturdivant Hall in Selma.

5. On the coast of Alabama, the inner quarters of Fort Morgan are a beautiful and enduring example of flying buttresses.

6. The Convention Center in Mobile.

7. The McWane Science Center in Birmingham.

8. The Montgomery Mall.

9. In Tuscumbia, the Colbert County Courthouse.

10. Two theatres of note: in Birmingham, there is the Alabama Theatre. In Mobile, the Saenger Theatre is just as beautiful.

11. On the campus of Auburn University, Hargis Hall.

12. On the campus of The University of Alabama in Tuscaloosa, Gorgas Hall (see the story about Dr. Gorgas in Chapter 4).

13. The one example of Frank Lloyd Wright's architecture in the state of Alabama is the Rosenbaum House in Florence.

14. In Tuskegee, you can see Grey Columns, which is home to the president of Tuskegee University.

15. In Fairhope, you can see the "Fairhope Castle." It was created mostly from items artist and architect Craig Sheldon, Sr. found on the beaches after storms. The castle is complete with a moat, a bridge and a "Fairytale Cottage."

The famous "Fairhope Castle." My friend Palmetto Panitchiwakul visited from Thailand and is on the bridge. Photo by the author.

DID YOU KNOW?

The first European settlement in what became Mobile, Alabama was Fort Louis de la Louisiane, in 1702.

TIME-TRAVELLING IN ARAB ... SORT OF

In the lovely and charming small town of Arab, you can do a "virtual time-travel" by visiting their Arab Historic Village. It is a tribute to, in the words of their web site, "a pioneer-spirited people who settled, and built this area into the prosperous, community-minded place it is today."

I remember when the Historic Village was just an ambition for the people of Arab back in 1991. This lovely historic village comes to life—literally—several times a year. Currently, ten buildings have been finished and are furnished and decorated as they might have been in the early settlers' and farmers' days through the 1940s (my favorite is Boyd's farmhouse—you MUST check this place out!).

On the last Saturday in April, Arab hosts the "Back When Day." On this day, volunteers show their quilting, blacksmithing, cornmeal grinding and other skills. Gospel singing groups are also featured. On the second Saturday in September, the village hosts an "Arab Community Fair," during which time crafters come from all over, selling their wares. My personal favorite, though, is Christmastime, when the Historic Village hosts "Santa in the Park" and the village is all aglow with Christmas lights.

You will love spending a half-day or more at this historic village! It will be a kind of going back in time.

GREECE IN ALABAMA? ABSOLUTELY!

In Greensboro (Hale County) lies the lovely Greek Revival house known as Magnolia Grove. Built around 1840, the house was the childhood home of Richmond Pearson Hobson, a Spanish-American War hero and U.S. Congressman. It is beautifully restored to the way it might have been in the 1840s. The most fascinating thing to me is the exhibit of the slave quarters, where you can understand more about the lives of the people who lived behind the main house.

You can tour Magnolia Grove almost any time during the year, but I recommend you take in their "Porches and Parlors" event they hold every December. Magnolia Grove is under the auspices of the Alabama Historical Commission.

VICTORY TEACHING FARM: BACK TO THE ROOTS OF INCREASING INDEPENDENCE AND REDUCING HUNGER

Victory Teaching Farm is located in Mobile, Alabama. It began with a nod to World Wars I and II, when men were off to serve in the war effort and food was rationed. During these times, gardens begun by individual citizens and families sprouted up, not only in garden plots but on rooftops, in front yards, and even in schoolyards. They were called "Victory Gardens" back then.

Some visionary people established Victory Teaching Farm in Mobile because they saw a need for people to eat more healthily and have less dependence on commercially grown fruits and vegetables.

I caught up with Tarrant Lanier, Director and one of the founders of Victory Teaching Farm to "dig a little deeper" into the story.

"We are currently only open on certain days and times for tours," Lanier said, "but we work with the community and schools." She said they were established in 2010 as a non-profit, starting with a small community garden. They then began working with a local food bank (Bay Area Food Bank) and schools while looking for land to implement the teaching farm. They broke ground in 2013.

"Cathy O'Neal, my co-founder, and I both had always worked with the non-profit sector and I was working with the child nutrition program for the state of Alabama," Lanier explained. We wanted to help families work toward self-sufficiency to learn more about being healthy with a good quality of life. One day we were talking and decided to begin a community garden, and the teaching farm just kind of grew out of that. We're both very passionate about health and organic gardening while being respectful of our environment."

Victory Teaching Farm welcomes visitors and school groups. They also have an annual fundraiser they call "Down to Earth FarmRaiser," every October that includes a sit-down dinner under the stars (weather permitting), with dishes prepared by local chefs and from produce grown by local farmers.

GAINESWOOD: A STEP BACK IN TIME

In the heart of the city of Demopolis stands the lovely plantation home known as Gaineswood. It was established by Nathan Whitfield in the early 1800s, when he and his family moved from North Carolina. It took Nathan Whitfield nearly 20 years to complete the construction of the plantation home, one of the most significant examples of Greek Revival architecture in the state of Alabama.

The home is called "Gaineswood" in honor of Indian agent George Gaines, because it was on the grounds of what is now Gaineswood that he met with Choctaw Nation Chief Pushmataha to negotiate a treaty (it was under an old post oak tree where this happened, and the tree is known today as the "Pushmataha Oak").

Gaineswood is operated under the auspices of the Alabama Historical Commission and is a National Historic Landmark.

POND SPRING

Also known as the Joe Wheeler Plantation, Pond Spring was originally held by the family of John Hickman, who were among the earliest settlers of Lawrence County. The land was purchased in 1827 by the family of Benjamin Sherrod. When Joe Wheeler came to Alabama to serve the Confederacy during the Civil War, he met Daniella Sherrod whom he married when the war was over. They built the mansion now known as Pond Spring. This lovely 50-acre site includes the Wheeler home and 12 historic buildings. The land has archeological features that date back nearly 5,000 years. Open to the public for tours, Pond Spring is operated under the auspices of the Alabama Historical Commission.

Many interesting architectural features accent the plantation home and the outbuildings. The house is decorated as it might have been when Daniella Sherrod Wheeler was its mistress. My favorite features of the house are two things: the hand-made bricks of the plantation home and the uniforms worn by "Fighting Joe" Wheeler (from both his service to the Confederacy during the Civil War and, as a U.S. General, during his service during the Spanish-American War) that are on display.

Located in Hillsboro just three miles east of Courtland and 15 miles west of Decatur on alternate US Highway 72, the Pond Spring Plantation is available for special events such as weddings. Some of the Pond Spring annual events include a spring plant sale, Joe Wheeler Birthday Celebration (in

September), and Christmas at Pond Spring during the month of December. See "Virtual Alabama" for websites.

Q & A

Q. Where in Alabama can you see more examples of "Steamboat Gothic" architecture than anyplace else?

A. In Huntsville in the Twickenham Historic District.

Q. What is the name of the Huntsville-based event in which children live for a week as pioneers of the 1819 time period?

A. Young Settlers Week.

Q. Where, just outside Tuscumbia, can you see one of the few examples of Palladian-style homes, not only in Alabama but in the entire southern portion of the United States?

A. Belle Mont Mansion. It is under the auspices of the Alabama Historical Commission and the rare home is available for tours (currently Thursday through Sunday), special event rentals, and is open (and decorated) for certain times of the year, such as during the Christmas season.

Q. Where in Alabama are the famous "Forks of Cypress" columns, which is all that remains of a plantation there?

A. In Florence.

Q. What Mobile native and award-winning author is perhaps best known for his architectural history books?

A. John S. Sledge.

CHAPTER 6

NATIVE AMERICAN, COWBOY, AND RODEO TALES

CHIEF TUSKALOOSA AND THE BATTLE OF MAUBILA

Somewhere north of Mobile, Alabama, in the 1500s there was a thriving, walled Native American village with a sizeable population. Although archeologists and historians spell it in different ways, many people spell it as Maubila. When Spanish Conquistador Hernando de Soto came through the area, he was intent upon subjugating the native people he encountered. Chief Tuskaloosa is said to have lured de Soto into an ambush. In an ensuing battle which historians say lasted about nine hours, de Soto emerged victorious. When the battle was over, he had his soldiers burn the village. The remaining native survivors fled and scattered. Hernando de Soto left and headed toward the Mississippi River, where he died of a fever.

Although he himself survived the battle, Chief Tuskaloosa never regained his former power. What remained of his tribe was absorbed into what is now known as the Choctaw Indians. Over the next hundred years, the Tuskaloosa, Coosa, Plaquemine Mississippian and other indigenous people formed a confederacy that became known as the Choctaw. The city of Tuscaloosa and the Black Warrior River that runs though it are both named after Chief Tuskaloosa. Today, the city of Tuscaloosa's Hands-on Museum has an exhibit of what a Choctaw village might have looked like in the 1700s.

T. Jensen Lacey

DID YOU KNOW?

One man who fiercely fought against the Creek Indians was a man named Samuel Dale. Nicknamed "Alabama's Davy Crockett," he, along with Justin Austill and a handful of other brave settlers, fought against nine fierce Creek warriors when they came upon them in canoes on the Alabama River. *The Encyclopedia of Alabama* refers to this as "the Canoe Fight." Dale County is named in honor of Samuel Dale.

NO BULL: ALABAMA IS BIG INTO RODEOS

Alabama and its people are about as "big" into rodeos and bull-riding competitions as anybody from Texas or Montana might be. Just about any given month, you can go to a rodeo and/or bull-riding competition somewhere in the Yellowhammer State. See "Virtual Alabama" for websites.

ALABAMA'S RODEO QUEEN

Robertsdale native Ashleigh Clukey is the current Miss Alabama HS Rodeo Queen. The Rodeo Queen state finals are held every June with competitions state-wide. Competitions include speeches, interviews and impromptu questions. There  is also a Horsemanship portion of the competition. This is Clukey's second time to win the title. She competes in barrel racing, pole bending, breakaway roping, goat tying, cutting, and the Queen Competition. She competed in the national High School Rodeo Queen Competition in Wyoming this past July and was in the top 10. See more about cowboys and rodeos at the MOOseum mentioned in the previous chapter.

GERONIMO! YES, HE WAS IN ALABAMA, TOO
The great chief of the Apaches, Geronimo, was held for a time in Mount Vernon, in Mobile, Alabama. He and more than 400 Apache prisoners of war were held in Mount Vernon after they surrendered to U.S. soldiers in Arizona in 1886. The Alabama Department of Archives and History (ADAH) has on exhibit a photograph of the famous Apache war leader when he posed for a picture while being held in Mount Vernon.

WHEN IN ORANGE BEACH...
You and your family must make a stop in to the Orange Beach Indian and Sea Museum on John Snook Avenue. Housed in a renovated old 1918-era schoolhouse, the museum tells the story of Indians indigenous to the area as well as that of how people from this area made their living, either by eking out an existence from the sea, or by the farms or the many turpentine stills that existed in this area "back in the day." Some of the Native American artifacts include spearheads, arrowheads, gaming pieces and pottery. My favorite thing in the museum is a 35-foot-long dugout cypress canoe, used by Native Americans of long ago.

ANOTHER DARK TIME IN ALABAMA'S HISTORY: THE BATTLE OF HORSEHOE BEND
It was early in the 1800s when white settlers who were expanding into the Southern states and territories complained to the U.S. government about an obstacle to their settling of the area: it was still populated by Native Americans.

Specifically, this part of the country had long been home to the Choctaw, Creek, Cherokee and Chickasaw. From the white settlers' point of view, these Indian nations stood in the way of progress and advancing civilization. The settlers began to pressure the government to help them out by ridding the area of these indigenous peoples.

Andrew Jackson, who ultimately became the 7th President of the United States, had long been a factor in what they referred to then as "Indian Removal." In 1814, in what

This is the grave of William Weatherford, also known as "Red Eagle," who lies interred beside his mother. Photo by the author.

came to be called "the Creek War" (but they were joined by the Chickasaw and Choctaw), Jackson led the U.S. military to defeat the Creek nation.

The Creeks were divided in whether they should fight Jackson and his soldiers. The ones who did not want war were known as "The White Sticks"; those who did were called "Red

Sticks." The first Creek battle was at a place called Burnt Corn in Escambia County. Then William Weatherford, a Red Stick known as "Red Eagle," led an attack on Fort Mims. He and his warriors attacked and killed roughly half of the 500 settlers and soldiers inside, including women and children. Approximately 100 of the Red Sticks also died—so fear gripped the new frontier. There was a call for more military support to protect the settlers.

A Choctaw Chief named Pushmataha, who had sided with the American Colonies during the American Revolution, came to Mobile to lend aid to punish the Red Sticks. In a speech to a Choctaw council, he declared that the Choctaw "friends were not the Creeks but the people at St. Stephens," which was then the Alabama territorial capital. His Choctaw warriors agreed and formed the Pushmataha Battalion to help fight against the Red Sticks.

The Red Sticks were supposed to have support from Spain and England by way of weapons and supplies, but these never arrived. Led this time by Creek Chief Menawa, the band of roughly 1,000 warriors settled in for battle, first creating a fortification in a bend in the Tallapoosa River. We know this area now as Horseshoe Bend. As Andrew Jackson with his roughly 3,300 soldiers prepared their attack, upon seeing how the Red Sticks were penned in on three sides, it is said he declared, "They have penned themselves up for slaughter."

He attacked from the north with the Choctaw Battalion, while General Coffee's Cherokee allies and Tennessee Militia attacked from the south. Cherokee warriors, meanwhile, swam across the river and stole the Creek warriors' canoes, making escape virtually impossible.

It is said that more than 800 Creek warriors were killed in the day-long battle. Witnesses said that for hours after the battle, the river ran red with blood. Although severely wounded, Chief Menawa somehow managed to escape; Jackson's and Coffee's losses were minimal.

This was the last battle of the Creek War. Following this battle, most Creeks signed the Treaty of Fort Jackson with Andrew Jackson. Creek Chief William McIntosh was among those who were White Sticks, who helped Andrew Jackson's soldiers fight against the Red Sticks. In the treaty, William McIntosh and other chiefs who signed the treaty received $200,000 to cede Creek lands to the United States. In May 1825 a band of vengeful Creek warriors, led by Chief Menawa, attacked McIntosh at his home and killed him.

William Weatherford himself never suffered for his role in the Fort Mims massacre. Many of his family members had sided against the Red Sticks, and said that Weatherford had been forced to take part. Some witnesses said that he tried to stop his warriors from the slaughter and left the fort when they would not listen. Red Eagle's family went on a kind of campaign, extolling his virtues, his excellent horsemanship (including leaping with his horse, Arrow, off a cliff into the Alabama River near the end of a Creek battle known as Holy Ground), and his willingness to make peace.

When Red Eagle attended the signing of the treaty at Fort Jackson, he promised to be peaceful. He was pardoned by Andrew Jackson. He retired from his warring ways and went to live on a plantation near St. Stephens, Alabama. He also went on to marry three different women and had a total of nine children. He died in 1824 and is buried next to his mother in the Little River community off Highway 59 near the Monroe-

Baldwin County line in the community known as Old Montpelier (incidentally, the gravesites are well-maintained and easy to find).

Andrew Jackson went on to become the 7th President of the United States.

Today, you can visit several places where this decisive and historic battle is commemorated. A painting of William McIntosh hangs in the Alabama Department of Archives and History in Montgomery (ADAH). Also at ADAH is a miniature, 3-dimensional model of the battle that depicts Jackson forces charging the Creek fortifications at Horseshoe Bend. In Dadeville on Broadnax Street, you can visit the Tallapoosee Historical Museum that has exhibits relating to this battle and its aftermath.

In addition, you can visit two major sites in Alabama to experience this conflict for yourself. The first is located in Stockton, where a replica of Fort Mims stands at the site of the old fort, complete with a staked-log fence and a log lookout tower. It's open all year and there is a re-enactment of the massacre every August.

As for the Battle of Horseshoe Bend, you can go visit the battle site located in Daviston (Tallapoosa County). Horseshoe Bend National Military Park is now part of the U.S. National Park Service. The park has an indoor museum with exhibits of artifacts from the battle, and occasional re-enactments of the conflict. The park also offers guided and self-guided tours.

When you go, remember these are places where people died for their beliefs, their families, their freedoms, and their lands.

DID YOU KNOW?

You might have noticed some rather "un-Native American" names in this passage about the Creek War. Names like Weatherford and McIntosh were names of the native men's fathers. In the decades leading up to the Creek War, many Creek women married Scots traders, who came to the area trading European goods for deerskins and other animal furs. In Creek society, they have a matrilineal culture, so the offspring of these Scots-Creek marriages were considered Creek, regardless of the ethnicity of the fathers.

One such person of Scots-Creek descent was named Hoboi-Hili-Miko, known to whites as Alexander McGillivray. He rose to prominence as a diplomat; in this position, he negotiated the 1784 Treaty of Pensacola, in which the country of Spain acknowledged Creek sovereignty in a dispute over three million acres of contested lands. When President George Washington sent McGillivray and other native diplomats to New York for a conference in 1790, the result was a treaty between the Creeks and the United States—the first ever to be ratified under the Constitution.

The medal Washington conferred on McGillivray for this achievement is in the Alabama Department of Archives and History; as of press time, it was on display in their "Alabama Voices" exhibit.

BENJAMIN HAWKINS AND THE CREEK INDIANS

One of the tenets of the Treaty of New York, which Creek diplomat Alexander McGillivray helped negotiate, was that the Creek Indians would adopt a more agrarian way of life. The majority of the Creeks were opposed to this sudden change in their lives and culture. In 1796, when President George

Washington appointed Benjamin Hawkins to be the General Superintendent for Indian Affairs in the southeast, Hawkins seized it as a great opportunity. He developed an especial affection for the Creek way of life in particular: he learned the Creek language, married a Creek woman, and wrote about Indian culture. Although he was unable to head off the Creek War of 1813-14, he was well-respected by the Creeks as a whole.

Today, you can see his image in the Alabama Department of Archives and History Museum of Alabama in the form of an etching. A large, free-standing 3-dimensional display of a Creek village as it might have appeared during Hawkins' tenure is also there.

THE TRAIL OF TEARS: DARK DAYS FOR NATIVE AMERICANS
After their defeat in the Creek Wars, the Creeks (and other Native Americans, such as the Cherokee, Choctaw, and Chickasaw) were forced to give up 22 million acres (some accounts say 25) of land in central Alabama and southern Georgia.

When President Andrew Jackson signed the Indian Removal Act of 1830, he cleared the way for voluntary or forced removal of all Indians living in the U.S. up to west of the Mississippi River. Between the years 1831 and 1837, approximately 46,000 Native Americans were forced to leave their homes in the southeastern United States and relocate to Oklahoma. Countless indigenous people died on the enforced march, many due to exposure from wintry weather.

Today, the Poarch Creek Indian Reservation near Atmore, Alabama, is the only Indian reservation recognized by the Federal government (and this group was NOT forced to remove). Another band, the MOWA (a band of Choctaw

Indians) has been recognized as a tribe by the state of Alabama but not by the federal government. Read more abut the Poarch Creek Indians in Chapter 10.

OSCEOLA, SEMINOLE LEADER?

A Creek warrior named Osceola (or sometimes Asseola) was born in the Creek village of Talisi, near modern-day Tallassee, Alabama. He was the son of a Creek woman and her Scots-trader husband, James McQueen. After the Red Sticks' defeat at the Battle of Horseshoe Bend, Osceola and his family fled to Florida, where he joined and became a leader of the Seminole nation there.

During the Second Seminole War, newspapers sold many copies of their periodicals, with their colorful tales of Osceola's exploits in his fights against the U.S. Army. Osceola's stories grew along with his fame; some people said he was invincible, and he became something of a legend.

He was finally captured, and quickly became ill with something that no bullet had been able to do. Osceola was "done in" by a mosquito that gave him malaria. He is buried in Franklin in Monroe County, in the Indian cemetery there, since as at that time (at least in Franklin) Indians were buried separately from whites. You can see paintings of him at the Alabama Department of Archives and History and at the Museum of Alabama, both of which are in Montgomery. Near the town of Franklin, the Alabama River Museum has a wonderful exhibit of what Creek life might have been like for Osceola before he became a Seminole.

THE LEGEND BEHIND NOCCALULA FALLS

In Gadsden at Noccalula Falls Park there is a statue of an Indian girl based on a legend. The legend begins something like this: Back around the turn of the 19th century a young Indian princess named Noccalula was in love with a dashing brave in her tribe. When she learned her father, the chief, had made arrangements for her to marry someone else, the young princess decided to throw herself over the falls. She fell 90 feet to her death on the rocks.

Today, the park is enjoyed by kayakers, especially after a heavy rain, as the falls have been compared to Niagara after such precipitation. At the top of the falls stands a beautiful statue of a young Indian maiden. It appears she is just about to take her fatal leap to the rocks below.

Q & A

Q. The city of Tuscumbia's name comes from what Native American phrase?

A. Tashka Ambi, meaning "Warrior who kills."

Q. On a similar note, the town of Sylacauga translates to mean what in Native American?

A. The word means "buzzard roost."

Q. What is the meaning of the two Choctaw Indian words "Tushka" and "Lusa," which formed the town name, Tuscaloosa?

A. Tushka means "warrior" and Lusa means "black."

Q. Near what fort on the Tallapoosa River was the famous Seminole chief Osceola born?

A. Fort Decatur.

Q. What town was established on land purchased from the Creek Indian chief Ladiga in 1833?

A. Jacksonvilllle.

Q. What former trading town used by the Upper Creek Indians was established at the confluence of the Little Cahaba and Cahaba rivers?

A. Mad town.

Q. The term "Alabama" comes from what Native American term?

A. "Alabamu," which means in Choctaw "I open" or "I clear the thicket."

Q. Where is the largest Indian mound on the Tennessee River situated?

A. Florence.

Q. The Indian Sequoyah, who gave his nation its first syllabary and printed language, lived part of his life in what north Alabama Cherokee town?

A. Willstown.

Q. In 1811, what famous Shawnee leader traveled to north Alabama to persuade the Creek Indians to side with British forces against the Americans?

A. Tecumseh.

CHAPTER 7
RELIGION AND UTOPIAN COMMUNITIES

Over the course of Alabama's history, many areas of the state have been settled by people who had a vision of what the ideal kind of life could be for them. Some of those communities were short-lived; others continue to exist and even thrive, today. Here are some of those stories.

THE "FAIR HOPE" OF OUR SUCCESS
The village of Fairhope, on the Eastern Shore of Mobile Bay, was begun as a Utopian colony. The founders and settlers of this village arrived here from Iowa in 1894. The group of approximately 500 settlers decided on the area for its mild weather, fertile land and scenic beauty. They were called "Single-Tax colonists" because of the philosophy of economist Henry George, who held the belief that there should be no taxes imposed on citizens, with the exception of a single land tax. Legend has it that one of the colonists declared their venture had a "fair hope of success," thus the name Fairhope stuck.

The colonists' vision of Utopia was revealed in every aspect of their lives. Education was highly regarded, and the first school to be established, the School of Organic Education, was led by founder Marietta Johnson. She believed that young people should advance in school as they mastered certain concepts, thus the "organic" name.

Since the first settlers came, Fairhope continues to attract people from all over the world. Many free-minded folks have fallen in love with the village. Artists, writers and other creative individuals have made Fairhope their home. Most of the original homes and cottages in Fairhope are marked with a historical designation, as the town continues true to the original colonists' vision. Many concepts the original settlers put in place, such as the Single Tax and the School of Organic Education, still exist. The streets themselves epitomize the

This early educator in the Utopian village of Fairhope, Marietta Johnson, is honored in a sculpture which sits on a bluff looking out over Mobile Bay. The sculptures were created by sculptors France J. Neumann, Barbara Casey and Richard Arnold. Photo by the author.

idyllic vision of the original settlers: as you drive, walk or bike through the city, you will see streets with not only original settlers' family names, but also ideals such as "Liberty," "Equality," and "Freedom." For such a relatively small town,

Fairhope has an active recycling program. The city website says that more than 70% of the 16,000+ citizens do some sort of volunteer work.

Today, you can tour the original Colony Cemetery in which many of the first settlers lie interred, stroll the beachfront park and other places given to the City of Fairhope by the Single Tax Colony, and see many fascinating exhibits at the Fairhope Museum of History, located in the heart of downtown.

... AND THE "POET OF TOLSTOY PARK"

One of Fairhope's settlers, who arrived later than the rest—in the 1920s, was Henry Stuart. His doctor had given him a diagnosis of tuberculosis—what they used to call "consumption"—and Stuart was told he had only a few months to live (unless he moved to a better climate). When others might have gone home to die, Stuart packed his most treasured belongings, left his children and home in Idaho, got on a train, and headed to Fairhope.

He made his home, not in Fairhope proper, but built a round-house in nearby Montrose. He dubbed it "Tolstoy Park" after Russian author Leo Tolstoy and tried to live like a hermit. Over the course of the years he lived there, though, he was visited by thousands of people. From his little hut, he became a well-known and respected writer and philosopher. Locals still refer to Stuart as the "Hermit of Montrose."

His round-house still exists; you can visit "Tolstoy Park," just off Scenic 98 and Greeno Road. For inspiration, many local writers and artists visit Stuart's little round-house, which is decorated with period furniture, books, and other artifacts. By the way, Stuart lived on for many years, much longer than his doctor predicted, dying peacefully in 1946. He would be pleased to know that his round-house is now listed on the National Register of Historic Places.

You can read more about Stuart and his life in a book by Fairhope resident and author Sonny Brewer, *The Poet of Tolstoy Park*.

THE ANNUAL BLESSING OF THE FLEET: IT'S THIS AND SO MUCH MORE!

Every year—usually the last weekend in April—the city of Bayou La Batre and nearby Coden hold the "Blessing of the Fleet." Being situated as they are on the coast of Alabama, many families in this area catch fish or haul in shrimp for their livelihood.

This two-day event includes a cook-off, a parade (this one's on land), a Blessing of the Fleet Queen and her Court, lots of food, music, and, of course, the blessing itself, which is usually given by a Catholic Bishop. According to their website (see "Virtual Alabama"), this is how the official blessing goes: "May God in heaven fulfill abundantly the prayers which are pronounced over you and your boats and equipment on the occasion of the Blessing of the Fleet. God bless your going out and coming in; the Lord be with you at home and on the water. May He accompany you when you start on your many journeys; may He fill your nets abundantly as a reward for your labor; and may He bring you all safely in, when you turn your boats homeward to shore. Amen."

Even if you are unable to attend both days of this event, the Blessing of the Fleet itself is something to see with all the fishing-boats gathered, the crews all onboard, and the bishop offering up a blessing for a good, safe and productive fishing season.

DID YOU KNOW?

The First Baptist Church in Montgomery is the oldest, continually-operating African-American Baptist Church in the state of Alabama (founded in 1867). It is the site where the "Freedom Riders" Civil Rights protesters took shelter and where Dr. Martin Luther King, Jr. came and offered the protestors words of encouragement. See more about this story in Chapter 9, "From Civil Wrongs to Civil Rights." Contact the church ahead of time to schedule a tour.

THE STORY OF SKYLINE FARMS

The young schoolgirl looked down the road and saw the outline of the sky at the end. "Skyline Farms," she said aloud. That name would become the winning name in a school-wide contest to name a town that was a governmental social and economic experiment.

Skyline Farms was one of several new homesteading colonies formed by the Federal Relief Administration (FERA) in 1934. Skyline Farms was originally named The Cumberland Mountain Farms Project, one of 43 such colonies FERA began in 1934.

Skyline Farms was established to help farmers in dire economic straits who were suffering in the wake of the Great Depression. This relief program was designed to offer families a path to self-reliance and home ownership. The program was in no way a handout to these famers and their families. The people worked the land, planted and harvested their crops, and built structures such as a school, a commissary, a warehouse and factory, a cotton gin, and the colony office building. They also constructed half of the original houses. The houses were quite modern for the times: they included one to three bedrooms (depending on the size of the family taking possession), a kitchen, living room and a porch.

The property was provided by a local judge and members of the Jackson County Rehabilitation Commission, who were offered a deal for 8,000 acres of land that had been used by a coal-mining operation that had played out.

The colony was a success from the start, with the children getting their education at the Skyline Farms School. This school was at that time the only one in Alabama that offered instruction in agriculture and home economics.

The colony also formed a band that performed for First Lady Eleanor Roosevelt, who invited the Skyline Farms Band, with its attendant square dancers, to a White House garden party. In 1939, electricity came to the Skyline Farms colony, and it seemed that nothing bad could ever happen to this thriving community. But in 1944, some members of Congress began to complain that the colony was promoting Socialism and demanded the liquidation of all the colonies founded as part of the New Deal. They called for families to make payments on their homes; only one family was able to do so, so many families left the area.

But the proverbial pendulum has a way of swinging back, and so it happened with Skyline Farms. After some decades, the colony has seen a resurgence in population and growth. After the town of Skyline was incorporated in 1983, many of its original inhabitants moved back to their hometown. The old school is now Skyline Elementary School. The colony office, originally called Rock House, is under renovation through the auspices of the Skyline Farms Heritage Association. It will be put to use as a research library.

The spirit of the original Skyline Farms colony continues to show itself in the people who now inhabit the town of Skyline. In the words of Heritage Association's Cindy Rice, "Skyline Farms was built by people with vision, faith in the future, and a willingness to put in the hard work and cooperation necessary to create a community."

DID YOU KNOW?

When it comes to churches, two of the most beautiful examples of architectural brilliance are accessible for those who want to see them for themselves. One is the St. Bernard Abbey in Cullman; another is the Cathedral Basilica of the Immaculate Conception in Mobile. The Cathedral is the oldest Catholic parish in the state of Alabama; both the Abbey and the Cathedral are open for tours.

THE FRENCH EXPERIMENT THAT "WITHERED ON THE VINE"

In 1817, a group of French refugees passed through St. Stephens on their way to some lands granted them by the U.S. government. They fled France after the overthrow of Napoleon Bonaparte; others with them were refugees from Haiti in the wake of the slave rebellion of 1791. Thomas Jefferson had granted these settlers 92,000 acres in what is now Marengo County (near present-day Demopolis) on the condition that they cultivate grapes and olives so the new country would not have to depend on Europe for their wines and could enjoy domestically-grown olives.

While the venture began optimistically enough, obstacles soon developed. One was that these settlers were unprepared for the rough, oftentimes perilous, life of the frontier. Another was that these settlers knew more about ballroom dancing and battle tactics than they did about agriculture. Yet a third was that one of the leaders of their "Colonial Society," Charles Lallemand, turned out to be a swindler, who sold acreage right out from under the Vine and Olive colonists. He had his own plan of invading Texas with those funds (he failed).

Before they ever produced any wine or olives, the majority of the colonists left the area, moving to places like New Orleans and other more settled parts of the U.S. Others who remained merged with the cotton-growing farm culture of Alabama.

Today, you can tour Demopolis and the Marengo County Museum and learn more about the colony that, as the Alabama Department of Tourism's Vacation Guide says, "withered on the vine."

"BROTHER" BRYAN: WALKING THE TALK

Born James Alexander Bryan in 1863 in South Carolina, Bryan studied theology at Princeton University then moved to Birmingham, Alabama, in 1941. He became part-time pastor of Third Presbyterian Church, at that time only a tent, while still a student at Princeton. After his graduation, he became an ordained minister and served full time at the Birmingham church.

He preached not only in the church but also to groups throughout the town and that region of Alabama. He gained the moniker "Brother" because this was how he addressed people (as "brother" or "sister"). He was an ardent and tireless advocate for racial reconciliation, the homeless, and poverty-stricken. He was memorialized by author Hunter B. Blakely in the book *Religion in Shoes: Brother Bryan of Birmingham* (1953, John Knox Press).

His life and contributions to Birmingham are further commemorated by a statue of "Brother" Bryan kneeling in prayer. The white marble statue, sculpted by artist George Bridges, can be found at the corner of 20th Street South and Magnolia Avenue in the area of Birmingham known as Five Points.

His life's work is carried on by staff and volunteers of the "Brother Bryan Mission," that was founded in 1940 and now serves the homeless and those addicted to drugs. According to the website www.Al.com, in 2015 the mission began a 1.4-million-dollar expansion to further continue the work begun by "Brother" Bryan.

POURING SPIRITS AND SAVING SOULS: THE FLORA-BAMA BAR AND CHURCH

Situated on the Florida and Alabama state lines on the Gulf Coast is an unusual and iconic bar known as the Flora-Bama. It was originally started because of a trade deal made between the states of Alabama and Florida: the "Sunshine State" wanted land on which to build the Perdido Pass Bridge and in return gave the state of Alabama two miles along the Florida beach front.

That was back in 1962. Shortly afterward, a family by the name of Tampary (the dad, Ted, along with children Connie and Tony) decided to open a package store on the border of the two states, and so the Flora-Bama officially opened in 1964. Since then, the iconic Flora-Bama has enjoyed an international reputation, offering patrons a place on the beach overlooking the Gulf of Mexico where they can people-watch and enjoy good music and their favorite libation while straddling two states. The Flora-Bama has always been a basic, laid-back bar. Most of the establishment still has a sand floor, so after a severe storm or hurricane, they're up and running in short order.

They continue to enjoy success: In 2017, they were voted by CNN Travel as "One of the World's Best Beach Bars." But nowadays there's more to the Flora-Bama than just that. The owners decided to give their establishment a new twist.

On July 3, 2011, the owners of this huge and constantly growing entertainment venue decided to begin offering worship services on Sunday mornings. Current pastor Dan Stone said the church began as an outreach to what is a diverse community of people in the area. The Church at Flora-Bama, affiliated with Central Christian Church out of Las Vegas, Nevada, wanted to get the word of God out to folks who might not attend the usual kind of church. This church would be different.

They were originally hoping to get a few dozen attendees. The number has now increased so much, that pastor Stone said they have an average of 2,300 attendees who come for one of the two services (which they refer to as "Experience Times"). The Church at Flora-Bama touts itself as, in pastor Dan Stone's words on the website, "a place where it's okay not to be okay."

He said people have thronged to this "Just as I am" gathering, and the Easter "Experience Times" of 2018 saw a total of 6,000 attendees throng the church doors.

Do some people originally come for the bar, yet stay for the service? Stone said that yes, many do. The Flora-Bama Church welcomes everyone, even in beach attire, and children are allowed if they're with adults. One manager, Mark Ainslie, told me that one of the "coolest things I've seen are baptisms on the beach, right on the Gulf." For more on all things Flora-Bama, see "Virtual Alabama."

"BROTHER JOE'S" LABOR OF LOVE: AVE MARIA GROTTO

Just off Interstate 65 on Highway 278 east in Cullman, you can see a place that's like nothing else you might experience in the world. This is the place of Alabama's only Benedictine monastery, Saint Bernard Abbey. The abbey is home to a fantastic collection of miniature replicas of famous spiritual shrines and buildings, and some that are the object of pure fantasy. These were created by Brother Joseph Zoettel, who came to the abbey in 1892 from Bavaria with an original goal to study for the priesthood.

Young Zoettel was assigned many tasks for the monks at the abbey. At first, it was housekeeping, a chore for which, apparently, he was ill-equipped. Then he was given the duty of cooking, but apparently his cooking was so bad that one of the monks called his food "poison." After he became a monk, one of his fellow monks gave him some cement. "Brother Joe" enjoyed working with his hands, so around 1918 he began creating replicas of famous religious shrines, using materials that were left over from construction of the buildings of the monastery.

As his replicas grew in number, the monks moved them from the monastery's outdoor recreation area to the limestone quarry nearby. The quarry had been used to obtain the limestone blocks to create the abbey and other buildings, and it was given the official name of "Ave Maria Grotto" in 1934.

Of all the 125 replicas on the property, my favorite is of St. Peter's Basilica, which is so accurate of a re-creation of the original that it's amazing to think that one monk made it with his own hands. Another is "Brother Joe's" last miniature creation: the Lourdes Basilica Church, which is a perfect, miniature representation of the church in Lourdes, France. In 1984, Ave Maria Grotto ("grotto" means "cave" in Italian) was named to the National Register of Historic Places.

This is a great place to spend an hour, or even a day or two. If you want, you may enjoy a retreat on the grounds of the abbey for families or groups to stay the night. Also, the monks offer dining facilities. "Brother Joe" died in 1961 and is buried on the abbey grounds, if you want to visit and pay your respects.

I can't help but wonder—if "Brother Joe" had been a great housekeeper or a better cook, would Alabama ever have had Ave Maria Grotto?

TWO BEAUTIFUL CHURCHES YOU WON'T WANT TO MISS!

Malbis, Alabama, was founded by Greek settlers (the Malbis family). They put their hearts into getting established in Alabama, and one of the first things they did was build a large and lovely church—and they paid for its construction themselves. Without a doubt, the Greek Orthodox Church in this coastal community is a sight to behold, with its Byzantine-style structure, wood carvings and artwork inside, and on top, a lovely, gleaming gold dome. Malbis church is a privately owned church (still owned by the Malbis family). It is open for tours, and if you're as lucky as I was, your tour will be led by Gertrude Malbis herself!

Approximately 50 miles south in the town of Gulf Shores, you'll find the St. Athanasios Greek Orthodox Church. In looking at its gleaming walls and classic Greek-blue dome, you might feel as though you are on the Greek island of Santorini.

SAVING SOULS FOR MORE THAN 200 YEARS: HUNTSVILLE'S FIRST PRESBYTERIAN CHURCH

In June of 2018, Huntsville's First Presbyterian Church celebrated its bicentennial. It is the oldest Presbyterian church in continuous service in the state of Alabama. The church was originally founded by The Reverend Gideon Blackburn. Today you can tour the church. Adjacent to it is the Gideon Blackburn House, built in 2004, and is available for wedding receptions and other life celebrations.

THE "SLEEPING PREACHER" OF NORTH ALABAMA

While you may know the oldest incorporated town in Alabama is Mooresville, there's more to it than just this fact. In the mid-1850s, there was a preacher there by the name of Constantine Blackmon Sanders who had an unusual talent. He would go into a sleep-like trance and, while in this state, make predictions that were remarkably accurate.

Although he is, of course, long gone, the Athens-Limestone County Tourist Association gives guided walking tours of Mooresville (and also the county seat of Athens), every spring. Part of the walking tour includes seeing the Old Brick Church of Mooresville, where Preacher Sanders, who signed many documents with the mysterious moniker "X+Y=Z," gave many sermons to his followers.

THIS PLACE GIVES NEW MEANING TO THE TERM "ROCK OF THE CHURCH": THE MEMORIAL CHAPEL IN MENTONE

If you want to see a really unique place in which to worship, it would have to be Mentone's Sallie Howard Memorial Chapel. Built in 1937 by Col. Milford Howard as a memorial to honor his wife's memory, the most unusual aspect of this chapel would be that it was built around a boulder. The boulder, in fact, juts out into the pulpit area. Services are held every Sunday.

Q. & A.

Q. The well-preserved, pioneer Claybank Church made with hand-made shingles still stands in what community?

A. Ozark.

Q. The town of Reform was initially settled by pioneers from what other state?

A. South Carolina.

Q. What town is named for Anna Milner, daughter of a Baptist preacher from Georgia?

A. Georgianna.

Q. What federally-subsidized homestead project near Gardendale was founded in the 1930s by the Resettlement Administration?

A. Mount Olive Homesteads.

Q. What federally-sponsored farm resettlement project begun in 1935 became the first of its type in the U.S.?

A. Coffee County Homesteads.

Q. Where did Baptists establish Judson College for Women in 1839?

A. Marion.

Q. What was the first public building constructed in Opelika?

A. The Lebanon Methodist Church.

Q. The colorful African-American religious leader, known as "Sanctified Sarah," headquartered her congregation in what town?

A. Uniontown.

Q. What social welfare program was begun in Jackson County in 1923 by Augusta B. Martin?

A. The House of Happiness.

Q. What religious group in 1808 became the first to send an official missionary to Alabama?

A. The Methodists.

Q. What ethnic group of settlers from the Carolinas first brought the Presbyterian Church to Alabama?

A. Scotch-Irish settlers.

Q. Who was ordained as the first Anglican priest in Alabama in 1763?

A. The Reverend Nathaniel Nash.

Q. Internationally-famous Gospel singer Jake Hess, who was given the moniker "Mr. Gospel Music," was born in what part of Alabama?

A. Near Athens in the community of Mt. Pisgah. He's an inductee of the International Gospel Music Hall of Fame in Detroit, Michigan.

Q. For what two famous singers' funerals did Jake Hess sing?

A. Elvis Presley and Hank Williams, Sr.

Q. How many Grammy Awards did Hess win over the course of his six-decades-long career?

A. Four.

Q. What Birmingham-born poet wrote, "For His Mercy Endureth Forever," a poem for which she received second place from the National League of American Pen Women?

A. Rosamond Henderson.

CHAPTER 8
SPORTS, RECREATION, AND AMUSEMENT STORIES

I was not surprised to learn that, across all sports, Alabama leads most U.S. states in champions and championships. From basketball to gymnastics to golf and, of course, football, the Yellowhammer State is one people talk about when they talk sports.

DID YOU KNOW?

Alabama has its very own "Grand Canyon." The Yellowhammer State's Little River Canyon, whose nickname is "The Grand Canyon of the East," is an outdoor enthusiast's paradise.

Part of the 15,288-acre Little River Canyon National Preserve, the Little River Canyon is in Fort Payne in north Alabama. According to the website OnlyinYourState.com/Alabama, the canyon runs approximately

Cheaha State Park has in its boundaries the highest point in the state of Alabama, offering hikers many scenic vistas like this one. Photo courtesy Cheaha State Park

12 miles long and the river gorge itself is as deep as 600 feet in some places. The canyon and the surrounding countryside are always beautiful, even in the dead of winter, when Jack Frost engraves his name on the forests and the canyon walls, or when the land is covered in snow (it does happen in north Alabama).

The other seasons are optimal times of the year for camping, hiking, rappelling, swimming and fishing. Furthermore, rock climbers from all over the country come to Little River Canyon to take on the formations within the canyon (they even have names such as Jungle Gym, Concave, Lizard Wall and Toomsuba, each with its own unique challenges).

... AND ANOTHER GRAND CANYON IN ALABAMA

For hiking enthusiasts, you can't beat the Walls of Jericho for a fascinating place to spend a day or a weekend. Nicknamed the "Grand Canyon of the South," the Walls of Jericho offers hikers, horseback riders and nature lovers nearly seven miles of trails of unspoiled wilderness. The trail is a bit arduous at times, with hikers crossing creeks via tree-bridges, and steep terrain bordered by high limestone bluffs and waterfalls. The Walls of Jericho's trailhead is located off Alabama Highway 79 outside Scottsboro. *Reader's Digest* recently named the Walls of Jericho as one of the top 20 hikes in the entire United States.

NICK SABAN: HERO OF "T-TOWN"

Anyone with internet access can look up the facts about this stellar head coach of The University of Alabama's football team. They can read about his early days, where, as quarterback for the Monogah High School football team (in his hometown of Fairmont, West Virginia) they had a 30-game winning streak and went on to win the 2A State Championship.

Saban graduated from Kent State in 1973 after marrying his high school sweetheart, Terry Constable, in 1971. After earning a Master's in Sports Administration, Saban returned to Kent State where he was the linebacker coach. In 1983, he was defensive back coach at Michigan State University, then coached the Houston Oilers for two seasons. After a brief stint at Toledo (Ohio) University, Saban hired on with the Cleveland Browns in 1991, this time as defensive coordinator. During his years with the Browns, the team allowed the fewest points on the opposition team and made it to the NFL playoffs.

Returning to Michigan State in 1995 as head coach, Saban led the team to bowl games in four out of their five seasons. By the time Saban accepted the job as head coach for Louisiana State University (LSU), he was more than well-seasoned. Within two years, LSU won their first SEC Championship (2001); in 2003, they won their second conference championship. That same year, LSU won the BCS National Championship—it was their first national championship since 1958. After Saban's five seasons with this team, they had a record of 48 wins with only 16 losses.

Apparently, Nick Saban loves a challenge: In 2004, he left LSU to be head coach of the Miami Dolphins, who, like LSU, were also at a low point. Under Saban's coaching, the team seemed to improve, but at the end of the 2006 season Saban resigned, having accepted the offer of head coach at The University of Alabama.

I remember the years before Saban, when the U of A football team struggled, and when Saban took the reins, he was the fifth head coach to be hired in six years. Under his guidance, the team still struggled initially, suffering a sixth straight loss to the Auburn Tigers (which, as any Tide fan knows, is THE one team Alabama HAS to beat). The team turned a corner in 2008, and finally seemed to get their "mojo" going. In 2009, their regular season record was 13-0, and with a 37-21 win over the Texas Longhorns, Alabama earned its first national title since 1992.

In the team's SEC Championship game against the Georgia Bulldogs in December 2018, their win was described as a "storybook ending" by sports journalists. In January 2018, Alabama had gone up against Georgia for the National Championship, and the team was struggling. Saban pulled quarterback Jalen Hurts to the sidelines and put in Tua Tagovailoa, who led the team to victory. Eleven months later, a struggling Alabama team under Tua's leadership saw him pulled from the game, and Jalen put in. His famous "quarterback sneak" stunned Georgia and made Alabama SEC Champs. Under Saban's tutelage, both these players have always supported each other, cheering each other on even from the sidelines.

Saban remains the only coach in the history of college football to win a national championship with not one, but two division 1 schools.

Now, Nick Saban and the Crimson Tide football team have become synonymous with great college football; they're always a part of the conversation when anyone talks about the game.

Many people may not be aware, however, of what Saban tries to instill in his players' characters. Once he arrived at the U of A, Saban started a program he called the "Peer Leadership Council" that he hoped would inspire responsible behavior among the players. Saban also instills a sense of compassion among his players in many ways. In the aftermath of the tornadoes in Tuscaloosa in the spring of 2011, for example, he and his players worked to help those devastated by the disaster. Also, since 1998, Saban and his wife Terry have run the charity, Nick's Kids Fund, which helps disadvantaged children.

Today, you can learn more about this remarkable and caring man. On The University of Alabama campus, at the Walk of Champions, a lifelike statue of him stands. Saban was inducted into the Alabama Sports Hall of Fame in 2013. At the Paul Bryant Museum in Tuscaloosa, you can learn more about Saban's life and his contributions to Alabama football. The museum is often open early just before a home game. See "Virtual Alabama" for websites.

DID YOU KNOW? Condoleezza Rice is a Football Aficionado!

Most people think of politics when they think of Condoleezza Rice. She was, after all, the first female African-American Secretary of State, among her other accomplishments. But you may not know that Rice is an avid golfer; in 2012, she was one of the first two women admitted to the Augusta National Golf Club (in Georgia). Rice also loves football, especially University of Alabama football. She's been such a devotee to the sport that in 2015, the National Football Foundation (NFF) named her their Gold Medal Recipient. She was the first woman ever nationally recognized in its 70+ year history.

THE TIDE'S OFFICIAL FIGHT SONG'S HISTORY

The University of Alabama's official fight song was written by a student named Ethelred (nicknamed "Epp") Sykes. He entered the lyrics for what would become the official fight song in a contest sponsored by the humor magazine, *Rammer-*

Jammer, and won $50. He gave that money to Alabama's Million Dollar Band.

UNION SPRINGS: "BIRD DOG FIELD TRIAL CAPITAL OF THE WORLD"

If you're a bird-hunting enthusiast and a dog lover, you might consider heading to Union Springs in February, where every year Sedgefields Plantation hosts the National Shooting Dog Championship. This competition was inspired by L. B. Maytag (yes, of washing machine and other appliances fame), who had purchased the 14,000-acre property for quail hunting and wanted to compare his bird-dogs with those of his friends'.

The Field Trial Hall of Fame, located in Grand Junction, Tennessee, began inducting honorees in 1954 and has had more inductees from Bullock County, Alabama, than any other place in the U.S.

To commemorate the members and their dogs, in Union Springs there is a large, colorful mural on the north side of what is currently a Napa Auto Parts store at 140 North Prairie Street. The mural was dedicated in February of 2017. Also, sculptor Robert Wehle created a life-size bronze statue of an English Pointer that stands at the intersection of Prairie Street and Hardaway Avenue on top of a granite pillar. The pillar has engraved on it the names of the 12 Field Trial Hall of Fame members; their dogs' names are on the south side of the pillar.

The sculpture of the English Pointer is frozen in the ideal position for when the dog indicates it has sniffed out quail: its tail is straight upward at 12 o'clock, head high, standing tall.

Locals call their annual February event "Bullock County's Mardi Gras." Even if you're not a hunting enthusiast, just going to enjoy the party scene makes for a pleasurable weekend.

A LITTLE ABOUT "SHUG" JORDAN

Before 2010, the Auburn Tigers had a single national championship to their credit. The year was 1957, and Ralph "Shug" Jordan was head coach. That year was the Tigers' best season to date, and with Shug as head coach (he started coaching the Tigers in 1951), they earned, and enjoyed, a stellar year. Their record that year was 10-0, including a 40-0 shutout win against their biggest rival, the Crimson Tide. Under Shug Jordan's tutelage, Auburn player Pat Sullivan won the Heisman trophy (in 1971). When Shug Jordan retired in 1975, the Auburn Nation mourned. Today, you can see more about Jordan's accomplishments at The Lovelace Athletic Museum located on the campus of Auburn University.

... AND COACH PAT DYE

It was under Pat Dye's coaching that Auburn Tigers' running back Bo Jackson earned the Heisman trophy (in 1985) and the team won the SEC Championships in the years 1983, 1987, 1988 and 1989. Pat Dye's team's best season was the year 1983, when they came close to being national champions (they lost to the Texas Longhorns, 20-7). Dye probably would have continued to be their coach, had it not been for an unfortunate NCAA scandal which behooved him to step down. His accomplishments are also on display in exhibits at The Lovelace Athletic Museum.

"THE STRIP"

It was at the Sugar Bowl and the national championship for The University of Alabama's Crimson Tide football team. The year was 1993; their opponent, the Miami Hurricanes. Miami was favored to win by more than a touchdown.

The underdog Tide team met Miami in the New Orleans Superdome. Gene Stallings, Tide coach, had conceded his team was probably not ready to overtake No. 1-ranked Miami, that the Tide was "about a year away" from being that prepared.

But prepared they were: the Tide's player, George Teague, made what coach Bill Oliver, in an interview with Jimmy Bryan of the *Birmingham News*, called "a play for the ages." Teague's play stunned everyone who was watching.

It was in the fourth quarter when the dramatic play happened. Miami's fastest receiver, Lamar Thomas, caught a pass, and to everyone watching, he was headed for an 89-yard touchdown. Teague ran down the field, and at the Tide's 6-yard line, stripped the ball from Thomas's hands. Although Alabama was flagged for an offside call, the play kept Miami from scoring and they never recovered. Alabama won the national championship in this, their hundredth year of playing football.

This play has become such an epic one that it even has a name: The Strip. Also, sports writers continue to comment on it. For example, Don Kausler, Jr. wrote for Al.com in a 2011 article, "[the play] was the ultimate moment in Alabama football history."

He added, "Other plays might have been bigger—the goal-line stand in the 1979 Sugar Bowl, Van Tiffin's game-winning field goal in the 1985 Iron Bowl, Kenny Stabler's run ... to beat Auburn in 1967 ... but no moment was more spectacular on such a big stage."

Final score: 34-13. Taking the wind out of the Hurricanes: priceless.

Oh, by the way, Teague later signed with the Miami Dolphins—and Thomas was his teammate.

"TOUCHDOWN, ALABAMA!" THE VOICE OF CRIMSON TIDE FOOTBALL

I had graduated from college and was long gone from The University of Alabama campus, when Eli Gold took the mike in 1988 and began sports casting Crimson Tide football games. Honestly, I'd always preferred to watch the games (in person or on TV) but until I heard Gold's rich and energetic voice calling the plays, I hadn't really cared to listen to the games on the radio. Gold changed all that with the very first game I heard his voice calling the plays, and now he has made a name for himself in the field of sports announcing.

When in 2014 he was inducted into the Alabama Sports Hall of Fame, he was probably more astounded than anyone else. In an interview that spring with *Southern Jewish Life Magazine* reporter Lee J. Green, Gold quipped that he never dreamed that a "Jewish kid from Brooklyn with zero athletic talent would make it into the Alabama Sports Hall of Fame."

"GIVE ME A SECOND": THE 78TH IRON BOWL

It was November 30, 2013; the so-called "Iron Bowl" was being played in Auburn's Jordan-Hare Stadium. The contestants were the Alabama Crimson Tide, who were ranked Number 1 (and the two-time defending national champion), and Number 4-ranked Auburn Tigers. The Tide was a 10-point favorite over the Tigers. The result of a win for either team would give them a spot in the 2013 SEC (South Eastern Conference) Championship Game, and from there, a shot at the national championship.

Alabama scored a whopping 21 points in the 2nd quarter, and 7 in the 4th, for a total of 28 points. Auburn had fallen behind in those quarters but rallied and tied the game at 28-28.

There were 32 seconds remaining on the game clock. After the kickoff, the Tide moved to the Tigers' 38-yard line, and with the game clock at zero, it seemed the Alabama and Auburn teams were bound for overtime with the score still at 28-28. But Alabama coach Nick Saban called for a video review of the timekeeping call, which resulted in one single second being put back on the game clock.

With one second left to play in the game, the Tide players lined up on the field for what they thought would be a winning 57-yard field goal. But the kick was short and an Auburn player by the name of Chris Davis (who was near the goal line) caught the ball just ahead of the goal posts. Davis ran the ball to the opposite end of the field as players on both sides were frozen, stunned by this turn of events. In that last second, Davis scored a touchdown, giving an extra six points to the Tigers and making the score 34-28 in Auburn's favor.

Alabama fans sat, stunned, as did the players. Then the Auburn fans went wild, stomping their feet so hard on the stands that their reaction registered on seismographs across the state. Some sports writers claimed that Davis's play was the greatest single moment in college football history, ever.

THE ONES THAT DIDN'T GET AWAY!

In Thomaston, Alabama, you can tour The Alabama Whitetail Records Museum that has exhibits all related to deer hunting in the state. They opened the museum in the fall of 2017, and as of press time are currently only open Thursday through Saturday. High-tail it to Thomaston to check out this interesting new museum! See "Virtual Alabama" for websites.

DID YOU KNOW?

Rickwood Field in Birmingham is the oldest continuously operated baseball park in the entire U.S. Since its opening in 1910, it has hosted such baseball greats as Babe Ruth, "Shoeless Joe" Jackson, Jackie Robinson, Ty Cobb, Lorenzo "Piper" Davis, Mobile-born Hank Aaron and Birmingham native Willie Mays.

PAUL "BEAR" BRYANT

The young boy in Fordyce, Arkansas, wasn't going to let the bear get the best of him in a wrestling match; he had to win the $5.00, and he did. After this match, he wound up being called "Bear" as a new moniker.

The man who most people recognized by his signature hounds-tooth fedora as he prowled the sidelines of the stadium was more than stellar: His football coaching career remains as one of the best in the business.

During Bryant's 25-year tenure as Alabama's head football coach, this man with a vision led the Tide to amass six national championships and thirteen conference championships. Born in Arkansas in 1913, he played football while in high school there (Fordyce High School). Once at The University of Alabama, he earned his B.S. degree in 1936 and played as blocking end for the Tide. While playing for the Tide, the team won the Rose Bowl against Stanford University in 1935. After serving as assistant coach at Vanderbilt University, Bryant appeared headed to the University of Arkansas, until the U.S. entered into World War II and changed his plans.

Bryant then joined the Navy, after which time he was head coach at the University of Maryland. He resigned his position there after a dispute with the university president.

After this, he coached the football team at the University of Kentucky, resulting in the team winning their first SEC championship.

He left Kentucky in 1953, and in 1954 Bryant coached at Texas A&M. That first year was rough: The team lost 9 out of 10 games but they managed to come back and win a Southwest Conference Championship in the seasons following.

Bryant returned to The University of Alabama in 1958. In 1971 he not only recruited the first African-American player for the team, but also helped promote integration at Alabama and other southern universities.

It was during his tenure at Alabama that his coaching talents came shining through. Under his coaching, Alabama won six national championships (in 1961, 1964, 1965, 1973, 1978 and 1979). Bryant was named National Coach of the Year three times and won 24 bowl games. His final game was the Liberty Bowl on December 29, 1982. There was hardly a dry eye in the stadium as Tide fans watched "The Bear" being hoisted, for the last time, on his beloved team's shoulders at the end of the victorious game.

In all, Bryant led the Tide to 28 bowl games. The team's winning average of 9.28 victories a year was unmatched by any other football college coach. His career coaching record of 323 regular season wins stood as most games won by a college coach (until it was broken by coach Eddie Robinson in 1985).

Also, without his coaching talents, players such as Joe Namath, George Blanda and Kenny Stabler would never have become such household names as they did. When he died on January 26, 1983, at the age of 69, Tide fans around the world mourned. The funeral procession was the longest one ever experienced by those who lived in Alabama. "The Bear" was interred at Elmwood Cemetery in Birmingham, and his grave is regularly visited by fans who wish to pay their respects. Shortly after his death, President Ronald Reagan awarded "The Bear" with the highest award a U.S. citizen could receive, the National Medal of Freedom.

"Bear" Bryant is remembered and honored in many ways today. In Tuscaloosa, you can tour the Bear Bryant Museum; outside the Bryant-Denny Stadium is a statue of Bryant, wearing his signature hounds-tooth fedora. You can also see more about Bryant at the Alabama Sports Hall of Fame in Birmingham.

JESSE OWENS, THE "NATION'S GREATEST OLYMPIAN"

The young track and field athlete, son of sharecroppers and the grandson of slaves, stood at the line, ready for his first competition in the long jump. He was in Nazi-ruled Berlin, Germany. It was 1936. He was an African-American and surrounded by a sea of Caucasian faces.

This young man, born in 1913 in Oakville (Lawrence County), faced his fears in the Olympic competitions in which he competed, for Germany's ruling Nazi Party had as one of their founding principles that white people were supreme (called Aryan superiority) in everything. Born James Cleveland Owens, his family called him "JC," but when he went to school his teachers thought he said "Jesse" when asked about his name so the moniker stuck.

In the words of the *Encyclopedia of Alabama*, Jesse Owens "shocked the world" when he won not only one track and field competition, but four. He took gold in not only the long jump, but also the 100-meter and 200-meter dashes and the relay race. He was the first African-American athlete to win four Olympic gold medals in track and field.

His other, post-athletic, accomplishments included heading up a national fitness program for African-Americans through the Office of Civilian Defense and acting as liaison for Ford Motor Company for its black employees. In the 1950s, President Dwight D. Eisenhower sent the affable and inspiring Owens on international goodwill tours. His other accomplishments included being spokesperson for Quaker Oats, Johnson and Johnson, and Sears and Roebuck.

This picture of Jesse Owens (courtesy of the Library of Congress) shows him in intense concentration as he competes in the Berlin Games.

His longtime hero, Booker T. Washington, had inspired Owens to achieve racial equality through means other than aggression. In his book, *Blackthink* (1970, William Morrow Press), Owens condemned the Black Power movement of that time as being out of touch with the majority of African-Americans of the day. His last years were spent giving lectures and serving as a member of the Board of Directors of the U.S. Olympic Committee. He died of lung cancer in Tucson, Arizona, in March of 1980. He was 66.

Owens' life and accomplishments were commemorated on two U.S. postage stamps (showing young Owens in mid-jump and in running stance). In 2016, an incredible movie, "Race" was released about his experience in the Olympic games in 1936 Berlin (and in the movie, actor Stephan James, who portrays Owens, says "There is no black or white; there is only fast or slow."). Author Alson Pierce wrote about his personal experience of witnessing Jesse compete in the 1935 Big Ten meet at Ann Arbor, Michigan. That day Jesse's performance set three world records and tied another in less than an hour - a feat that has never been equaled and continues to be known as "the greatest 45 minutes ever in sport history."

This sculpture depicts track star Jesse Owens leaping through the Olympic logo. Photo by the author.

After returning victorious from the 1936 Olympic Games and being an international celebrity, Jesse Owens had to have been disappointed at his treatment in the U.S. President Franklin D. Roosevelt not only did not invite Owens and the other 17 African-American athletes to the White House, but did not even send them a congratulatory telegram. This snub was somewhat corrected when in 1976, President Gerald Ford presented Owens with the Presidential Medal of Freedom, the highest award given to a civilian. In 1990, Jesse was posthumously awarded the Congressional Gold Medal by

President George H. W. Bush. In 2016, President Barack Obama met with the families of the 18 African-American athletes of the Olympic Games in Berlin in 1936 to praise and properly honor them for their courage to successfully compete in a time of Nazi-ruled Germany and a segregated U.S.

A 2016 documentary, "Olympic Pride, American Prejudice," honors Owens and the 17 other African-American athletes of the 1936 Olympic Games. A stretch of Highway 36 that runs between Hartselle (near Huntsville) and Danville to the Morgan-Lawrence County line is called the Jesse Owens Parkway.

This sharecropper cabin, similar to one in which Jesse Owens was born and raised, is at the back lawn of the Jesse Owens Museum. It is furnished much the way it would have been in the early 1920s. Photo by the author.

Today you can tour the Jesse Owens Museum, which was built in Owens's birthplace of Oakville. Three people who worked to put together a plan to raise money for the museum to honor the track and field star were James Pinion, volunteer Curtis Cole, and Oakville resident Therman White; they were featured in a *Southern Living* issue (2008).

James and Nancy Pinion, who with a handful of other local visionaries began the museum and opened it in 1998, continue to actively work to perpetuate Jesse Owens' legacy and to properly honor his accomplishments. On the grounds of the museum is a fully restored and refurbished sharecropper's cabin. It looks much like it might have when Jesse Owens and his family would have lived in a place like it. As you tour it, his brother Sylvester's recorded narrative tells you what life was like for a family of twelve living in a three-room cabin. Outside the museum is a large statue depicting Owens in a running position, running through the Olympian 5-ring symbol (this sculpture was created by Birmingham native Branko Medenica.

Also on the grounds is a full-size replica of the Berlin long-jump pit (where you can compete against Jesse if you dare) and a replica of the 1936 torch. Inside the museum itself are interactive exhibits; in the theater section of the museum, you can also view actual footage of the Berlin games narrated by Jesse himself, see Hitler cringe at the sight of Owens' winning competitions, and watch sports announcer Howard Cosell praise this young and brave athlete. Many photographs of Jesse Owens with more exhibits about his life are also here.

In 1996, the Olympic torch was carried through parts of the South at the beginning of the games in Atlanta, Georgia. James Pinion met with the head of the Olympic Committee and asked that the torch be routed through the Jesse Owens Museum birthplace. The grandson of Jesse Owens, Stuart Owen Rankin, carried the torch into the park and Owens's widow, Ruth, lit the "eternal flame" in the park's replica of the 1936 Olympic torch.

Owens is remembered and honored in other ways, too: in Jesse Owens Park, you can see a monument of Owens. It was made possible through funding by Governor George C. Wallace, who paid for the monument of Jesse Owens to be created (it was meant to be set on the lawn of the Lawrence County Courthouse in Moulton, but in 1983 that was voted down by the county commissioners, thus its final home is in the park.

Owens is still remembered as, in the words of the *Encyclopedia of Alabama*, the "nation's greatest Olympian."

... AND ANOTHER SPEEDY ALABAMIAN

Birmingham-born (1961) Carl Lewis actually beat Jesse Owens' track and field gold medal record. Lewis won nine Olympic gold medals in four different Olympiads, and a total of eight World Championship medals during his track and field career, which spanned the years 1979 to 1996. According to latest information, Lewis still holds the world record for the indoor long jump that he set in 1984. Also in 1984, the four gold Olympic medals he won that year were on par with those of Jesse Owens, reported to be Lewis's hero according to the *Encyclopedia of Alabama*.

Lewis received many awards and honors for his notable achievements, including being named *Sports Illustrated*'s "Best Olympian of the 20th Century." In 1999, the International Olympic Committee named Lewis "Sportsman of the Century." You can see more about Lewis's achievements at the Alabama Sports Hall of Fame, as he was inducted in 1999. In December 2001, he was inducted into the National Track and Field Hall of Fame (in New York City). He currently is living in California and is serving the United Nations as one of their Goodwill Ambassadors.

BE QUICK TO TOUR THIS MUSEUM!

George Barber was a race car driver who took first place 63 times. He began collecting and restoring classic cars such as Porches in the 1980s but also developed an affinity for motorcycles. Then he realized that there was no place in the world that was a showcase for motorcycles of all kinds.

Thus, he founded the Barber Vintage Motorsports Museum. Located in Birmingham, this museum has employees who do motorcycle restorations on the premises. A motorcycle racing crew (the Barber Vintage Motorcycle Team) also has its base of operations under this roof.

Originally located in the Southside area of Birmingham in 1995, in 2003 the museum moved to its new location at Barber Motorsports Park near Pine Tree Country Club. For racing and motorcycle aficionados, this museum is a great place to spend a day. It houses more than 900 vintage and modern-day motorcycles on display, ranging from early 1900s models to present day.

FOR THOSE WHO LOVE ALL THINGS NASCAR

For NASCAR fans, your race-fan Paradise just might be found in Talladega. Besides watching the races, there are two tours you can take to get up close and personal with all things NASCAR. The International Motorsports Hall of Fame offers a self-guided walking tour where you can easily spend several hours learning more about racing, motorsports, and the legendary personalities of the competition. The Motorsports Hall of Fame is open most days (except major holidays) and has extended hours during race days.

For those who would like to actually get out on the track, there is a Talladega Superspeedway Tour especially with you in mind. This is approximately a 20-minute long tour, offered every half-hour beginning at 9 a.m. and ending at 4 p.m., with the van driver offering narration and answering questions. While you're a passenger, ask the driver about the "Talladega Jinx."

DID YOU KNOW?

Mobile native Robert Brazile, nicknamed "Doctor Doom" for playing in all 147 games for the Houston Oilers in his 10 years with the NFL, has 185 tackles on his record during that time, and was inducted into the National Football Hall of Fame in Canton, Ohio, in August of 2018.

Terrell Owens, another Alabama native, was also inducted into the hall at the same time although he was not present at the ceremony in Canton. He played for the Cincinnati Bengals.

FOR SPELUNKERS: ALABAMA COULD BE CALLED "THE CAVE STATE"

For decades, my family members and I explored caves. Of course, it has its risks, but every time I'm underground, I forget about any dangers and get lost in the exploration of these secret (and not-so-secret) places underneath the soil of Alabama.

Alabama could well be called "THE Cave State": According to the Alabama Cave Survey, there are more than 4,400 caves in the Yellowhammer State. The city of Huntsville has more than its share of caves as does the city of Florence and surrounding area. Just two counties in Alabama—Jackson and Madison—are home to more than 2,000 caves. This enormous number of caves caused the National Speleological Society (NSS) to relocate its offices from its home base in Washington, D.C. (where it had been since its inception in 1941), to Huntsville in 1971. The NSS has now grown to more than 250 chapters referred to as "grottoes" across the U.S. There are currently eight such "grottoes" in Alabama.

Two of the more popular caves that spelunkers like to explore are Cathedral Caverns (in Woodville). Inside this commercial cave is a huge, 45-foot-tall stalagmite they call "Goliath." Beyond that, you can see a sprawling and awe-inspiring forest of stalagmites.

Another cave is located in Jackson County. Named "Green's Well," the only way into this vertical cave is by rappelling. Those who dare to do so are rewarded with a thrilling, 227-foot drop onto the cave's floor.

The current president of NSS is Geary Schindel. See "Virtual Alabama" for websites.

FOR THE ADRENALINE JUNKIES: THE PARK AT OWA

In July of 2017, Alabama's newest amusement park opened in Foley, Alabama (just north of Gulf Shores). This 520-acre amusement park currently has 22 different rides, as well as various food venues and gaming facilities. For the diehard thrill-seekers, though, probably the biggest attraction is the ride called "Rollin' Thunder," which has a 165-foot vertical climb (with a subsequent drop) and loops and twists. Its top speed is 65 mph.

THE BANKS-WOODLAWN GAME: THE BIGGEST HIGH SCHOOL FOOTBALL GAME EVER PLAYED IN ALABAMA

It was on the night of November 8, 1974, at Legion Field in Birmingham when a historic high school football game was held. It was between major rivals--the Woodlawn High School Colonels and the two-time defending champion, the Banks High School Jets. Bob Carlton wrote about the historic game on its fortieth anniversary in 2014 for AL.com.

The main rivalry was between the Colonels' player "Touchdown Tony" Nathan and the Jets' player Jeff Rutledge. Carlton wrote that as time has gone by, "the details [about the game] have gotten fuzzier and the legends have grown larger." He wrote that no one could seem to remember the final score. What they could remember was people came in such numbers that the start of the game had to be delayed. Carlton also wrote that Legion Field was packed with a whopping 42,000 people in attendance! This number remains as the highest to attend a high school football game in the state of Alabama. Legion Field Stadium, which locals affectionately refer to as "the old gray lady," is still currently in use for sports events, entertainment venues and other large-capacity events.

By the way, about the two football players—Banks High School quarterback Jeff Rutledge would go on to play at The University of Alabama (Tuscaloosa) and lead the team to a national championship, then play on two winning Super Bowl teams. Woodlawn running back Tony Nathan, who was one of the Miracle City's first African-American superstar athletes, wound up playing with, rather than against, his former rival Jeff Rutledge, playing for The Crimson Tide. He also played in two Super Bowl matchups. At that time, according to Carlton, these two players were "the most sought-after high school recruits in the country."

Both Rutledge and Nathan are Alabama Sports Hall of Fame inductees—Nathan was an inductee in 1999 and

Rutledge in 2011. You can see more about them at the all-things-sports venue located in Birmingham.

WHO KNEW?

You might know that Tuscaloosa native Deontay Wilder has been the World Boxing Council's World Champion every year since 2015, but what you might not know is how big of a Crimson Tide football fan he is and that he has been a motivational speaker to the team. For example, before the Tide's kickoff game against Louisville in the fall of 2018, Wilder gave the team a pep talk. Nicknamed "The Bronze Bomber," Wilder said to the team in a televised motivational speech, "You combine yourselves, you think like y'all are supposed to think on a team—nobody will stop you. I'm rooting for y'all. When y'all are knocking people out, I'm knocking them out, too."

… AND ANOTHER BOXING STAR

Atmore-born Evander Holyfield has led an amazing boxing career. Born in Atmore in 1962, Holyfield is the only holder of the World Heavyweight Champion—FIVE TIMES. In the Summer Olympic Games of 1984 (in Los Angeles), Holyfield took the Bronze Medal in boxing competition. In the year 2015, he was inducted into BOTH the Alabama Sports Hall of Fame (in Birmingham) AND the International Sports Hall of Fame (in Chicago). Talk about a one-two knockout!

YOU'LL BE "TEED OFF" AT YOURSELF IF YOU DON'T PLAY THESE AMAZING COURSES

When most people outside Alabama think about the state, the first thing that may come to mind for them might be the sugar-white beaches of the coast or the great fishing to be had in Mobile Bay, the Delta or the Gulf of Mexico, or the state's many fantastic museums and entertainment venues. But one of the state's biggest attractions is golf.

The internationally-famous Robert Trent Jones Golf Trail began as a vision held by the CEO of the Retirement Systems of Alabama, Dr. David Bronner. It was in the late 1980s when Bronner wanted to diversify the RSA pension funds while also helping bring more tourism to Alabama. Bronner commissioned the well-known and respected golf course architect Robert Trent Jones to design a series of 18 golf courses sprinkled throughout the state of Alabama.

The RTJ Golf Trail currently comprises 26 golf courses across 11 places in Alabama for a total of 468 championship holes. Jones' achievement remains the largest single golf design contract in history. With their iconic slogan that says, "World-class golf, that's not a world away," you're within chipping distance of any one of the golf courses in the state when you're in Alabama. The trail has been hailed by such notable publications as the *New York Times*, who proclaimed it as "some of the best public golf on Earth," and the *Wall Street Journal*, who hailed it as "the biggest bargain in the country."

There is something unique about each of the golf courses—for example, at the Ross Bridge golf course, every evening at sunset they have a man dressed in a kilt play the bagpipes (in the Ross Bridge hotel lobby) as a nod to the "game of kings'" Scottish roots. Further, most of the golf courses offer golf lessons for those who want to learn to play or to improve their game. Even if you don't play, there are other amenities offered by the RTJ Trail, such as relaxing spas, lovely resorts, beautiful views and fine dining. See "Virtual Alabama" for websites.

DID YOU KNOW? THIS BOXER CHALLENGED THE PGA—AND WON

Lafayette native Joe Louis became famous through his fantastic boxing career (his nickname was "the Brown Bomber"), but he also became the first African-American to play a PGA-sanctioned golf tournament. It happened in 1952 when Louis was invited to play the San Diego Open that year. At the time, there was a Caucasians-only clause in the Professional Golfers of America's constitution. Louis's celebrity status obliged the PGA to remove this clause, so he paved the way for future African-American golfers.

You might say he "beat 'em to the punch." By the way, there is a statue of Joe Louis (in boxing stance) in front of the Chamber County Courthouse in Lafayette, Alabama.

MAKING HISTORY A "PAIGE" AT A TIME

Mobile-born Leroy Robert "Satchel" Paige first became well known as the greatest pitcher among the African-American teams. He was also one of the first African-American baseball players to be a part of the integration of the game. The 1981 movie, "Don't Look Back," was based on Paige's life. There is a statue of Paige in Cooper Park, Cooperstown, NY; also, a street near Hank Aaron Stadium in Mobile is named after one of the fastest pitchers in baseball history.

… AND THEN THERE'S "HAMMERIN' HANK" AARON

Another Mobile native, Henry "Hank" Aaron, who played for the Braves, broke Babe Ruth's homer record in 1974 with 715 homeruns. He also won three Golden Gloves. In 2010, his boyhood home was moved from Toulminville to where it now stands, on the grounds of Hank Aaron Stadium in Mobile. The home is full of memorabilia from Aaron's and his family's life and his baseball career. My personal favorite is hearing Aaron's own recorded voice, reminiscing about his childhood growing up in Mobile. It's a fitting tribute to "Hammerin' Hank." Currently it is open five days a week (and on game days).

Q & A

Q. What 1938 University of Alabama football player (and letterman) became blind, then went on to become an internationally-famous golfer?

A. Charley Boswell. There is a golf course on the Southside area of Birmingham named in his honor.

Q. What lake in Alabama is known as "The Bass Capital of the World"?

A. Lake Eufaula. The 45,000 acre lake has produced monster large-mouth bass. The lake record is a little more than 14 pounds! Mayor Jack Tibbs told me there are roughly 100 bass tournaments held at Lake Eufaula every year. There is a large statue of a bass in front of the Eufaula Chamber of Commerce on East Broad Street.

Q. What was the field position Hank Aaron played during the majority of his baseball career?

A. Right field.

Q. Out of his 71 boxing matches, how many did Lafayette-born Joe Louis, aka "The Brown Bomber," win?

A. He won 69 matches. There is a life-size statue of the boxer-turned-legend in the Chambers County Courthouse Square in downtown Lafayette.

Q. What football team was the first shutout team in their fall to The University of Alabama in 1892?

A. Birmingham High School. The score was 56-0 in Alabama's inaugural game.

Q. Who introduced football to The University of Alabama?

A. William Little in 1891.

Q. Born in Alger, what Auburn track star and halfback coached Bessemer High School for 30 years?

A. Euil "Snitz" Snider.

Q. What Alabama coach, on the night he was scheduled to be inducted into the Alabama Sports Hall of Fame, died of a heart attack?

A. Hank Crisp, in 1970.

Q. Stevenson native Sanders Russell became nationally famous for racing what kind of horse?

A. The trotting horse.

Q. What sportswriter and editor for the *Birmingham News* was the driving force behind the Alabama Sports Hall of Fame?

A. Zipp Newman.

Q. In what city is the Alabama Sports Hall of Fame located?

A. Birmingham.

Q. What is the seating capacity for the Bryant-Denny Stadium in Tuscaloosa?

A. As of 2018, it was 101,820.

Q. The year 1926 was The University of Alabama football team's first-ever bowl game (the Rose Bowl). What team was their opponent?

A. The Washington Huskies. The score, incidentally, was 20-19 in Alabama's favor; this was the Tide's first National Championship.

Q. Tannehill State Park holds what event every October?

A. The Black Powder Muzzle Loaders' Rendezvous.

Q. Before coaching at Alabama, Paul "Bear" Bryant was coaching at what other university from 1954 to 1957?

A. Texas A & M.

Q. Which Alabama coach (1950s era) was named to six different halls of fame: Alabama, Tennessee, North Carolina, Brown University, Helms and the National Football Hall of Fame?

A. Wallace Wade.

Q. What long-running sailboat race still brings sailors from all over the world to the Alabama coast?

A. The Dauphin Island Regatta, which began in 1958 and is held every spring.

Q. What native of Wilsonville became internationally famous for his archery skills by winning 196 tournaments in a row and was inducted into the Alabama Sports Hall of Fame in 1971?

A. That would have to be archery expert Howard Hill. Some of his memorabilia is on display in the Alabama Sports Hall of Fame in Birmingham.

Q. During what years did John Heisman, for which the Heisman Trophy is named, coach at Auburn?

A. 1895-1899.

Q. What coach was head coach of the Crimson Tide football team in its first untied and undefeated season?

A. Wallace Wade, in the year 1925.

Q. More than $30,000 in prizes are awarded at what equestrian event, the largest American Saddlebred horse show in the South?

A. The Alabama State Charity Horse Show. It's held every October in Priceville, Alabama.

Q. Joe Louis recorded how many knockouts in his boxing career?

A. Fifty-four.

Q. What Auburn football coach, born in Selma, has recorded the most wins to date?

A. Ralph "Shug" Jordan, with 176 wins under his belt. Jordan-Hare Stadium is partially named in his honor.

Q. What Alabama player holds the individual record for the most career rushes?

A. Johnny Musso. Statistics show he had 574 rushes in the three years from 1969-1971.

Q. Where is English-born Sir Malcolm Campbell's land speed record-setting Bluebird racecar on display?

A. It is on display in the International Motorsports Hall of Fame in Lincoln, Alabama, adjacent to the Talladega Superspeedway.

Q. Who founded the National Association for Stock Car Auto Racing (NASCAR)?

A. Bill France, Sr.

Q. What coach led the Crimson Tide to its first-ever SEC Championship in 1933?

A. Frank Thomas.

Q. What award is given to the outstanding player of the annual Red vs. White ("A Day") each spring?

A. The Dixie Howell Memorial Award.

Q. What is the seating capacity of the Jordan-Hare Stadium in Auburn?

A. After its latest renovation (2007), Auburn's website has the stadium's seating capacity at 87,451 as of 2018.

Q. What famous sportswriter wrote two books on Alabama football: *War Eagle: A Story of Auburn Football* and *The Crimson Tide: A Story of Alabama Football*?

A. Clyde Bolton.

Q. Andalusia hosts what world championship competition?

A. The World Championship Domino Tournament. It is held every July.

Q. What former Crimson Tide player and NFL football star penned the book, *Snake*?

A. Kenny Stabler.

Q. What Auburn head basketball coach was awarded SEC Coach of the Year three times, and still holds the record of 213 wins during his career from 1949 to 1963?

A. Joel Harry Eaves. He was inducted into the Alabama Sports Hall of Fame (Birmingham) in 1978.

Q. Why did the Crimson Tide become associated with the elephant as a mascot?

A. The enormous size of the 1930 varsity team caused someone to refer to them as elephants. According to the official Crimson Tide website, upon seeing the team in their red jerseys running out onto the field, one excited fan yelled, "Hold your horses, the elephants are coming!" Atlanta Journal sportswriter Everett Strupper heard this and began to refer to the team as "the red elephants."

Q. What play did Coach John Heisman originate at Auburn?

A. He originated the center snap. He also legalized the forward pass.

Q. What Crimson Tide tackle became the school's first All-American?

A. W. T. "Billy" VandeGraaf, in 1915.

T. Jensen Lacey

CHAPTER 9
THE CIVIL WAR AND ALABAMA

THE CONFEDERACY'S "FIRST WHITE HOUSE"

In Montgomery, on Washington Avenue just off I-85, you will find the First White House of the Confederacy. This home was the residence of President Jefferson Davis and his family during the time the capital of the CSA (Confederate States of America) was located in Montgomery in 1861. In May of that year, the Confederate capital was moved to Richmond, Virginia.

The White House Association gave the completely restored home to the people of (in the words of their tour brochure) "Alabama, the South and the Nation." It has been open for tours since it was given to the people in 1921. Inside you will find many personal items of the only President of the CSA, Jefferson Davis, and his wife, Varina Davis.

"SUB OF DEATH": THE STORY OF THE HUNLEY

The first submersible vessel to be *successfully* used in wartime was constructed in Mobile, Alabama. Marine engineer Horace Lawson Hunley had drawn out the plans for the vessel, thus the submarine was named in his honor. The *Hunley* was a 40-foot-long cylinder of iron, a steam boiler tapered at both ends. It was manufactured in Mobile, then successfully tested on the Mobile River, and finally taken by rail to Charleston, South Carolina's harbor in August of 1863. The submarine was the symbol of the Confederacy that, with this vessel, they could successfully break the Union blockade of the Confederate-held ports (including Mobile).

The sub was nicknamed the "Sub of Death" when, during its testing in Charleston Harbor, five of the nine crewmembers drowned because someone gave the order to dive while the *Hunley*'s hatches were still open. The *Hunley* was brought back up and salvaged, but two months after the fatal incident, the second eight-member crew, including Hunley himself, all died in a similar incident.

Lieutenant George Dixon then took command of the *Hunley*. It was November of 1863, and Dixon may have thought himself under a kind of charm: his lady-love Queenie Bennett had given him a golden coin, saying it would protect him from harm. The gold coin in his uniform pocket had protected him from a Union soldier's bullet in the Battle of Shiloh. In Charleston Harbor, on February 17, 1864, the *Hunley* and her crew managed to get close enough to a Union vessel, *The Housatonic*, and shot it with a spar torpedo, causing the Union ship to sink.

The crew of the *Hunley* probably had no time to celebrate this first Confederate submariner's victory; most likely due to what coroners referred to as "blast lung," the crew became incapacitated due to their proximity to the explosion. The *Hunley* sank shortly after the Union vessel went under, with her brave crew on board.

Dixon and his crew of seven brave Confederate sailors died, and they remained interred in their water tomb until the year 1995, when preservationists discovered her in Charleston Harbor in only 30 feet of water. With funding provided in part by author Clive Cussler, in August 2000 the *Hunley* and her crew were brought up, out of Charleston Harbor. In sifting through the soldiers' remains and artifacts inside the vessel, researchers did find Dixon's gold coin, inscribed on one side with his initials and "Shiloh" (the coin, along with other artifacts, are in safekeeping in Charleston, according to *National Geographic* staff).

In the spring of 2004, in what *National Geographic* writer Willie Dye called the "Last funeral of the Civil War," the remains of the soldiers, including Dixon, were re-interred in Magnolia Cemetery in Charleston with full military honors (even their pall-bearers wore dress Confederate uniforms). The burials were attended by thousands of people from all over the world.

Now, the *Hunley* itself is on display in a water tank at Warren Lasch Conservation Center in Charleston. In Mobile, Alabama, where the *Hunley*'s story began, you can see a memorial in Magnolia Cemetery in the "Confederate Rest" portion of the graveyard, honoring the crew of the *C.S.S. Hunley*. You can also learn more about the story of the *Hunley* and her crew in a museum in Mobile. There is a partial replica of the *Hunley* in the GulfQuest Maritime Museum in downtown Mobile. When you sit inside the vessel, a wonderful visual exhibit comes on before you, and you can hear all about the *Hunley*, Dixon and his lady-love. See "Virtual Alabama" for websites pertaining to the Hunley.

DID YOU KNOW?

"Fighting Joe Wheeler" was the ONLY Confederate general to be made a Union general after the Civil War. Wheeler National Wildlife Refuge just outside Huntsville is named for him.

FORT MORGAN IN THE CIVIL WAR

Finished in 1834, this Pentagon-shaped fort across from Fort Gaines was named after Revolutionary War hero Daniel Morgan. Prior to its construction, a lesser fort, called Fort Bowyer (named after Colonel John Bowyer), saw action in the War of 1812. Eight days before Alabama formally seceded from the U.S., four companies of volunteers under the command of Colonel John B. Todd captured the fort early in the morning of January 3, 1861. They proceeded to place 18 of the fort's largest guns to bear on the channel leading into Mobile Bay. To impede Union soldiers from attacking by land, they put up redoubts and trenches east of the fort. They had a small flotilla to aid in defending the fort; these vessels (the Tennessee, a ramming vessel, and three gunboats) were under the command of Admiral Franklin Buchanan.

Civil War re-enactor Ralph Oalmann shows visitors at Fort Gaines how blacksmiths used to make tools and other metal items for the fort. Photo by the author.

The soldiers at Fort Morgan successfully aided a total of 36 vessels to elude capture from Union vessels attempting to blockade the mouth of the bay (some were coming in, some heading toward the Gulf of Mexico).

During the Battle of Mobile Bay, Admiral Farragut and his Union fleet were able to get past Fort Morgan and enter

Mobile Bay (see more about him in the story on Fort Gaines). After Farragut and his men sank one warship and captured two others, they were able to capture Fort Gaines.

They then set their sights on laying siege to Fort Morgan. After two weeks of this, the commander of Fort Morgan, Major Richard L. Page, surrendered on August 23, 1864.

Once Fort Morgan was under Union control, they used the fort as a base from which to attack Spanish Fort and Fort Blakely to the north.

Today, Fort Morgan is open for tours, and occasionally puts on re-enactments. In 1960, it was designated a National Historic Landmark and, like its neighbor across the water, Fort Gaines, was listed by the Civil War Preservation Trust as "one of the most endangered battle sites."

Fast-forward to the year 2008, when workers doing some repair work on the east wall of the fort uncovered something no one knew about or expected: it was an unexploded, 90-pound ordinance called a Parrott cannon ball. The area was cleared of workers and tourists for about an hour, while experts determined whether it presented a danger to anyone around it. Kenny Smith, who wrote about this finding for AL.com, said it was the "only intact shell that can be confirmed as having been fired at Fort Morgan" during the Battle of Mobile Bay. Site curator Mike Bailey expressed amazement that, for 144 years, this 90-pound, unexploded ordinance lay under the sand at the east wall. "It's amazing," he said in Smith's article, "how it was there all this time and was never found when the fort was being repaired in 1866, or during all the work the Army did here, right up to World War II."

In May of 2018, I caught up with Fort Morgan Historian Dylan Tucker to get an update about this unexploded ordinance. It's currently not on display, but anything is possible, he indicated.

Fort Morgan offers guided tours during the months of March, April and May, and candlelight (ghost) tours in October. There is also a boat launch and picnic area on the premises.

THE BLOCKADE AND ITS RUNNERS

On April 19, 1861, Union President Lincoln announced a blockade of all southern ports. His decree demanded naval monitoring and warships halting maritime trade of more than 3,000 miles of coastline. At the outbreak of the Civil War, ten ports were deemed to be of utmost significance to the success of the Confederacy. The port of Mobile was among them (the others were Norfolk, Virginia; Beaufort, New Bern and Wilmington, NC; Charleston, Savannah, Pensacola, New Orleans and Galveston).

Initially, since the Union Navy was ill-prepared and ill-equipped for this task, blockade runners skillfully evaded engagement and capture by Union warships. As time went on and the Civil War continued, the Union Navy grew to be able to detect and deter blockade runners. In particular, the port of Mobile was, in the words of author Hamilton Cochran (*Blockade Runners of the Confederacy*), "securely bottled up." For the people of south Alabama especially, this meant they were obliged to do without things they'd come to depend on that had been produced elsewhere. For example, for shoes, they began to make their own out of pigskin!

DID YOU KNOW?

When General Robert E. Lee surrendered to Ulysses S. Grant, the standard-bearer ceremoniously handed the flag of truce to Grant on Lee's behalf.

That flag-bearer was an Alabamian. He would become better known as the Honorable T. (Thomas) H. (Heard) Herndon, who served the CSA first as a major then colonel of the 36th Alabama Infantry. He later became governor of Alabama (1890-1894). You can learn more about him and other Alabama governors in Montgomery's Alabama Department of Archives and History (ADAH).

JOSEPH SANDERS, THE TURNCOAT OF DALE COUNTY

Born in 1827 in North Carolina, Joseph Sanders was brought to Newton in Dale County as a child. When the Civil War broke out in 1861, Sanders was an early enlistee for the Confederate State of America's (CSA) Army. He served well and quickly rose to the rank of captain. He fought bravely in several battles, including Antietam, in which he was wounded. While on furlough to recover from his wounds, he began construction of a gristmill that was sorely needed. The citizens of Newton began a petition to have Sanders released from the army, and it was finally approved by CSA President Jefferson Davis.

In 1864, the U.S. Army formed the First Florida Cavalry—and one of the first to enlist was none other than Joseph Sanders. In early 1865, he took the men under his command and set them to raiding and terrorizing the citizens of Holmes and Walton Counties in northern Florida. He even led an attack on the town of Newton, which locals successfully repulsed. When he finally became a citizen again and returned to Dale County, the people there made it clear he was no longer welcome; he left to settle in Georgia in DeKalb County. He was killed there in 1867; no one knows for sure who committed the murder, but many people in Dale County say it was an act of revenge, done by someone who signed the petition to have Sanders released from the CSA.

There is a historical marker in Newton that mentions the Sanders raid and also a Civil War Memorial in town.

TANNEHILL IRONWORKS HISTORICAL STATE PARK

Just south of Birmingham in the town of McCalla, you will find this lovely, sprawling, 1,500-acre state park. Spreading across three counties, Tannehill Ironworks was used to make iron for the Confederate cause. The furnaces, which are still there, are among the best-preserved among all Civil War landmarks in the U.S.

The Gott House at Tannehill Ironworks Historical State Park is a wonder to see. Courtesy Tannehill Ironworks Historical State Park.

Within this state park, you can hike, do some bird-watching, ride the horse trails, stay in cabins, tour the Alabama Iron and Steel Museum, and more. The park has a "Pioneer Farm," which includes a fully-functioning blacksmith shop (along with a working 'smith at the forge), and many of the hiking trails follow the old ore miners' and furnace workers' routes. During the weekends of the months of March through November,

Tannehill is host to "Crafts Cabins." These cabins, all from the 1800s era, were brought here some years back especially for what I call Tannehill's Artisans weekends. On these weekends, the cabins are filled with artisans making and selling their wares, from art work to pottery, cane chairs, quilts and more. Many of them are dressed in period clothing, adding to the fun. Also in this park is the famed "Gott House," a log cabin built by noted Appalachian Mountain cabin builder Peter Gott.

TALLASSEE'S CLAIM TO FAME: THE TALLASSEE ARMORY

When, in the spring of 1864, the war threatened the Richmond, Virginia armory, Colonel Josiah Gorgas, Ordnance Chief with the CSA, had a carbine (short-rifle) shop moved from Richmond to Tallassee, Alabama, located northeast of Montgomery. The armory machinery was set up and began operations inside one building of an operational cotton mill there. When Union General Lovell Rousseau, who was under orders from General W. T. Sherman, went on a raid to destroy as much Confederate military production and transportation capabilities as he could find in East Alabama, his raiding party bypassed the armory at Tallassee, due to a small force of unseasoned cadets and old men Governor Watts sent by train to oppose Rousseau and his soldiers.

Sherman had ordered Rousseau not to fight any pitched battles; his sole mission was one of destruction of any manufacturing or military supply-making facilities that he could find, and to destroy the vital rail line connecting Montgomery, Alabama, and West Point, Georgia. Rousseau encountered CSA troops (some of whom were 16- and 17-year-old cadets on furlough from The University of Alabama), who engaged him in battles at Chehaw Station and nearby Franklin. Threats of CSA General Nathan B. Forrest and his men being on the proverbial trail obliged him to give up his quest to destroy the armory at

Tallassee. After his troops destroyed large portions of railroad track and burned supplies, Rousseau moved on toward Georgia.

The Tallassee Armory continued working in an attempt to bring its production of carbines to 6,000 a year. Meanwhile, in the spring of 1865, U.S. General James H. Wilson with his 13,000 well-seasoned, war-hardened and well-armed soldiers raided through Alabama. One of Wilson's reports read, "We encountered a superior enemy [CSA] force at Franklin and were forced to rejoin our command at Auburn."

According to Bill Anthony, Sutler Coordinator for the Tallassee Armory Guards (Sons of Confederate Veterans Camp 921) and member of the Tallassee Historical Preservation Society, Wilson had in his possession an old map that showed the location of the Indian village of Tsali and mistakenly thought this was the town of Tallassee and the armory. Wilson forced an African-American to guide him and his troops to what he thought was the location for Tallassee. When the guide told Wilson that his map was wrong and that Tallassee and the Confederate armory were on the opposite side of the river, Wilson, thinking this was trickery, had the poor man shot. Wilson and his men continued their march and stumbled upon Franklin, where, like Rousseau, they were also engaged by a superior Confederate force. Like Rousseau, Wilson and his men turned away.

In case you have in mind a question such as "What of the carbines?" surviving records show that there were only 500 guns actually produced at the Tallassee Armory. They are now among the rarest of weapons produced by the Confederacy.

Today, you can take tours of the Confederacy's ONLY carbine armory still in existence. Every autumn, the town reenacts the historic "Battles for the Armory," which they began doing in 1997, according to Bill Anthony. This weekend-long event includes field exhibits, a working blacksmith shop, an operational period field hospital, battle re-enactments, artillery demonstrations, guided tours of the Confederate Armory and a living-history school program (on that Friday) so children can see what life was like during the era. As of 2018, they also added an Arts and Crafts Fair.

CAHAWBA AND ITS CIVIL WAR GHOST

You can read the story about "Old Cahawba" and its attractions today; but back during the Civil War, a ghostly image haunted the area. Known to locals as "Peque's Ghost," the story goes that it was around 1861 that two lovers, a Confederate soldier and his lady, were strolling in the gardens behind General Peque's house. He had raised the Alabama 4th Infantry, and some soldiers were on leave at this time. The lovers were startled to see a large, luminous orb in front of them in the walkway. When the soldier tried to touch it, the orb disappeared into a thicket. Thinking that the orb was caused by the full moon that night, the lovers turned to go in the opposite direction—and the orb reappeared right in front of them!

It was shortly after this sighting that General Peque was wounded in battle and died two weeks later. Now, you can tour Old Cahawba, which is an archeological park—and hope that you don't see Peque's Ghost! *Alabama Pioneers* website blogger and Alabama historian Donna Causey says Old Cahawba is one of the most haunted places in Alabama.

DID YOU KNOW?

Many cities and communities in Alabama were occupied by Union troops in the last days and just after the end of the

Civil War. For example, the city of Guntersville was shelled on more than one occasion, without warning, killing citizens as they were attempting to flee for their lives. In January 1865, Union troops attacked the city and burned every building except for a few. According to the magazine *Alabama Confederate* (July 2018 issue), Guntersville may hold the record for being the longest-occupied city in Alabama—it was under Union occupation from 1865 to 1877!

THE LARGEST-SCALE CIVIL WAR BATTLE FOUGHT IN NORTHWEST ALABAMA: THE ENGAGEMENT AT LITTLE BEAR CREEK

The biggest Civil War battle to be fought in northwest Alabama was the engagement at Little Bear Creek, approximately three miles west of Tuscumbia in the autumn of 1863. Although it's not as well-known as the Battle of Athens or the Battle of Decatur, more soldiers on both sides were engaged on the field. The Confederates assembled to check the advancing Union Army were led by Jeffrey Forrest, the brother of General Nathan Bedford Forrest. Although it was a bit of a "draw," the Confederates were able to stop the Union soldiers in their attempts to complete the rail line. The Union army's mission was to rebuild the Memphis & Charleston Railroad from Corinth, Mississippi, so they could ship supplies and soldiers by rail to Tuscumbia and from there to Decatur, where they could cross the Tennessee River and continue on into Tennessee.

They were obliged to leave the area and the railroad, their mission unfinished. Due to the Confederates' relentless attacks, the Union soldiers were forced to march on to Tennessee via Huntsville and Florence. You can see more exhibits about this and other Civil War battles fought in northwestern Alabama through Tuscumbia's "History and

Haunts" tour, held every October. During this time, you can see Civil War re-enactors and take a tour of the battlegrounds, which are said to be haunted.

RAPHAEL SEMMES: WOLF OF THE DEEP

Born in 1809 in Maryland, Semmes served in the U.S. Navy from 1826 through 1860 (he also studied law and was admitted to the bar). When the Civil War broke out in 1861, he gave up his commission and went to serve in the Navy of the Confederate States of America (CSA). Initially, he was put in charge of overseeing the lighthouses, an assignment which was said to have chafed him. Finally, he was given a naval appointment and sent to New Orleans to oversee the conversion of a steamer into a ship capable of commerce raiding. The ship, christened the *CSS Sumter*, was the vessel which launched Semmes' career and reputation as the greatest commerce raider captain in naval history.

His reputation was a global one, as his ship ranged from the Caribbean to the Atlantic. He and his crew successfully sank 18 merchant vessels, while also avoiding Union warships. He and his crew were obliged to disband when, getting the vessel repaired in neutral Gibraltar, U.S. Navy vessels kept vigil outside the harbor. His ship was disarmed and sold at auction.

Semmes traveled to England, which was sympathetic to the Confederacy. It was there he was given a new command and a new ship: This one was outfitted to be the commerce raider, the *CSS Alabama*. He and his ship would make international news in the years 1862 to 1864. During these years, Semmes and his new crew captured 65 merchant vessels, ever eluding Union warships. Interestingly enough, the *CSS Alabama* never touched waters in either Mobile Bay or the Gulf of Mexico. Semmes captained his ship to far-flung ports around the globe, as far as Africa, Australia and Europe.

It was in June 1864 when the *CSS Alabama* met her fate. Semmes had the ship in the port of Cherbourg, France for much-needed repairs when he found himself blockaded by a Union warship, the USS *Kearsarge*, under the command of Captain John A. Winslow. Semmes took the CSS *Alabama* out to meet and engage the *Kearsarge* in what would go down in history books as the most famous naval engagement of the Civil War. The captain and crew of the *Kearsarge* won the battle; Semmes was forced to surrender but defiantly threw his sword into the sea, depriving Captain Winslow of the traditional surrender ceremony of receiving it as victor. Semmes and his surviving crew were taken to England, where they were celebrated as naval heroes, in spite of the loss of their ship.

Semmes eventually made his way to the Confederate capital. In Montgomery in 1864, he was promoted to Rear Admiral and given command of the James River Squadron. When he heard of the fall of Richmond, Semmes destroyed his fleet and brought his crew to Virginia; he and his men escorted the fleeing president south to safety. After the surrender of the Confederacy, Semmes was arrested, charged with piracy, treason and other war crimes. After being held for three months, however, the charges were dropped and Semmes was freed without being brought to trial.

After spending some time in Louisiana, Semmes returned to Mobile, where he was editor of a small newspaper, practiced law, wrote his memoirs and gave speeches. In 1877, he died in a way no one would have thought: not in a battle, but from food poisoning. He is buried in Mobile's Catholic Cemetery.

Today, there is a bronze statue of Raphael Semmes in downtown Mobile and also a street named in his honor. The bridge over the Tensaw River (just east of Mobile) is named after him, as is a road on Dauphin Island. Pierre Manet painted his first work of historical art by depicting the battle between the *U.S.S. Kearsarge* and the *C.S.S. Alabama*. The original hangs in the Philadelphia Museum of Art, and a beautiful replica is on display in the Alabama Department of Archives and History in Montgomery. The lovely hotel The Admiral, also in downtown Mobile, is named after the man they called "The Wolf of the Deep."

CIVIL WAR GOLD, YOURS FOR THE FINDING

Many treasure seekers and just plain lucky folks have come across gold that was buried or sunk in a ship at sea, because of rumors (and some true stories) about gold, especially Confederate gold, that never made its way to its destination or that was buried to keep it out of the hands of invading Union soldiers. In 1926, a man named Gayus Whitfield found gold worth $200,000 (worth $2.6 million today), using a map his father, Boaz Whitfield, left him. Boaz Whitfield, whose father was General Nathan Bryan Whitfield, had been said to be one of the wealthiest of Alabama's citizens before the Civil War (and built Gaineswood plantation).

Other people have discovered gold and silver when they've found a coin or two after a heavy rain has uncovered them, and have gone to digging for more.

What are you waiting for? Get out that metal detector! LEGAL DISCLAIMER: you are hereby informed that looking for gold and historical artifacts is prohibited in many places of historic or archeological value. This author advises you to check with property owners as to the legality of taking your metal detector on their site.

ONE OF THE NEWEST THINGS ON THE CIVIL WAR TRAIL

In October of 2014, there was a grand opening of a new, permanent exhibit at the Morgan County Archives. Called "The Civil War in Morgan County, Alabama," it was the culmination of several years of planning and working to finally open the exhibit to the public. According to the website www.AppalachianHistory.net, many of the citizens of Morgan County objected to Alabama's seceding and disliked the idea of going to war. Some of the farmers in the county joined with Union military forces, becoming the mainstay of the Union's First Alabama Cavalry.

The town of Decatur was strategically located due to its railroad links and its position north of the impassable Muscle Shoals; when Union forces occupied Decatur in 1862, General R. S. Granger evicted Decatur's citizens and leveled their city. He had a fortress constructed where the buildings and homes of the people of Decatur had once stood.

As a result of these Federal forces that had evicted the people of Decatur and leveled their city, bitter citizens joined up with Confederate forces, leaving to go out of state because, at the time, Alabama was unable to equip its volunteer soldiers.

Confederate General John Bell Hood attacked Granger's fortress with a force of 30,000 soldiers of the Army of Tennessee against a few thousand Union troops but was unsuccessful. Historians say that this loss of Decatur may have also cost Hood the Battle of Franklin, Tennessee, later.

African-American men had a role in the Civil War here. There were so-called "contraband camps," that recruited slaves who escaped their captivity and were willing to join in the Union effort against the Confederacy. It was one of these camps that formed the 106th U.S. Colored Infantry, or USCI, which was the only such unit formed in Alabama. Another unit, the 14th USCI, attacked Confederate artillery positions at Decatur on October 28, 1864.

Incidentally, the aforementioned First Alabama Cavalry were what aided Union Colonel Abel Streight to raid the area in 1863. Known as "Streight's Raid," he met Confederate General Nathan Bedford Forrest, and their ensuing battle was a furious one.

Today, you can see a monument erected for the brilliant Confederate General N. B. Forrest; it's at the site where Streight surrendered on Highway 9 three miles east of Cedar Bluff. The M1848 ("M" stands for "Military-issue") sword that Streight relinquished to Forrest (in keeping with the surrender tradition) is on display in Montgomery at the Alabama Department of Archives and History. Also, the Cullman County Museum (in the town of Cullman) has a fantastic exhibit with audio and video displays, telling more about what they refer to as "The Lightning Mule Brigade." You can also see more about this interesting part of Civil War history at the Morgan County Archives.

WOMEN IN THE CONFLICT

Emma Sansom was a young and courageous Alabamian during the Civil War. Although this teenage girl never donned a Confederate soldier's uniform (as quite a few courageous and determined women did then), she was nonetheless a heroine to the Confederacy. When General Nathan Bedford Forrest was in pursuit of Colonel Streight and his Union forces, she helped Forrest and his men find a clear passage across Gadsden's Black

Creek to overtake, engage and capture Colonel Streight and his 1,466 men.

Her story has been romanticized and glorified in ways that live beyond her. For example, newspaper journalist and poet John Trotwood Moore immortalized her brave efforts in his poetic work, "The Ballad of Emma Sansom." On Walnut Street in Gadsden there is a monument to Emma Sansom, honoring her heroism and bravery. The monument depicts a teenage girl pointing the way for Forrest and his army. In addition, there is an exhibit with a daguerreotype of Emma Sansom at the Alabama Department of Archives and History in Montgomery, which includes Streight's surrender sword when he capitulated to Forrest.

Other Alabama women were formidable forces during the Civil War. Mobilian Juliet Opie Hopkins went to the front lines in Virginia to nurse wounded Confederate soldiers. Kate Cumming went to the battlefield at Shiloh, Mississippi, to nurse injured CSA soldiers there.

A NEW CIVIL WAR MUSEUM

In April and May of 1863, Colonel Abel Streight was in charge of a raid. The track of his raid was from Nashville, Tennessee, to north Alabama. His infantrymen were short on horses and were obliged to use mules, pressed into service from surrounding farms. The soldiers had no training as cavalry. As most people know, mules can be extremely stubborn, so it probably made for some challenging times for the soldiers.

Streight was hounded by General Nathan Bedford Forrest; their fighting lasted for days. Similar to the trick detailed in the story below this one, Streight was purposefully misled to believe that Forrest's numbers were much more than they were in truth. He surrendered his approximately 1,700

Union soldiers to Forrest's 500 or so. After Streight's surrender, he was imprisoned in Virginia for nearly a year before escaping.

The so-called Battle of Crooked Creek is now commemorated in a fairly new museum located at the battle site. The Crooked Creek Civil War Museum, which opened in 2006, is located in Vinemont (just outside Cullman proper), is open most every day and home to many fascinating artifacts from this facet of Civil War history.

Gazing over the 40-acre property of this museum, you can see where the ground is uneven because that is where soldiers are buried (Fred Wise, proprietor, says paranormal researchers have come to visit and talk to the ghosts of these valiant dead). See "Virtual Alabama" for websites about this.

ONE BRILLIANT MILITARY TACTICIAN or SUCCESSFULLY TRICKING THE ENEMY

In late September 1864, General Nathan Bedford Forrest rode into Alabama with 4,500 of his soldiers and eight pieces of artillery. Their mission: to destroy the Tennessee and Alabama Railroad, for it would be this means by which Sherman and his soldiers, in his "March to the Sea," would invade Alabama. Along this railroad line, the Union had built forts and blockhouses to defend the rail-line from destruction. One fort was located north of Athens at the Sulfur Branch Trestle; another was located in Athens.

On the night of September 23, 1864, Forrest and his men surrounded the Athens fort and placed their artillery in position from which they could fire on the fort from three sides. The fort in Athens was under the command of Union Colonel Wallace Campbell; the men under his charge included 418 African-American soldiers and the 3rd Tennessee Cavalry, a total of roughly 600 men.

Early in that morning of September 23, Forrest and his soldiers began a barrage of the fort. It lasted approximately two hours. At that point, Forrest sent one of his soldiers bearing a white flag to demand surrender of the Athens fort. Campbell turned down Forrest's offer. Forrest then requested a parley with Campbell; during this talk, Forrest told Campbell that he had plenty of men to cause Campbell's forces to be completely wiped out. In the words of an article about this in *Alabama Heritage* magazine, Forrest told Campbell he was offering the Union general an opportunity to save his men. Forrest said he was doing this for "the sake of humanity" that would be lost if Campbell did not surrender.

Campbell wanted to review the forces under Forrest's command to assure himself that Forrest did, indeed, have more than sufficient men to annihilate Campbell's forces. When Campbell was allowed to review Forrest's soldiers, he had no idea that the Confederate general had planned this trick well in advance. Saying he had 10,000 soldiers and nine cannons ready to attack the fort, Forrest had his men mount, remount, and dismount, moving about to make Campbell think that Forrest's cavalry was more than twice its true size.

Seeing these "10,000 men" ready to attack, Campbell capitulated and surrendered the fort.

As Campbell negotiated the terms of surrender, he heard gunfire near the fort. It was Union reinforcements from the 18th Michigan and 102nd Ohio Infantries trying to reinforce the fort. When these soldiers arrived at the fort, they were compelled to surrender as well!

Today, you can see artifacts and relics from this Civil War engagement at the Athens-Limestone Chamber of Commerce.

... AND THE STORY OF WILSON'S RAID

It is not a well-known fact, even among Civil War historians, that the largest cavalry raids happened in Alabama. In the spring of 1865—from March through about April 15 of that year—a Union general by the name of James H. Wilson led his forces to raid the area of northwestern Alabama, his target mainly being Selma and her arsenal.

Much like he did with Streight, Confederate General Nathan Bedford Forrest harassed Wilson and his troops from Montevallo and Tuscaloosa to Selma. When he realized he and his troops were too few and too poorly equipped to stop Wilson, Forrest and his men set the cotton warehouses to the torch before fleeing the city. Unfortunately, much of the rest of Selma burned, as well.

Today, you can see many reenactments of skirmishes and battles such as what might have happened in those cities. For example, Confederate Memorial Park (in Marbury, Alabama) usually has at least one reenactment in the spring.

THE "FREE STATE OF WINSTON"

Winston County has long been known for its citizens who consider themselves to be quite independent thinkers and very free-willed. Such was the case just at the time when Alabama seceded from the Union. In Winston County, the people were divided as to whether they were pro-Union or pro-Confederacy. Many of the people living in this rugged, hilly terrain in northwest Alabama said that the county should secede from the state of Alabama, much like the state had seceded from the Union.

There was much infighting among Winston County's citizenry as to how to handle their given situation. In addition, there was political infighting, fence-sitting and side-taking.

Some people supported a Democrat named John Breckenridge for president, since it seemed he was much like the ever-popular Andrew Jackson. Others, very pro-Union, supported a 22-year-old schoolteacher named Christopher Sheats to represent the county at Alabama's secession convention. Sheats refused to sign the secession document; for this, he was expelled from the state legislature and imprisoned for treason. Men in the militia units and home guard groups refused to serve in the Confederacy and defended themselves against Confederates.

The dates vary as to when pro-Unionists got together (either 1861 or 1862) at a place called Looney's Tavern (near Addison, Alabama). They made three resolutions while there: one praised Sheats for his bravery and resolve; another stated their right to secede from the state of Alabama; and a third stated that all members of this group should refuse to fight for either the Confederate *or* the Union side. As *Encyclopedia of Alabama* author and Auburn professor David McRae stated, the men present wanted to "work out our own political and financial destiny." It is said that upon hearing the second resolution, someone shouted "Winston secedes! The Free State of Winston!"

The men who supported Alabama's right to secede, and the Confederacy, also had a meeting. Theirs was held November 30, 1861. They wrote and signed a petition requesting Alabama Governor John G. Shorter to make all the county's residents take an oath of fealty to the Confederacy, and to give the county more than 200 Confederate soldiers. Shorter wrote out arrest warrants for those residents who were passionate and vocal Union supporters. He also demanded that militia commanders who refused to take the oath of loyalty to the Confederacy resign their commissions.

Many pro-Union men fled their homes when faced with being drafted to fight for the Confederacy. They hid out in the woods (and Natural Bridge was also a place where they took refuge--read more about that in Chapter 13). Others joined forces with the Union military. With these farmers gone, their farms and families suffered; to make matters worse, Confederate agents seized many farms' livestock and food, to feed their soldiers. Throughout the duration of the rest of the war, Confederate soldiers, Union soldiers, and some just plain thieves marauded, raiding, stealing and killing their way through the county. After the war, there was still much unease in the county. This led to occasional outbreaks of violence.

Now, you can see a statue of a half-Union, half-Confederate soldier in the town of Double Springs in front of the Winston County Courthouse. It is an iconic allusion to when the county experienced divided loyalties and called itself "The Free State of Winston."

In 1991, the Alabama Legislature passed an act, making a musical play, "The Incident at Looney's Tavern" Alabama's official musical drama. The play is held in Double Springs every April. See their website(s) in "Virtual Alabama" for more information.

THE BATTLES OF SPANISH FORT AND FORT BLAKELY

After the Battle of Mobile Bay, Union forces led by Major General Edward Canby turned their attention to Spanish Fort and Fort Blakely to the north. These two battles happened from April 2 to April 9, 1865, in the waning days of the conflict.

At Spanish Fort, it didn't take long before Union soldiers had their Confederate counterparts surrounded on all sides. Turning their attentions to Fort Blakely, Union forces built three rings of earthen ramparts (also called redoubts), allowing them coverage from fire so they could get ever closer to Fort Blakely. With his 4,000 troops defending Fort Blakely, Confederate Brigadier General St. John R. Liddell held out until Spanish Fort fell on April 8; Canby then turned his force of 16,000 troops on Liddell's forces. Surrender was inevitable, and Liddell surrendered in less than an hour after the battle had begun. It was April 9, 1865, the same day that saw Lee's surrender at the Appomattox Courthouse, so Liddell probably surrendered to save what troops were still alive and uninjured. He and his men had put up a valiant fight. According to the May 27, 1865, article in *Harper's Weekly*, "It was probably the last charge of the war and as gallant as any on record."

Today, Fort Blakely is a State Park under the auspices of the National Park Service. You can go tour Fort Blakely and see the earthworks that were made there. The park offers camping facilities and pamphlets for self-guided walking tours. Very knowledgeable park rangers are at the park entrance, and usually at least one battle re-enactment is held every year. See "Virtual Alabama" for more.

DID YOU KNOW?

In Point Clear, Alabama, the Marriott Grand Hotel, Resort and Spa was once used as a Civil War hospital to care for the wounded soldiers in the aftermath of the Battle of Vicksburg (Mississippi). Near the hotel, there is a cemetery for those who died despite medical care. Confederate Rest Cemetery has within its gates more than 300 Confederate soldiers' graves. Unfortunately, the records of those interred within the cemetery gates were destroyed by a fire in 1869. The cemetery is open for those who want to go by and pay their respects.

ALABAMA'S OWN ARLINGTON

When Union-mounted forces led by General James H. Wilson made their way through the area of Elyton (now a part of Birmingham) in March 1865, they used an antebellum home (called Arlington) owned by William S. Mudd as their headquarters while they planned their next move. Wilson divided his forces and sent part of his troops on to invade Tuscaloosa, while the majority of his troops went on to Selma.

Today, the Arlington Antebellum Home and Gardens is a delightful place in which to spend a day. It is now a living history museum, complete with historic artifacts and décor as it would have been during Wilson's "visit." Incidentally, Arlington is not simply an antebellum home: it is Birmingham's *only* antebellum home.

The owner of Arlington at the time of Wilson's possession (William Mudd) went on to help establish the city of Birmingham.

THE ONES WHO SAVED THE UNIVERSITY OF ALABAMA FROM THE TORCH

After Wilson's divided forces went their separate ways as mentioned above, one group of troops went to Selma and one to Tuscaloosa. When word came to Tuscaloosa that Wilson's troops were headed there, many of its citizens evacuated. There were some, though, who stayed behind to defend the campus of The University of Alabama.

Those brave young men were The University of Alabama military cadets. Although much of the campus was burned down by Wilson's troops, the cadets kept them from completely destroying the campus.

Today, the university's Commons Area (where Denny Chimes is located) has on its grounds a large boulder; inscribed on it are the names of those cadets who defended against the Union troops in 1865.

DID YOU KNOW?

Tannehill Ironworks Historical State Park supplied iron for the Confederacy during the Civil War. You can visit the area today, hike the trails, see Civil War-era cabins and tour the Alabama Iron and Steel Museum, located in McCalla, near Tuscaloosa.

... AND SPEAKING OF IRON

Other furnaces in Alabama produced iron to supply the Confederacy during the Civil War. The Cedar Creek Furnace in Franklin County was among the oldest, founded in 1818. Near Montevallo, the Mahan Forge was built in 1836. In Bibb County, a forge named Little Cahaba Iron Works was established in 1846. The Bibb County Iron Company in Brierfield was built in 1862. Two of these were destroyed by Union soldiers led by General James H. Wilson in 1865. Tannehill, however, is one of the best-preserved examples of a 19th century iron producing site. This ushered in the era of Birmingham being a leader in the iron and steel industry.

Q & A

Q. What teacher at the Judson Female Institute in Marion designed the Confederate flag and uniform?

A. Nicola Marshall.

Q. What vessel received a letter of commendation for running the blockade at the

Port of Mobile "in actively cruising against and destroying the enemy's commerce"?

A. The sloop *Florida*, under the command of Captain Maffitt.

Q. Until the Civil War, what town was the county seat of Conecuh County?

A. Old Sparta.

Q. Where was the second-largest Confederate prisoner-of-war camp in the South situated?

A. Cahaba. The first was the infamous Andersonville (Georgia).

Q. In what building were smallpox cases quarantined in Eufaula during the Civil War?

A. The Oyster Shell House.

Q. Where is the grave of the Confederate officer known as "Gallant John Pelham"?

A. Jacksonville.

Q. What Corinth, Mississippi, munitions company relocated in May, 1962 to Columbiana, Alabama, to avoid Union forces?

A. C. B. Churchill Company.

Q. The grave of the Confederate Unknown Soldier lies in what Chilton County park?

A. Confederate Memorial Park, Mountain Creek.

Q. What memorial, unveiled in 2017, commemorates the unknown soldiers of Crenshaw County?

A. It's a modest stone marker at the Confederate Memorial Park about three miles outside Brantley.

Q. At the onset of the Civil War, what town was the largest inland cotton market in Alabama?

A. Claiborne.

Q. What was the first Alabama county to be invaded by Union troops during the Civil War?

A. Limestone.

Q. From what base did General Sherman begin his infamous "march to the sea" in 1864?

A. Battery Hill, at Bridgeport.

Q. What Alabama city was the first capital of the Confederate States of America?

A. Montgomery.

Q. Because of its role in the history of the Confederate States of America, what nickname was given to Montgomery?

A. "The Cradle of the Confederacy."

Q. Jefferson Davis unveiled what monument in Montgomery's Capitol Hill on April 29, 1886?

A. The Confederate Monument.

Q. Who was the first governor of Alabama after the Civil War was over?

A. Robert M. Patton.

Q. What man was given credit for raising troops and garnering war materials for the Confederacy in its first year?

A. Leroy Pope Walker.

Q. Alabama ranked where in its seceding from the Confederacy?

A. Alabama was the fourth state to secede from the Union.

Q. On February 18, 1861, who was inaugurated in Montgomery as President of the Confederate States of America?

A. Jefferson Davis.

Q. The six-pointed brass star on the portico steps on the west side of the capitol building commemorates what event in Alabama history? (Hint: it has to do with the previous question)

A. It is the spot where Jefferson Davis took the oath of office as provisional President of the Confederate States of America.

Q. What general in charge of the Confederate Department of the West forces surrendered his troops at Citronelle on May 4, 1865?

A. General Richard Taylor.

Q. Who was the youngest brigadier general in the Confederacy?

A. Auburn's Brigadier General James H. Lane.

Q. Who was commander of the famous 10th Alabama Infantry Regiment during the Civil War?

A. General John H. Forney, C.S.A.

Q. What was the nickname of Confederate General Joseph Wheeler?

A. "Fighting Joe."

Q. The prisoner-of-war prison in Cahaba was given what nickname?

A. "Castle Morgan."

Q. What building in Selma has on display munitions manufactured in the town during the Civil War?

A. The Old Depot Museum.

Q. In what building in Selma can you find all kinds of Civil War artifacts and art?

A. The Vaughan-Smitherman Museum. It also served as a school, a Civil War hospital, and was the first Freedman's Bureau hospital in the area.

Q. Which prison camp treated its prisoners better than any other Civil War camp?

A. Cahawba, also known as "Castle Morgan." According to locals who shared this tidbit with me, one of the ladies in town felt so sorry for the prisoners-of-war that she brought them vegetables from her garden and books from her library. At the end of the war, physicians who checked on the returned prisoners of war remarked that never had they seen such healthy former POWs!

Q, What Union outpost in north Alabama was manned by two companies of African-American soldiers?

A. Sulfur Trestle Fort.

Q. After the Confederacy's surrender, who did then-President Andrew Johnson appoint as Alabama's provisional governor?

A. Lewis E. Parsons.

Q. During the Battle of Gettysburg, Colonel William H. Forney of Jacksonville had how many horses shot out from under him?

A. Six!

Q. What Huntsville native was the first to serve the Confederacy as Secretary of War?

A. Leroy Pope Walker.

Q. What senator in a resolution introduced the phrase, "The War Between the States," as the proper term for the Civil War?

A. Senator Lister Hill.

Q. Who was appointed Life President of the Alabama Division of United Daughters of the Confederacy in 1952?

A. Jacksonville native Annie Rowan Forney Daugette. She is honored and her many achievements commemorated at the Alabama Women's Hall of Fame in Marion, Alabama, on the campus of Judson College in A. Howard Bean Hall.

Q. What flag did Ms. Daugette petition to obtain from Iowa in 1939?

A. She was successful in her efforts to bring the flag of the Independent State of Alabama to its home state; it had been in Iowa since 1865. Its new home is at the State Department of Archives and History, Montgomery.

Q. The Alabama Legislature in August of 1863 set what age limits for the drafting of soldiers for the Confederacy?

A. The youngest age was 16; the oldest, 60.

Q. The anti-slavery faction in north Alabama selected what name for a proposed pro-Union state in 1861?

A. Nickajack.

Q. When did Alabama pass legislation to secede from the Union?

A. January 11, 1861; the document was The Ordinance of Secession.

Q. Alabama was the biggest supplier of iron to the Confederacy during the Civil War; what was the state's yearly output at that time?

A. 40,000 tons.

Q. By what name were Alabama soldiers called during the Civil War?

A. Yellowhammers.

Q. What sculptor created the Confederate Rest monument, which is in the Magnolia Cemetery in Mobile?

A. Matthew J. Lawler.

T. Jensen Lacey

CHAPTER 10
FROM CIVIL WRONGS TO CIVIL RIGHTS

MARTIN LUTHER KING, JR.: THE DREAM LIVES ON

I remember watching King's televised, now-iconic "I have a dream" speech in 1963, as he stood in the shadow of the Lincoln Memorial in Washington, D.C. I was only eight years old at the time but watching him make this speech was something that stunned me. Until that moment, I had been unaware that people were not treated equally in this country.

Born in Atlanta in 1929 as Michael King, Jr., his father changed his son's name (as well as his own) to Martin. King's father, Michael King, Sr. (who was a pastor to Atlanta's Ebenezer Baptist Church), had traveled to Germany and was inspired by the speeches and essays of the Protestant Reformation leader, Martin Luther.

Young King graduated from Morehouse College, then attended Crozer Theological Seminary and then Boston University, where he earned a PhD in Systematic Theology. He married Coretta Scott in 1953, became pastor of Dexter Avenue Baptist Church in Montgomery, Alabama, and was there from 1954-1959.

King became a nationally recognized figure during the Montgomery bus boycott of 1955-56, which ended when it was declared that segregation on public transportation was unconstitutional. The boycott, that began after Rosa Parks refused to give up her bus seat to a white person, was a success. As a result, both King and Parks became famous icons of the Civil Rights movement.

Jailed for coordinating marches and sit-ins to protest racism in Birmingham, King wrote eloquently of the need for nonviolent protest, something he said was inspired in him by Mahatma Gandhi of India. Called an "outsider" by white ministers, King protested by writing his famous statement, "Injustice anywhere is a threat to justice everywhere. We are caught in an inescapable network of mutuality, tied in a single garment of destiny. Whatever affects one directly, affects all."

Martin Luther King, Jr., helped shape the freedoms all Americans enjoy today. Photo courtesy National Archives.

His famous "From Selma to Montgomery March" in 1965 has since been re-enacted by Presidents, including George W. Bush and Barack Obama on the anniversary of this nonviolent protest to make all people equal under the law.

In 1964, King was awarded the Nobel Peace Prize, making him the youngest person to receive the award at that time. He continued to preach and work tirelessly for equality for all people, especially minorities. The entire nation mourned when King was assassinated in Memphis, Tennessee.

His accused killer—James Earl Ray—denied his guilt, and conspiracy theories have abounded as to exactly who really killed King.

King has left all Americans with a lesson in what one person can do to change the world. The impact he made on Alabama history, global politics, and social justice is remembered throughout the state. Virtually all of Alabama commemorated the 50th anniversary of his assassination on April 4, 2018. It seems that every city of any size in Alabama has a Martin Luther King, Jr., Boulevard. His church in Montgomery (now Dexter Avenue King Memorial Baptist Church) commemorates his work and welcomes visitors. You can also tour the Dexter Avenue King Memorial Legacy Center located on Washington Avenue.

In Birmingham, there are several exhibits and sites you can see to learn more about King's life and the Civil Rights Movement. For example, you can stroll Kelly Ingram Park, where you can take a "Freedom Walk" and admire several sculptures depicting the opposition to racial discrimination. There also is a statue of King facing the Sixteenth Street Baptist Church. There is a historical marker on Sixth Avenue South, telling the story of King's arrest in April 1963 and his now-famous "Letter from the Birmingham Jail," in which he explained why the Civil Rights movement was not only important but necessary. The Civil Rights Institute is an amazing, inspiring and sometimes sobering array of exhibits pertaining not just to the Civil Rights movement in the United States, but to the endeavors of people worldwide, striving for

"TIRED OF GIVING IN": THE ROSA PARKS STORY

Born Rosa Louise McCauley in Tuskegee in 1913, she was the daughter of James McCauley, a stoneworker and carpenter, and Leona Edwards, a teacher. She received a fairly good education until family illness obliged her to quit school, after which time she supported herself with housekeeping and sewing for white people. When she was 20, she married a Randolph County native, Raymond Parks. In her late 30s, Rosa Parks became active in the Montgomery chapter of the NAACP or the National Association for the Advancement of Colored

Rosa Parks sitting in the front of the bus, at the victorious end of the Montgomery Bus Boycott. Photo courtesy National Archives

People. In this capacity, she encouraged young African-Americans to become politically involved and helped educate them as to their voting rights.

On the night of December 1, 1955, Rosa Parks' life would suddenly be forever changed when she boarded a city bus after work. As more whites boarded the bus, the driver asked her to give up her seat and move to the back. Rosa Parks politely refused, and the driver hailed two police officers, who arrested her. Local activists in the Montgomery chapter of the NAACP bailed her out of jail. In the trial that followed, she was fined $10.

This mistreatment of a human being sparked outrage and garnered international attention. Montgomery's African-American population began a boycott of all city buses. The boycott lasted a year. As a result, the law of segregating public transportation was challenged all the way to the Supreme Court. After the highest court in the U.S. supported a district court's ruling, public transportation was integrated.

In 1956, the bus boycott ended and Rosa Parks, who had become the "mother of the civil rights movement," took a symbolic bus ride—this time, at the front of the bus. She devoted the rest of her life to fighting against inequality and injustice.

In 1996, President Bill Clinton awarded Parks the Presidential Medal of Freedom. In 1999, she received the Congressional Gold Medal. The Rosa Parks Library and Museum opened in Montgomery in 2001, and, although she was frail due to advanced years, Parks attended the opening (after the bus boycott, she and her husband had moved to Detroit due to receiving a number of death threats).

Although Rosa Parks passed away, you can read her autobiography, *Rosa Parks: My Story*. The Rosa Parks Museum is now sponsored by Troy University. According to Museum Director Georgette Norman, the boycott lasted 382 days, not just a year. At the Rosa Parks Museum, you can see the very bus in which Parks took her historic stand, exhibits of Martin Luther

King, Jr., a peek inside the church where African-Americans met after Rosa Parks said, in Ms. Norman's words, "The NO! heard around the world." The strong-willed young woman who once explained why she had refused to give up her seat that night was because, as she was once quoted in an interview, "I was tired of giving in."

THE FREEDOM RIDERS OF 1961: PROTESTING INEQUALITY ON WHEELS

"Dear Mom and Dad," a letter from a Freedom Rider might have begun, "I am writing to tell you what I'm doing and why, and because of this, I may be killed. I want you to know that I love you both." Letters such as this one were written by 21 young people. Some of them also wrote wills in the event that their nonviolent protest resulted in their demise.

It was in the year 1961 that young people protested the fact that the laws regarding interstate transit and the integration of passengers were being all but ignored, although the Supreme Court had ruled for integration three years prior. To create an increased focus on this inequality, 21 young people, both black and white, and all under the age of 22, loaded into buses in Washington, D.C. and rode them to various places in Alabama to press their point (this protest, incidentally, was organized by future Congressman John Lewis).

These so-called "Freedom Riders," although protesting peacefully, received violence at the hands of segregationists in cities in Alabama. Arriving on Mother's Day of that year in Birmingham and Montgomery, the Freedom Riders were savagely attacked. Riders arriving in Anniston witnessed to their horror that someone had set their bus ablaze while they were still inside it (they survived). In Montgomery, Dr. Martin Luther King, Jr. addressed passengers who had taken sanctuary in the First Baptist Church there (their minister was Reverend Ralph Abernathy). Angry segregationists by the thousands were outside the church, and it took an order from Governor John Patterson to have police and National Guardsmen force them to disperse.

Calls to end the Freedom Rides seemed to further fuel the movement. The protests that began with a handful of young people increased to nearly 400 Freedom Riders, who were outraged at the violence that the initial peaceful protestors received. Dr. Martin Luther King, Jr. trained these protestors in non-violent resistance methods. Despite this training, the Freedom Riders upon arrival to their destinations were jailed by the hundreds, charged with "breach of peace" violations.

Finally, five months after the first Freedom Riders boarded buses heading South, U.S. Attorney General Robert Kennedy issued a new, tougher Federal order, which banned segregation at all interstate public facilities.

Alabama has changed a great deal since this terrible time, but as it has been said, "Those who do not remember the past are doomed to repeat it." Alabama commemorates this turbulent time in many ways. One of them is the Freedom Rides Museum, which is located at the former Greyhound Bus Station on South Court Street in downtown Montgomery. Another is the First Baptist Church in Montgomery, which incidentally is the oldest continually operating African-American Baptist Church in the state of Alabama (founded in 1867). The church welcomes everyone and is open for tours if you contact them in advance.

T. Jensen Lacey

DID YOU KNOW?

IN 1984, the Alabama Historical Commission (AHC) and the State Historic Preservation Office worked together to form the Black Heritage Council (BHC). The BHC was formed in order to advise and advocate for the AHC on preserving places of significance to African-American history and culture in Alabama. The BHC was the first such organization of its kind in the *entire United States*! Their Chair Emeritus and charter member, Louretta Wimberly, helped other states form their own such councils. The Alabama BHC has helped many communities throughout the Yellowhammer State identify, document, and preserve places in Alabama which are of significance to African-American history. One such place is the Selma-to-Montgomery National Historic Trail. Two others of significance are the First Baptist Church (in Selma) and Hobson City.

Membership is free and open to anyone.

DID YOU KNOW? MARTYRS WHO DIED FOR THE CAUSE

Today, when you think of the Civil Rights movement, you may initially think of Selma or Montgomery, and you'd be right—partially. The Civil Rights movement actually had its beginnings in the small west Alabama town of Marion.

It was during a peaceful protest on February 18, 1965, that a man named Jimmie Jackson was shot by law enforcement officers. The officers were beating demonstrators, and Jimmie Jackson, a war veteran, was simply trying to protect his mother (officers said they thought Jackson was armed). Jackson's death would soon prove not to be in vain.

Just a few weeks after this—on March 7 of that year—Reverend Hosea Williams left his lectern at Brown Chapel Church and led more than 600 Civil Rights marchers from Selma. They were headed to Montgomery. After only marching less than a mile, they were attacked by state troopers and deputies as the protestors tried to cross the Edmund Pettus Bridge. This peaceful protest and its violent end came to be known as "Bloody Sunday." It shocked the entire nation and helped solidify and galvanize people into action toward achieving justice and equality.

Just two weeks later, Dr. Martin Luther King, Jr. and approximately 300 marchers attempted the same Selma-to-Montgomery march. This time, these peaceful protestors were protected by Alabama National Guardsmen and U.S. Army soldiers. They marched the 54 miles in four days.

Jimmie Jackson wasn't the only martyr during this time. Shot while shuttling marchers back to their homes in Selma, a middle-aged white woman named Viola Liuzzo was another martyr for the cause of Civil Rights.

These people did not die in vain: in 1965 a bill which had long been stalled in the system, the Voting Rights Act, was signed into law by President Lyndon Johnson (who succeeded Kennedy after that president's assassination). Following this, more than 7,000 African-American people registered to vote in Dallas County (where Selma is located). They later helped defeat the sheriff who led the attack on protestors during the terrible "Bloody Sunday."

Today, you can visit Selma and stand on the Edmund Pettus Bridge, located at U.S. Highway 80 and Water Avenue (it's a great "photo-op"). When you're there, perhaps make a mental salute to those who were martyrs for this cause. Also in

Selma at the foot of the Edmund Pettus Bridge at 2 Broad Street is an Interpretive Center, which is now part of the National Park Service.

DID YOU KNOW?

There is a Civil Rights Memorial located at the Southern Poverty Law Center (on Washington Avenue) in Montgomery, designed by artist Maya Lin. It has inscribed on it the names of 41 people who died for the cause of Civil Rights.

A FIRST IN ALABAMA: HOBSON CITY

In Calhoun County, just south of Anniston, Alabama, is the town of Hobson City. Founded in 1899, Hobson City first began as a part of the town of Oxford. After the African-American population of Oxford was emancipated, they were moved to another part of town, which was originally called Moree Quarter.

The residents of Moree Quarter were allowed to vote in local (city and county) elections, so the white population soon looked for ways to prevent African-Americans' influence in their political dealings (and it irked the white population that an African-American man was elected to be Justice of the Peace.) In 1899, the mayor of Oxford asked the state government to change the boundaries of the town, making Moree Quarter separate from Oxford. That same year, in retaliation, the African-American citizens of Moree Quarter incorporated as Hobson City. The first school was founded in Hobson City in 1905, and by 1950 the town had a population of nearly 2,000 and several thriving businesses. The last census showed that the population had dwindled to around 800, probably due to a decline in the steel industry.

The town of Hobson City and its citizens are proud of the fact that they are known as "Alabama's First Black City." Hobson City is actually the second such city in the U.S. run by African-Americans (the first one is Eatonville, Florida, the early childhood home of author Zora Neale Hurston).

Now a quiet place, you can enjoy a weekend in Hobson City during their annual May Day celebration. There is also a lovely park there, Booker T. Washington Park. The town of Hobson City is under the auspices of the Alabama Historical Commission's Black Heritage Council.

REV. FRED SHUTTLESWORTH, FIGHTING HATRED WITH LOVE

Fred Shuttlesworth was a minister at Birmingham's Bethel Baptist Church. His church was "Ground Zero" for the Civil Rights movement in Alabama, serving as the headquarters for the Alabama Christian Movement for Human Rights from 1956 to 1961. Like King, Shuttlesworth also embraced social change through nonviolent means and urged equality and love against inequality, oppression and hatred. His passionate sermons focused on the city's unfair segregation laws, and during this turbulent time he invited Dr. Martin Luther King, Jr. to come and give a speech in his own eloquent way.

Those against Shuttlesworth and his sermons on segregation reacted violently: Bethel Baptist Church was bombed not once, but in the years between 1956 and 1962, three times. Although the congregation moved their church to a place a block away, the original building that housed Bethel Baptist Church has been named a UNESCO Heritage Site and is open for tours (but by appointment).

"SUFFER THE CHILDREN TO COME UNTO ME": THE 16TH STREET BAPTIST CHURCH BOMBING

In September of 1963, the Civil Rights movement was at its height as far as tensions went. Alabama cities such as Birmingham, Selma and Montgomery all sat like proverbial powder-kegs, for everyone knew something big would eventually happen.

On the evening of September 15 of that year, the 16th Street Baptist Church in Birmingham became the focus of the Civil Rights cause when KKK members bombed the church. Killed in the blast were four little innocent girls: Addie Mae Collins, Denise McNair, Cynthia Robertson and Carole Wesley. The slaughter of these little girls rocked the nation and served to further galvanize the Civil Rights movement.

The now-famous letter Martin Luther King, Jr. wrote after this, from his cell in the Birmingham Jail, was commemorated and celebrated 50 years after it was written in 1963. In 2013, a group of interracial and interfaith pastors met at the historic church and read parts of the letter to the group. The pastor of the church today, Rev. Arthur Price, Jr., said then (in an interview with Greg Garrison of al.com), "This is ... a historic and momentous occasion. Dr. King's letter was one of his most compelling works." He added, "[We can see] ... how far we've come as a people and, more importantly, as a nation."

The 16th Street Baptist Church is open for tours.

THE SAD HISTORY OF THE SLAVE TRADE IN ALABAMA

Besides the Port of Mobile, where the majority of kidnapped Africans were brought, the city of Montgomery was probably the busiest city of all when it came to dealing in the slave trade. The advent of the cotton gin and the steam engine both propelled this terrible business to new heights. More workers were needed to manage and harvest cotton crops, and the slave trade provided the demand. Between the years 1820 to 1860, the slave population of Alabama was roughly half of the total number of people living in the state. It wasn't just those living in plantation homes who owned slaves: yeoman farmers and even free blacks had slaves as well.

Today, in several places in Alabama, you can learn more about this sad time in Alabama history. One is the Museum of Mobile, which has a walk-through exhibit of what it was like to be on a slave ship. Another is the Legacy Museum and National Memorial for Peace and Justice in Montgomery. The latter museum first opened in the spring of 2018, and even young children who view these places come away with a new understanding of this time in history.

Finally, the Equal Justice Initiative has placed several historic markers throughout Montgomery to mark places that were formerly associated with the slave trade. Also, the Alabama Department of Archives and History in Montgomery has many artifacts, such as slave collars which identified enslaved people as to who claimed them.

THE CLOTILDA: GRIM HISTORY

In 1855, a shipbuilder by the name of William Foster began building a ship. This was no ordinary ship: its cargo was to be humans. It was built to be able to hold 190 people below decks. In 1860, Timothy Meaher bought the ship, had it loaded with food, casks of rum, dry goods and sundries, and $9,000 in gold, the latter of which was intended for the purchase of kidnapped Africans.

On March 3, 1860, *The Clotilda* set sail from the Port of Mobile in the darkness of night. It arrived in what is now Benin in the African nation of Guinea. Within a couple of months, the ship was fairly full of kidnapped Africans—mostly teenagers who had been sold by their own people to slave-traders—and, in July 8, 1860, the ship entered the Mississippi Sound, headed back to the Port of Mobile.

What the slave-traders on board didn't know was that their illegal wrong-doings had been discovered, and the law was out to get them (international slave-trading was declared illegal in 1808, and the slave-traders were committing an act of defiance). With them not having a way to make a profit from their ill-gotten human trafficking, the slave-traders sailed their ship into the Port of Mobile, took their human cargo to what is now known as Africatown, and dropped their young captives there, left to fend totally for themselves, in a strange, unrecognizable country. The slave-traders set torches to their slave-ship and left it to burn.

Fast forward to the 1930s. Mobile native Emma Langdon Roche, who was Alabama State Director for the Federal Art Project in the 1930s, spent time in Africatown interviewing and painting portraits of the last nine survivors of the slave ship *The Clotilda*. Roche shared these persons' stories in 1914 in a book, *Historic Sketches of the South* (Knickerbocker Press).

Also, Alabama-born African-American author Zora Neale Hurston traveled to Africatown to interview and get stories from the last living survivor of *The Clotilda*. Unwilling to speak with her at first, the elderly (late 80s, early 90s) man known as Cudjo Lewis was reticent; but Hurston was compassionate and patient, so finally Lewis opened up. She wrote what he told her, and in his own vernacular—as though he might be speaking one-on-one to the reader. At first, no one wanted to publish this book, saying the way she recorded him speaking would make it too difficult for the average reader to make out what

Lewis was trying to impart. It was after both Lewis and, later, Hurston were deceased that another African-American author by the name of Alice Walker took up the proverbial torch, taking Hurston's manuscript from publisher to publisher. It is now available from Amistad Press and is titled *Baccaroon: The Story of the Last "Black" Cargo* (the word "baccaroon" translates to refer to a holding place for kidnapped slaves).

Today, you can visit the Museum of Mobile to see a replica of what the inside of a slave-ship might have looked and felt like. It's not for the faint of heart, as it vividly paints a picture of a reminder of our sometimes-grim past.

Also, the community of Africatown is beginning to see an uptick in interest in improving and preserving this vital part of Alabama history. The National Park Service has been looking into making Africatown part of a series of interconnected canoe-and-kayak stops they call the "Blueway," with other improvements in the works. Africatown might be a place that will eventually come to be a destination for historians and tourists.

THE *AMISTAD* AND ITS ALABAMA CONNECTION

Most people know about the revolt in 1839 by captive Africans aboard the Spanish slave ship, *Amistad*. What you may not know is there's an Alabama connection. In 1938 artist Hale Woodruff painted three murals about the revolt and its African captives (who, after a trial which went to the U.S. Supreme Court, were returned to their home in Africa). *The Amistad Murals* are currently on display in Savery Library on the campus of Talladega College. The murals are vivid and historically-accurate depictions of the revolt, the trial and the Africans' victorious return home.

T. Jensen Lacey

THE INFAMOUS STORY OF THE SCOTTSBORO BOYS

It was back in 1931 that two white women accused nine African-American males, some of them only teenagers and the rest young adults, of raping them while they were all travelling by train through Alabama. The nine were charged, held, and tried in Scottsboro.

The trial received international and national attention, and the public outcry at the injustice the nine received, coupled with the outrageous fact that the nine were not represented by a jury of their peers (it was an all-white, all-male jury) had an explosive effect and a call for judicial reform. Two landmark cases (*Patterson versus Alabama* in 1932, and *Norris versus Alabama* in 1935) resulted in two decisions. One of them (from the first case) said that a defendant had a constitutional right to a competent defense. The other (from the second case) said that a defendant had a right to a jury of his peers. The circuit judge in the case, James E. Horton, Jr., cited a lack of evidence to uphold one of the women's charges, and he granted the men a new trial (he was later removed from the case). When Judge Horton ran for re-election, he was, unfortunately, defeated.

Eventually, in 2013 all those charged were pardoned by Governor Robert Bentley (although some were serving time then). Bentley didn't just do this paperwork from his office in Montgomery: he came to Scottsboro for a ceremonial signing of the piece of legislation that would exonerate (clear of all charges) the nine known as "The Scottsboro Boys." Although there were many who questioned, and rightly so, why it took 82 years for these nine to receive justice, it was a major turning point in the Civil Rights movement that this happened at all.

Today, there is now a museum in Scottsboro to commemorate this terrible time of prejudice and injustice.

Located at the former Joyce Chapter United Methodist Church just a few blocks away from the Jackson County Courthouse, the Scottsboro Boys Museum and Cultural Center has been a part of the Civil Rights Trail since it opened its doors in 2010.

As for Judge Horton, he is immortalized on a plaque which is inside the Limestone County Courthouse (where he served as judge) in Athens. The plaque has Horton's words thus: "So far as the law is concerned it knows neither native nor alien, Jew nor Gentile, black nor white. This case is no different from any other. We have only to do our duty without fear or favor."

In October 2017, another item of interest was added to a spot in downtown Athens. Due to efforts by the Judge Horton Monument Committee, the city unveiled a life-sized, bronze likeness of the judge, as he appeared during the time he sat on the bench during the "Scottsboro Boys" case. Garnering funds for the statue was a five-year-long labor of love that retired Circuit Court Judge Jimmy Woodruff spearheaded, but it was worth it all at the unveiling, which was attended by Judge Horton's granddaughter, Kathy Garrett. The sculpture was created by Mobile artist Casey Downey, Jr., with the limestone base of the statue coming from French Mill Stone, an Athens-based company owned by Mike Grisham. You can see the statue today; it's located on the lawn of the west side of the Limestone County Courthouse.

DID YOU KNOW? THE BIG STORY BEHIND THE LITTLE HOUSE IN TUSCALOOSA

On the corner of Paul W. Bryant Drive and Lurleen Wallace Blvd. in Tuscaloosa there is a house with more than its share of history. This olive-green, two-story bungalow type house is now the home for a ton of African-American history, not just in Alabama, but in modern society.

It began with a dream—to educate people about the contributions of African-Americans to history—and has now grown to where a grant in 2004 from the Alabama Historical Commission's Black Heritage Council allowed the museum's volunteers to renovate the old home. The bungalow was built in the early 1920s by an African-American contractor Will J. Murphy and his wife Laura, with salvaged building materials from Alabama's old Capitol in Tuscaloosa.

Besides being a contractor, Will Murphy was also the first licensed black mortician (and funeral director) in Tuscaloosa. His wife, Laura, was a principal at 20th Street Elementary School. The Murphys lived in the house for some years after completing the work, then sold it to a private individual. In 1986, the city of Tuscaloosa purchased the house in order to preserve it.

Now listed on the National Register of Historic Places in Alabama, the Murphy-Collins house has been restored to its grandeur and appearance as it might have been in the 1920s. My personal favorite room is Laura Murphy's bedroom with its collection of antique dolls. There are exhibits throughout the museum highlighting contributions made by African-American Alabamians, from jazz singer Dinah Washington to former NFL star John Stallworth. Many people who visit this museum say they come away with a new perspective of what African-Americans have contributed to Alabama history and culture. It is soon to be added to the U.S. Civil Rights Trail. See "Virtual Alabama" for websites.

CHAPTER 11

WHEELERS AND DEALERS IN ALABAMA (AMAZING ENTREPRENEURS)

A "PATCHWORK" COMMUNITY THAT RUNS ITS OWN BUSINESS—GEE'S BEND

Just outside Camden, Alabama, is the town of Boykin, which locals and many historians and artists refer to as "Gee's Bend." If you have never been there, it makes for a fairly easy day trip because it's a place where history, art and entrepreneurial talent come together.

It was here in 1816 that a man named Joseph Gee settled, arriving from Halifax County, North Carolina. With him he brought 18 African-American slaves. Gee's Bend was surrounded on three sides by the Alabama River, and Gee established a cotton plantation on this fertile ground. The slaves worked his land, hauled in the cotton, and tended his house.

In 1845, Joseph Gee sold his land, including his slaves, to a man named Mark Pettway. After the Civil War was over, the newly freed slaves took their last name as Pettway and founded their own all-black community in what they still refer to as Gee's Bend.

The people of Gee's Bend struggled for decades to eke out a living, for although they had their own property, they still were living in the middle of proverbial nowhere. They needed to find a way to earn some significant amounts of money, and so they cast about for a creative way to do this. Since the women were skilled in the art of making quilts, they began to build upon this talent.

Fast-forward to the mid-1960s. The women founded a quilting collective to nurture their community's development by selling the results of their labor. Then, an art collector named William Arnett saw a photograph of a Gee's Bend quilt. Arnett was working on a project about African-American art, and sought out the ladies of Gee's Bend. Soon, designers in New York noticed their work. Suddenly patchwork quilting became the latest trend. Since then, other famous museums have purchased their work. Smithsonian probably has the most expensive quilt: theirs came at a price of $20,000!

There are two ways to get to Gee's Bend. The way that is all by land takes longer, or you can go to Camden and take the ferry, which is the most scenic (and enjoyable) The roadsides in and around Gee's Bend have wooden artistic depictions of the most famous quilts made by the artisans of the now world-famous Gee's Bend Quilting Collective.

You will love visiting the warm and lovely members of the collective. They still teach quilting at the Collective and at the nearby Boykin Nutrition Center. If you call ahead, you might even enjoy a home-cooked meal at the Collective, lovingly made by one or more of the ladies.

The Collective and the people of Gee's Bend continue to show growing success in their lives: Auburn University's architectural students already have built a lively Senior and Nutrition Center, and they hope to have a learning center completed here before too long with a new quilting exhibition building and a retail shop.

DID YOU KNOW?

In 1997, the Alabama Legislature voted to name the Pine Burr Quilt as the Official State Quilt of Alabama. The Pine Burr Quilt pattern is rooted in the African-American community of Gee's Bend. Quilt Collective member Lorretta Pettway Bennett created a Pine Burr quilt and donated it to the State Archives in Montgomery, where you can see it for yourself.

A PARTIAL LIST OF SOME OF THE OLDEST BUSINESSES STILL BOOMING IN ALABAMA

When a business establishes itself in the Yellowhammer State, it usually stays. Here are some of the oldest, and still successful, businesses in Alabama:

HARRISON BROTHERS HARDWARE—This is the oldest hardware store in the entire state. I used to love to cruise its aisles as a kid growing up in Huntsville because you never knew what you might find. Located on Southside Square in downtown Huntsville, the hardware store has been a staple (pun intended) of the area since it opened its doors in 1879. Besides hardware, they sell art, crafts and some interesting (and locally-made) gifts.

FIRST BANK OF ALABAMA—This bank was first founded in Talladega in 1848 and remains as Alabama's oldest continually-operating bank. Originally named The Isbell National Bank of Talladega, it was renamed The First National Bank of Talladega. In 2015, its name was again changed to its current one. The First Bank of Alabama is on North Street East.

THE HISTORIC BATTLE HOUSE RENAISSANCE HOTEL AND SPA—This is one of my favorite hotels in the Yellowhammer State. Located in downtown Mobile and within view of the Port of Mobile, it was originally built in 1852 but burned in 1905. It was rebuilt to its former grandeur in 1908, and since it's located on North Royal Street, it is near the cruise terminal, the Maritime Museum, the Carnival (Mardi Gras) Museum, and other attractions.

THE "SHOCKING" STORY BEHIND ALABAMA POWER COMPANY

The oldest utility company in Alabama is Alabama Power. Headquartered on 18th Street North in Birmingham, Alabama Power began its business in 1906. It currently provides electricity for 1.4 million people in the Yellowhammer State.

But Alabama Power does so much more than just provide power for its people and businesses in the state: when there are disasters in neighboring states, they are quick to load up their trucks with extra equipment, supplies and employees, and go to assist in places where they are desperately needed. For example, as I was writing this book (in 2018), Hurricane Michael had wreaked terrible destruction in Florida cities like Mexico Beach and Panama City Beach. As soon as was possible, Alabama Power had sent its crews to those locations, working hard to restore power and a sense of normalcy to the people living there.

Alabama Power also hosts golf and fishing tours as charity fundraisers. Various plants are open for tours.

CONECUH SAUSAGE: A DELICIOUS HISTORY

Every time I pass through the town of Evergreen (south of Montgomery), I inhale deeply, but it's not the scent of pines I smell. It's the aromas emanating from the Conecuh Sausage factory located there. Since this family-owned business opened its door in 1947, their philosophy of making sausages with a patented blend of seasonings and without such unnatural additives as MSG has caught on with Alabamians. Today, you can get Conecuh Sausage at most grocery stores across the U.S., and, in keeping with modern times, Conecuh fans can also order online.

Although there are no plant tours, the Conecuh Sausage Factory has a fine gift shop on the premises, selling locally-made items, and offers samples of their food items.

YOU THINK YOU'VE GOT BAGGAGE? WAIT 'TIL YOU SEE THIS PLACE!

Hailed by the *Los Angeles Times* as "one of Alabama's most unique tourist attractions," the Unclaimed Baggage Center in Scottsboro was the brainchild of a man named Doyle Owens.

It was back in 1970 that Owens borrowed a truck, along with $300, and headed to Washington, D.C., to get his first load of unclaimed airline baggage. Initially, he sold what he brought back in the truck, displaying his unclaimed wares on folding tables in a rented house.

Owens' idea was an instant success. He, his wife Sue, and their two sons began running this business that is currently the only store in the entire U.S. to sell the contents of lost luggage.

Now, son Bryan Owens is running the store after taking over the reins in 1995. Located on Willow Street, the store now covers an entire city block. It's currently open every day except Sunday.

Bryan Owens says that they've had visitors from more than 40 countries, and people never know what they'll find. The shop has been featured on the *Oprah Winfrey Show*, *Fox News*, and *National Public Radio*. And the Unclaimed Baggage Center doesn't simply sell unclaimed luggage items. They give more than half of their merchandise to dozens of charities such as

The Lions Club (eyeglasses) and Salvation Army (clothing and linens go to underprivileged families).

IN THE SPIRIT OF HISTORY: JOHN EMERALD DISTILLING COMPANY

In the lovely town of Opelika (Lee County) is a place you'll want to visit that's guaranteed to lift your spirits. A rather new business, the John Emerald Distilling Company, was founded in 2015 by a father-and-son team, John and Jimmy Sharp. They named their company in honor of John's father. Established downtown on Railroad Avenue in an old cotton warehouse, the distillery is Alabama's first legal maker of whiskey since the Prohibition era. Their current best-selling product is "John's Alabama Single Malt," but they also distill corn-based vodka, gin, and rum, the latter of which has won awards. Staying true to their regional roots, the team uses locally harvested produce, such as juniper berries, to make their spirits. The distillery offers tastings, classes in cocktail-making and for those who want to stay over, a bed and breakfast is nearby.

... AND NOW ALABAMA HAS "BICENTENNIAL BEERS"

Acclaimed Alabama historian and Professor Emeritus at Jacksonville State University, author Harvey H. (Hardy) Jackson also writes a regular column in *Alabama Living* magazine. One article that he wrote for that magazine, and which came out in July 2018, covered the issue of the trend of "Bicentennial Beers." He wrote about how each capital, including the capital of the Territory of Alabama, was coming out with a unique, signature beer to commemorate the anniversary of the Yellowhammer State's 200th birthday.

Cahaba brewed their version they call "Mulberry Road"; St. Stephens' brew is called "St. Stephens Stout"; and other towns such as Huntsville, Tuscaloosa, Selma and Montgomery all followed suit. In his article about this, Jackson wrote, "Although I can't prove it, I am sure that holding the constitutional convention in a town where beer was brewed was not coincidental." He added that, "...ready access to beer influenced the writing of what has been judged to have been one of the most 'liberal' state constitutions of the time.'"

So go check out these "Bicentennial Beers." You'll be foaming with disappointment at yourself if you don't try at least one!

THAT'S NOT DIRT, THAT'S MONEY: THE STORY OF CLAY CITY

Back around 1902, a visionary settler named Frank "Fantastic" Loton Brown took note of the vast clay deposits along the banks of Fish River in Baldwin County and saw a business opportunity in the red clay (this large clay source dates back in geological time to the Miocene era, which began more than 24 million years ago). He started a business called Clay City Products, Inc. and, using this clay and his five large round kilns on Clay City Road, began the manufacture of all sorts of building materials.

There was plenty of clay for the manufacture of building supplies. According to my expert on all things Clay City, fellow author Alan Samry says that these clay deposits are said to be one of the largest in the country. European settlers came to Clay City and brought with them their pottery and brickmaking expertise.

The Clay City potters and brickmakers made such items as drain tile (for pipes), building blocks known as Structural Clay Tile, flooring, buttresses, arches and lintels. So-called "Clay City Tile" became very popular, because the hollow tile made homes fire-resistant, maintenance free, stable, dense and vermin-proof. Much of Baldwin County was made of this tile, and a majority of the buildings, including churches, schools, municipal buildings, community buildings and homes still stand today.

I tracked down Alan Samry, who has written several articles about all things related to Clay City. He imparted this tidbit: "Bart (Junior) and Beverly Jennings ran the company successfully for decades. Their sons, Bart (III) and Ralph Jennings, began running it in 1980. Bart (the Third)'s death in 1983 and that, combined with market forces, including brick-manufacturing competitors and rising gas prices (which fueled the kilns' operations), proved to be insurmountable."

Today, only a minute part of Clay City still exists. You can see the old site, which has a couple of the original kilns still standing, and there is a pottery company operating near the property (Tom Jones Pottery).

THE POARCH BAND OF CREEK INDIANS: CREATING SUCCESS FOR GENERATIONS

The indigenous people known today as the Poarch Band of Creek Indians have come a very long way since the Creek Indian War of 1813-14 and, later, the Trail of Tears. They are the only federally recognized tribe in Alabama. As such, they have their own sovereignty, their own system of government and laws. Today, they have on their reservation (eight miles northwest of Atmore) a casino (Wind Creek), which is doing very well; they also own two other casinos (also named Wind Creek); one is in Wetumpka and the other in Montgomery. Also located on the reservation is the Cultural and History Museum with interesting, interactive exhibits and educational videos so people can learn more about the history and culture of these indigenous people (admission is free).

In 2014, the Poarch Band of Creek Indians donated a half a million dollars to the University of South Alabama for the purpose of teaching a new, Native American Studies Program at the college. This is the only college in the state of Alabama that now offers a course on the culture, history and language of the Poarch Band of Creek Indians.

The Poarch Band of Creek Indians plays an active role as citizens of Alabama. They contribute to the economy of the state and offer cultural projects such as pow-wows during various times of the year (the biggest one is held during Thanksgiving weekend).

DANIEL PRATT: ALABAMA'S ORIGINAL INDUSTRIALIST WITH A MIDAS TOUCH

Born in 1799 in New Hampshire, even at a young age Daniel Pratt had a penchant for all things mechanical. He moved to Georgia at the age of 20, where he began to be fascinated with Eli Whitney's cotton gin—and he knew he could make improvements on it (a cotton gin removes the seeds from the boll, a very arduous and time-consuming task for human hands) He took a job in a factory that made Whitney's style of cotton gins and young Pratt set about tinkering with it to make it better and more productive.

In 1833, he purchased land in Autauga County, moved with his wife there (near Montgomery) and founded the town of Prattville. He built the town from his cotton mill and gin factory to adding a carriage factory, a saw-mill, a gristmill and other industrial buildings. He also built houses, a town hall, a library, four churches and two schools for his new town. His cotton gin industry, known as the Pratt Gin Company, ultimately became the largest manufacturer of cotton gins, not just in Alabama, but in the entire world.

When I caught up with Prattauga Museum Interim Director and head volunteer Barbara Gaston, she told me that the visionary Pratt put the proverbial Midas touch on many other ventures. "He started a newspaper, the *Autauga Citizen*; he also started a bank, and was active in politics," she said. She told me Pratt expanded his reach into the coal and iron industry in Birmingham and was a sponsor of itinerant artist George Cooke, building a gallery in Prattville especially to showcase his works.

Because of Pratt's vision, he brought industry and real progress to Alabama. Today, you can see the old gin shop, which is still on the banks of Autauga Creek in Prattville (the city has plans to convert the building into a complex containing shops, condominiums and restaurants). Near Heritage Park is the Prattaugan Museum that houses many items relating to the history of Prattville, including a full-size cotton gin that was made in Pratt's gin shop.

VIEWING THE WORLD THROUGH AN ALABAMA BUSINESS: SEE COAST MANUFACTURING, INC.

It was Fairhope resident Geoff Cain who had a vision: make faraway places accessible to everyone, regardless of where they are in the world. In 1960, he took that vision, manufactured some prototypes, and patented his coin-operated and non-coin-operated binoculars and telescopes.

His company not only continues to do well, but it's thriving. Although Geoff passed away in 2017, his company continues to hum away under the guidance of his wife, current president and owner of See Coast, Geraldine Cain. With only a tiny staff of seven or eight people including sales, production specialists and office workers, See Coast Manufacturing has its telescopes and viewfinders located all over the world. You may see them on cruise ships, on tall buildings, and in some exotic locales such as the Rock of Gibraltar, Chamundi Hills in India, Dubai, the Virgin Islands, Puerto Rico and the Verdon Gorge in France. See Coast was recently featured in *Business Alabama* Magazine as one company to watch—no pun intended! They offer tours if you give them advance notice.

INVENTORS AND AMAZING CEOs OF ALABAMA

What do Erskine Ramsay, Miller Reese Hutchinson, Mary Anderson, Waldo Semon, Jimmy Wales, Tim Cook, George Kirchoff, Andrew Jackson Beard, Percy Lavon Julian, Lonnie George Johnson, and Robert Van de Graaff have in common? They're all from Alabama and they all are either inventors or CEOs of large companies. Ramsay (1864-1953), a Birmingham native, invented devices to make mining safer. Green County native Mary Anderson (1866-1953) invented the windshield wiper. Hutchinson (1876-1944) of Baldwin County invented the car horn.

Demopolis native Semon (1898-1999) invented vinyl. Van de Graaf (1901-1967) of Tuscaloosa created the particle accelerator (also known as the atom smasher). Huntsville native Jimmy Wales (1966-) is co-inventor of Wikipedia. Another Baldwin native, Kirchoff (1931-) invented the automobile airbag. Mobile-born, but Robertsdale-raised Tim Cook (1960-) is CEO of Apple Corporation. Beard (1849-1921), a native of Jefferson County, invented several farming implements and a device to make coupling of railcars independent of human labor (and was a former slave). Montgomery native Julian (1899-1975) held more than 100 chemical and medicinal patents and was the first African-American chemist inducted into the National Academy of Science.

Finally, Mobile's Johnson (1949-) is most well known for creating the water toy, the Super Soaker. His real genius, though, lies in the arena of defense, energy, and aerospace. In this capacity he worked with NASA on *Galileo's* mission to Jupiter. You can learn more about these and other amazing Alabamians in various county museums of history as well as the Alabama Department of Archives and History in Montgomery.

LILY FLAGG WAS A WHAT??? OR, MAKING A DAIRY COMPANY FAMOUS

There once was a cow that, in 1892, set international records: in that year, she produced a record-breaking amount of dairy products, producing 1,000 pounds of butter and 1,375 gallons of milk. Her name was Lily Flagg, a Jersey cow. Owned by Meadow Gold Dairies (Huntsville's only dairy farm), Lily Flagg and her achievements were honored at a ball hosted by owner Samuel Moore, and developer Harry Rhett hosted a party in his home commemorating the bovine.

Meadow Gold Dairies first featured a cow on a billboard advertising their company. This work of art was called Bessie, or Elsie. During the 1960s, she stood at the corner of Governor's Drive and Memorial Parkway. Originally painted as a Holstein cow, she remained on the billboard for more than 25 years.

What do the two cows have to do with each other? Well, for his party Harry Rhett took the billboard-cow Elsie (which had been vandalized many times and stolen once), repainted her as a Jersey cow in honor of Lily Flagg, then after the party returned her to her original Holstein colors. For a time, Lilly Flagg/Elsie was at home on top of a water tower near Meadow Gold Dairies, but vandals continued to deface the bovine work of art. Over the years she had to have her tail replaced six times, and her hooves and one leg replaced.

When Meadow Gold Dairies closed, her image was moved to Constitution Village (part of the Early Works Museum complex) in Huntsville. The image of the famous bovine is outside on the grounds of Constitution Village.

I guess the city continues to "milk" the celebrity status of both cows.

THERE'S GOLD IN THE HILLS! THE STORY OF THE ALABAMA GOLD RUSH

It was in 1830 that gold was first discovered in East Alabama. The so-called "Gold Belt" covered 3,500 square miles within the state. Named the Arbacoochee Gold District, this area between the Georgia line and Alabama's Talladega Mountains contained gold in the form of alluvial deposits— along with small nuggets, there were gold flakes mixed with soil, sand and gravel. When word of the discovery got out, prospectors and alluvial miners poured by the thousands into East Alabama and established mines in places called Goldville, Ely Pits, Log Pits, Dutch Bend and Hog Mountain.

Towns such as Goldville and Arbacoochee sprang up seemingly overnight, and for a time, they flourished. With gold being found in such small nuggets and flakes, however, miners and other people who had come to "get rich quick" soon found this type of mining to be hard work. Two things signaled the death knell for the Alabama Gold Rush and the gold-mining towns: the standard U.S. rate for gold fell to below $35 per ounce, and in 1849 gold was discovered in California. Overnight, Goldville shrank from being the largest city in Alabama to practically nonexistent. The prospectors and miners moved on to those more productive California fields, and towns like Goldville and Arbacoochee became ghost towns.

There is an update to this story: the town of Goldville reincorporated in 1973. The last census showed the population to be a whopping 55. Just a few miles north of Goldville, Lineville is the site of a gold mining camp. People of all ages and ability can go and pan for gold in Lineville's "Alabama Gold Camp."

The lure of quickly getting rich lives on in Alabama! See "Virtual Alabama" for their website.

"MOON" OVER HOOVER: VULCAN, GOD OF THE FORGE

The statue of Vulcan, which sits atop Red Mountain, was first created in 1904 by (son of immigrants, but Alabama-born) Guiseppe Moretti to be originally displayed at the Louisiana Purchase Exposition at St. Louis, Missouri. The Roman "God of the Forge" was a tribute to the steelworkers of Birmingham and to the steel-making industry in the area.

After the exposition, the statue was brought back to the Birmingham area known as Hoover, where many residents protested its rather "unusual" placement. Those who lived in the south side of the statue had a view of Vulcan's partially exposed backside, and a number of people were unhappy over the prospect of this kind of view from their windows (the statue, the world's largest cast-iron statue, wears a welder's apron but no trousers). Nonetheless, Vulcan was placed where he now stands, towering over the city of Birmingham.

Vulcan stands at 56 feet tall from his toe to his upheld spear-point. He stands atop a pedestal of 124 feet, for a total of 180 feet, and weighs more than 100,000 pounds. Located at Vulcan Park and Museum, the statue and museum are available for tours. It's a great way to spend some time seeing this "ironic" part of Birmingham.

Incidentally, another cast-iron statue also "moons" Alabamians: it's a cast-iron sculpture in the Woods Quad Sculpture Garden located on the campus of The University of Alabama in Tuscaloosa. Created by sculptor Joe McCreary, "Goldie" is another tribute to Alabama's historic iron industry—and also has an exposed bottom! See "Virtual Alabama" for websites.

DID YOU KNOW?

In 1910, author Ethel Armes outlined Alabama's economic development in a published work titled *The Story of Coal and Iron in Alabama*.

SOME OF THE OLDEST COMPANIES IN THE YELLOWHAMMER STATE

Some of the things you see on shelves in Alabama stores are from companies that have existed in Alabama for generations. Here is a partial list:

RED DIAMOND TEA COMPANY—It celebrated its 100th anniversary in 2006, having been founded in Moody, Alabama in 1906.

GOLDEN FLAKE – Now the company which got its start in 1923 has branched out into a variety of snacks, but when it was first founded, Golden Flake made its specialty--potato chips. In my younger days of modeling and doing radio and TV ads, in 1984 I was in a Golden Flake commercial in Bryant-Denny Stadium in Tuscaloosa, with The University of Alabama team mascot, Big Al.

MILNER-RUSHING DRUGS—Established in 1853 in Florence, this drug store continues to help make folks around Florence feel better.

BROMBERG & COMPANY—This jewelry store, first established in Mobile in 1836, still sparkles.

ROYAL CUP COFFEE—Based in Birmingham, this coffee importer was founded in 1896. It roasts nearly 60 million pounds of coffee beans annually. The coffee company is on Cleage Drive.

Q & A

Q. Bessemer became home to what well-known railroad car manufacturer?

A. Pullman-Standard.

Q. Open for business in 1878, what was the South's first commercial tourist attraction?

A. Fort Payne's Manitou Cave.

Q. What Alabama businessman bought Key West, Florida, in 1821 for the price of $2,000?

A. John Simonton.

Q. How many other states in the U.S. have the natural resources such as dolomite, limestone, iron ore, and coal, all of which are required in the manufacture of iron and steel?

A. None. Alabama is the only state in the nation with all four natural resources. It is also the largest producer of steel pipe and cast-iron products. You can learn more about this at the Iron and Steel Museum at Tannehill Ironworks Historical State Park in McCalla, just south of Birmingham.

CHAPTER 12
FILM, MUSIC AND DRAMA OF ALABAMA

DID YOU KNOW?

The Mobile-based Excelsior Band, first established in 1883, is one of the most well-known jazz bands in the world. Its members, many of whom are descendants of the original band members, perform every year during Mardi Gras parades.

FUNKY ALABAMA: LIONEL RICHIE AND THE COMMODORES

They were only (mostly) freshmen when they met at what is now called Tuskegee University in 1968. They were there for a talent show, and they were originally two different musical groups: the Mystics and the Jays. They performed so well that they signed with Motown Records by 1972 after they played the opening act for the Jackson 5. The original members were Lionel Richie, William King and Thomas McClary (from the Mystics) and Milan Williams, Michael Gilbert and Andre Callahan (from the Jays).

Once the group formed, they needed a new name. Member William King picked up a dictionary, opened it at random and chose a word. He later joked that, luckily, he pointed to the Commodores instead of another word. "We almost became The Commodes," he reminisced in a 2014 interview with Graham Betts for an entry in *Motown Encyclopedia*.

In 1986 they won their first Grammy Award for their song "Nightshift." The last night The Commodores performed in concert together was in Tuscaloosa in 1984 (I was lucky enough to be there), and the crowd shed more than a few tears when the group sang their last song together.

When he went solo, singer Lionel Richie cut an album, "Truly," which was also the name of the hit song on it. That album became the best-selling Motown album in history (at that time).

Today, you can take a trip back in time to the Commodore Museum. Located in Tuskegee, the museum stands on the spot of the Commodores' previous recording studio. The museum is filled with memorabilia from the musical group's heyday, and contains a gift shop. The museum has all of the recording and stage equipment as it was when the group was at their height of popularity. The Commodore Museum is currently run by a former bodyguard of the group, Johnny Bailey, who has all kinds of stories to tell.

ONLY THE GOOD DIE YOUNG: HANK WILLIAMS, SR.

Growing up on my grandparents' farm in north Alabama (Union Grove), I listened to a lot of radio. Besides listening to Gospel music, one singer we regularly heard was this musical luminary. Although he passed away at a young age (at the age of 29 in 1953), the popularity of Hank Williams, Sr. continued to rise and even grow in popularity after his death.

The songs that Hank Williams Sr. made famous, such as "Your Cheatin' Heart" and "Hey, Good Lookin'" were two of the songs that many singers today know by heart. Williams' musical legacy was passed down to his son, Hank Williams, Jr., his grandson, Hank Williams III, and his daughter, Antha Belle Jett (who later changed her name to Jett Williams).

Hank Williams, Sr. paved the way for what used to be given the derogatory term, "Hillbilly Music" to be admired and even respected as "Country Music." Today, you can tour the Hank Williams Sr. Boyhood Home and Museum, located at 127 Rose Street in the town of Georgiana, Alabama. The Hank Williams, Sr. Boyhood Home and Museum pays homage to what is now known as country music's greatest legend. In Montgomery, you can tour the Hank Williams Museum, which has as its highlighted exhibit the so-called "Hank Williams' Death Car" (the car in which he died as he was being driven to a performance). Nearby this museum, you can see the statue of Hank Williams, Sr. Finally, part of I-65 is named "Blues Highway" in his honor. Williams is buried in Oakwood Annex Cemetery in Montgomery, and his grave is visited almost daily by his many fans.

NAT "KING" COLE: "UNFORGETTABLE"

"Unforgettable" was the first Nat "King" Cole song I learned. Like the singer himself, Cole's musical legacy left an unforgettable mark on the industry. Born as Nathaniel Adams Cole in Montgomery in 1919, Cole's family moved in 1923 to Chicago, where he began taking voice lessons. He rose to prominence and fame across races when in 1956 he began a television show called "The Nat King Cole Show," and people everywhere were enthralled by Cole's smooth-as-honey, baritone voice. He was inducted into the Alabama Music Hall of Fame in 1997.

In 2015, Cole's childhood home was relocated from its place on Saint John Street in Montgomery to the campus of Alabama State University. It opened in 2017 as a museum; there is a historical marker commemorating not only Cole's musical achievements, but also his efforts in the Civil Rights Movement of the 1960s. Like Hank Williams, Sr., Cole's legacy is being carried on through his daughter Natalie's singing. In 1991, she recorded her father's song, the famous "Unforgettable," putting her vocals with his, in one amazing duet.

YOU'D NEVER HAVE THE BLUES IF NOT FOR W. C. HANDY!

Florence native W. C. Handy was born under humble circumstances—in a log cabin to an impoverished couple—but he rose from this to become known around the world as "The Father of the Blues."

Born in 1873 as William Christopher Handy, his grandfather (a newly freed African-American slave) was a preacher at the local African-American Episcopal Church and had high expectations for his grandson to become educated. Although the Handy household encouraged music of a spiritual nature, they frowned on young Handy's interest in becoming a professional musician. In an interview with Handy, he quoted his father as saying, "Son, I'd rather follow you to your grave than see you become a musician."

Young Handy completed his high school education but went on to become an itinerant musician. At one point, he had to resort to sleeping under a bridge (Eades Bridge) in St. Louis, Missouri. Broke, discouraged, homeless and hungry, Handy decided to fight for his dream no matter the odds against him.

Eventually, he got a job as an orchestra leader (the Knights of Pythias Band) in Clarksdale, Mississippi. Here, he was exposed to the sound of African-American folk music, and he fell in love with it. He lived for two years in Mississippi, listening to what he called the "crude singing" of African-American songs and spirituals. He began to write the tunes to what he heard; this became known as "the Blues."

In 1903, Handy moved to Memphis, Tennessee, and found a job working as a band leader. His tunes began to be played all along Beale Street. His songs were picked up by such notable singers as Ella Fitzgerald and Mae West.

When no one would publish his tunes and songs, Handy formed his own musical publishing company, Pace and Handy, which was a first for African-Americans. The blues were quickly becoming all the rage in the music industry. Capitalizing on this, in the 1920s Handy moved his publishing company to New York City's Times Square. Handy's most well-beloved collection of music was his album, "Saint Louis Blues," reminiscent of the difficult first years struggling to become a professional musician (and his signature tune by the same name was part of that collection).

In 1954, Columbia Records produced an album that combined Louis Armstrong's music with W. C. Handy's blues. Although W. C. Handy passed away in 1958, the world, and especially Florence, did not forget him.

Today, Handy is celebrated in many ways in Florence. In 1954, Handy's birthplace log cabin, in danger of destruction, was moved to property that is now the W. C. Handy Birthplace, Museum and Library (Handy purchased the land on which the cabin was, and donated it to the city of Florence). The W. C. Handy Birthplace, Museum and Library is a part of the Mississippi Blues Trail. Every year since its inception in 1982, Handy's life and works are celebrated with the W. C. Handy Music Festival, which now is a 10-day-long celebration. The museum hosts a W.C. Handy Birthday celebration every November 16, with free admission and birthday cake. Also in Florence on the 200 block of Tombigee Street, you can see a statue of Handy (created by sculptor James W. Stoves), as if in the middle of playing his cornet.

Handy himself was inducted into the Alabama Music Hall of Fame in 1987. See "Virtual Alabama" for websites for more on this astonishingly talented musician.

Just think—if Handy hadn't had such an independent streak, we might not ever have had the Blues, and we might not ever have known "the Father of the Blues."

MUSCLE SHOALS AND ITS GROWING MUSICAL ATTRACTIONS

The area of Muscle Shoals and Sheffield, both in north Alabama, has many musically themed attractions. There's the "Father of the Blues," W.C. Handy Birthplace and Museum; FAME Recording Studio; and the latest jewel in the city's musical crown, the Muscle Shoals Sound Studio. The recording studio was originally founded in 1969 on Jackson Street by the band known as The Muscle Shoals Rhythm Section (whom locals and music-lovers affectionately refer to as "The Swampers"), in a cement-block building formerly used as a coffin shop.

The sound studio was moved to 1000 Alabama Avenue, and the old studio, now listed on the National Register of Historic Places, was sold to the Muscle Shoals Music Foundation in 2013. Because of a grant by Beats By Dre, the recording studio was able to reopen at its former address, 3614 Jackson Highway, as a museum. This is the place where musical greats such as Linda Ronstadt, Aretha Franklin, Bob Dylan and the Rolling Stones recorded some of their hits. Next time you're in north Alabama, swing by and see if you don't come away inspired!

"SWEET HOME ALABAMA"

The song which has become a part of Crimson Tide football games, a title of a movie starring Reese Witherspoon, and mentions the Muscle Shoals Rhythm Section ("The Swampers"), was written by a band out of Jacksonville, Florida, known as Lynyrd Skynyrd. The song came out in August of 1974 in response to Neil Young's derogatory song "Southern Man," which was an insult to many people who lived in and appreciated the Yellowhammer State.

Now, the state of Alabama has "Sweet Home Alabama" as its logo; it's on the Alabama Department of Tourism official website, and everyone who enters the state sees it on the Alabama welcome signs along highways and interstates.

ALABAMA: HOME TO THE WORLD'S LARGEST JUKEBOX

Located on the north side of Huntsville on 108 Cleveland Avenue is the world's largest jukebox. Standing a whopping 22 feet tall, the jukebox plays songs that were originally recorded in Alabama. You can go stand in front of it and it will play a tune for you! Visiting the jukebox is free and fun!

"COME HOME IT'S SUPPERTIME" IN BRUNDIDGE

The Official Folklife Play of Alabama is "Come Home It's Suppertime," which is performed at the We Piddle Around Theatre in the town of Brundidge, slightly southeast of Troy. The players perform authentic situations and will have you both laughing and crying as they portray events that your grandparents might have experienced, farming, picking cotton and growing up in Alabama. You'll have to make sure to catch these performances, which are only offered in the month of November every year.

THE FILM INDUSTRY IN ALABAMA: ALIVE, WELL AND GROWING

You might be strolling in downtown Huntsville, Decatur, Montgomery or Mobile and be witness to someone making some kind of film production. All kinds of films have been made in Alabama, and the Yellowhammer State continues to draw more movie- and documentary- makers to its welcome mat. The Q&A section of this chapter has a partial list.

GEORGE LINDSEY, WHO BECAME FAMOUS BY ACTING GOOFY

He became an iconic figure as the gas-station attendant and unsophisticated goofy guy, playing the character of Goober on the hit TV series, *The Andy Griffith Show*. Born in Fairfield, Alabama, in 1928, young Lindsey found his talent early as a jokester, and for a time was a stand-up comedian. He was raised by his grandparents and grew up in Jasper (Walker County). In college, Lindsey played football for The University of North Alabama and had a stint in the Air Force. While waiting to be accepted into the American Theatre Wing in New York City in 1956, Lindsey taught high school at Hazel Green, Alabama.

Once he finished acting school, Lindsey had many acting stints on TV shows, including *The Rifleman* and *The Alfred Hitchcock Hour*, before landing his hit role on *The Andy Griffith Show*. When the show was cancelled, a new TV series, *Mayberry R.F.D.*, came out. Lindsey continued to play the role of the slow-witted but comedic Goober until that show was also cancelled in 1971.

Lindsey continued to portray the role of Goober, this time on the syndicated country music show, *Hee-Haw*, where he played that character for twenty years (1972 to 1992). For his years in playing football in college, Lindsey was inducted into the Alabama Sports Hall of Fame in 1983. In 1995, Lindsey was the recipient of the Governor's Achievement Award from the Alabama Music Hall of Fame. His last celebrity appearance was a Christmas comedy special with "Larry the Cable Guy" in 2009.

Lindsey died of heart failure in Nashville, Tennessee, in 2012, and is buried in Oak Hill Cemetery in Jasper.

What many people may not know about this self-deprecating comedian was how big his heart really was: he was an avid fund-raiser for the Alabama Special Olympics and raised money for the Alabama Association of Retarded Citizens through golf tournaments in Montgomery. He established a scholarship under his name for promising but poverty-stricken students who wanted to attend his college alma mater (University of North Alabama, or UNA) in Florence.

Today, besides paying your respects at Lindsey's grave, you can celebrate his life achievements by going to the George Lindsey/UNA Film Festival held in Florence every spring. This film festival is HUGE; it is attended by filmmakers from places as far away as Europe and California, and they also have a panel of film supervisors. People on this panel include celebrity filmmakers. In 2015, for example, panel members included such notables as Dave Jordan (*Guardians of the Galaxy* and others); Julianne Jordan (*The Bourne Identity*); and Thomas Golubic (*The Walking Dead*). Also that year, the Awards Show was MC'd by actor Natalie Canerday (*October Sky* and *Sling Blade*).

In Jasper, locals are proud of the fact that the State of Alabama named Highway 78 "George Lindsey Highway" in his honor to commemorate his life and achievements.

Not bad for a guy who created fame and fortune by acting goofy.

THE SOUND OF ALABAMA: THE STORY OF SUN RECORDS

Born to poor tenant farmers in Florence, Alabama, Sam C. Phillips was the eighth child in the family. Most people would say that a bright future would be impossible for someone born in poverty, but Sam never let where he came from determine where he was going.

Phillips' early inspiration came not from a college career or even from listening to the radio, but from his experiences helping his tenant-farming parents pick cotton. Picking alongside other poor farmers, Phillips would listen to the singing of the African-American pickers. Later, on a trip to see a preacher in Dallas with his parents while in Memphis, young Phillips slipped away and headed to the famed Beale Street, which remains the core of the city's music scene.

He was smitten by the music bug, and that inspiration would affect the rest of his life.

When in 1941 his father died, young Sam was obliged to drop out of high school in order to support his family. He married in 1942 and had two sons. Although he tinkered with the idea of going into legal practice, his love of music overwhelmed everything else.

In Muscle Shoals, Alabama, Phillips was tapped to host a religious radio show; with this experience, he went on to be on radio stations WMSC (Decatur, Alabama), and WLAY (Nashville, Tennessee), the latter of which earned him recognition as host of a radio program called the "Afternoon Tea Dance." After this, he went on to be a radio host of Memphis-based WREC radio station.

Once in Memphis, Phillips began to notice a trend among musicians: they were obliged to go to other towns, such as Nashville, to record their music. If they didn't, because of financial hardship that made travel impossible, these musicians were doomed to obscurity. Phillips decided to fill the void: in 1950, he leased a building on Union Avenue and opened Memphis Recording Service.

By 1952, Phillips and his label Sun Records were doing so well that he could afford to quit his job at WREC and work the studio full time. He recorded such notables as B. B. King, Elvis Presley, Big Mama Thornton and Elvis Presley (the latter of whom he signed to a recording contract). In 1954, he sold Presley's contract to RCA, which allowed him to expand Sun Records and record even more musicians. Those who walked through his door included such musical icons as Johnny Cash, Carl Perkins, Roy Orbison and Jerry Lee Lewis. In 1961, Phillips had to expand even more, and moved Sun Records to a place on Madison Avenue in Memphis. In 1969, he sold Sun Studios but enhanced his income with the revenue from several radio stations he had purchased and other investments. He died in 2003 and is buried in Memphis.

According to the *Encyclopedia of Alabama*, Sam Phillips is "... so far, the only person inducted into the Rock and Roll Hall of Fame (1986), the Alabama Music Hall of Fame (1987), the Country Music Hall of Fame (2001) and the Rockabilly Hall of Fame."

Today, even if you can't get to Memphis to see the original Sun Studios on Union Street (which has been named a National Historic Landmark), there is a display on exhibit at the Alabama Music Hall of Fame in Tuscumbia about Sam Phillips and his contributions to Rock and Roll and the birth of

"Rockabilly." Also, the city of Florence, Alabama, holds a "Sam Phillips Music Celebration." It's celebrated every January. See "Virtual Alabama" for websites.

ALABAMA'S TWO MUSICAL HALLS OF FAME

Alabama has not one, but two, halls of fame that relate purely to music. The Alabama Music Hall of Fame (AMHOF) is located in Tuscumbia (so while you're there visiting Helen Keller's birthplace, make sure to stop in). They celebrated their grand opening in 1990, and more than 50 musicians have been inducted into the AMHOF for their contributions to the sound of Alabama. AMHOF recently completed an expansion project, so there's more to see and hear than ever. The Alabama legislature created a seven-member board of directors to oversee the AMHOF's activities. One of my favorite exhibits in the AMHOF is of Sam Phillips and his Sun Records exhibit.

In the fall of 1993 in Birmingham's renovated Carver Theater, the AMHOF created a museum to celebrate and honor the achievements of those Alabamians whose specialty was in the musical field of jazz. Located near the Sixteenth Street Baptist Church, the Alabama Jazz Hall of Fame (AJHOF) has exhibits related to such notables as W. C. Handy, Ella Fitzgerald, Nat "King" Cole, Dinah Washington and Duke Ellington. The AJHOF also hosts free jazz workshops and programs for schools.

THE PHENIX CITY STORY: A FILM

This film, which was made in the real town of Phenix City, is loosely based on the 1954 assassination of Albert Patterson, an Alabama lawyer and politician. At one time, Phenix City itself was so overrun with violence and corruption that General George S. Patton (then stationed at nearby Fort Benning) threatened to flatten the city using his armored vehicles. The film, released to theaters in 1955, was a hit thanks in part to the national attention the media gave the assassination. Alabama native Jonathan Rosenbaum, who wrote the book *Essential Cinema* (Johns Hopkins University Press, 2004), proclaimed the film the best ever made in the Yellowhammer State.

MOVE OVER, NASHVILLE & LOS ANGELES: FAME IS MAKIN' IT, BIG TIME!

In 1959, FAME got its start as a recording studio in Florence. With the acronym standing for Florence Alabama Music Enterprises, since its inception, the recording studio (and music label by the same name) has been the go-to studio for a long list of notable musicians and singers. The list includes bands such as Drive-By Truckers, Third Day, the Greg Allman Band, Anderson East, and more. Individual singers who've been at the FAME studio include Tina Turner, Aretha Franklin, Elton John, Janis Joplin and B. B. King.

Rick Hall was the founder of FAME studio. In his memoir, *The Man from Muscle Shoals: My Journey from Shame to Fame*, Hall reminisced, "For every hit I ever produced, I have given three pints of blood and one pint of sweat." When Hall died in January of 2018, New York Times writer Jon Pareless wrote in Hall's obituary, "Mr. Hall turned small-town Alabama into a crucible of soul, country, pop and rock."

FAME Studio is still actively recording and is open most days for tours. It was added to the Alabama Register of Landmarks and Heritage in 1997 and to the National Register of Historic Places in 2003.

ALABAMA SHAKES

Although they are a relatively new band, the Alabama Shakes has "shaken things up" with their style of music. It's gutsy, bluesy and definitely hard to pigeonhole. On their website, lead singer and Athens, Alabama, native Brittany Howard said that their music is "genre-bending"—it's difficult to categorize their music into one particular genre. Their debut album, "Boys & Girls," shot to the top of the music charts, and their next album, "Sound & Color," made it big as well. *Billboard Magazine* honored Howard in 2015 as one of the top women in music. The group tours internationally and in the U.S. Give 'em a listen when they're in your area.

THE "QUEEN OF SCREAM"

Birmingham native, actress Courtney Cox, may be best known for her role in the *Friends* series, but she also starred in one of the most popular horror-film series in history. If you've ever watched one of the *Scream* movies, you would have seen Cox starring in the role of journalist Gale Weathers.

GUESS WHO?

What Montgomery native and Auburn University graduate made her film debut in the 1996 drama, *A Time to Kill*, and has won an Academy Award, a British Academy Film Award, and a Golden Globe? If you thought, "Octavia Spencer," you'd be right.

DID YOU KNOW?

In 1955, a man named Clarence Steiner began a business in Bayou La Batre. It was originally meant to be a repair yard for wooden ships, but since that time, it has evolved into a full-service shipyard. Today, its specialty is in the manufacture, repair, and conversion of aluminum and steel naval vessels. Now owned and run by Clarence's son Russell Steiner, the ship repair-turned-manufacturing is booming. Many of the company's clientele have been with them for more than 40 years. One in particular, Sahlman Seafoods, entrusted Steiner to manufacture 179, 75-foot steel shrimp trawlers, an endeavor of 20 years.

But no one at Steiner saw their biggest "break" coming. In 2005, someone in the film industry sought out Steiner to ask if they could locate and fit out a special kind of ship for a movie. The ship was to be used for the wildly popular movie, *Pirates of the Caribbean*, and it was outfitted to be the *Black Pearl*. The movie crew came to Bayou La Batre to work with the Steiner shipyard employees, remaining there for months to get the ship ready for her film debut. The *Black Pearl* was captained by Jack Sparrow, played by Johnny Depp, in the second and third movies in the *Pirates of the Caribbean* Disney series.

"TOUCHDOWN TONY" AND THE FILM ABOUT THE BIGGEST HIGH SCHOOL FOOTBALL GAME EVER PLAYED IN ALABAMA

It was on November 24, 2014, and the Legion Field in Birmingham had been made to look much the way it had been in 1974, when it was the site of the historic high school football game between major rivals: the Woodlawn High School Colonels and the two-time defending champion, the Banks High School Jets. Tamika Moore, who covered the filming of the event for Al.com, wrote about it so vividly I felt as though I were there in person.

The main rivalry was between the Colonels player, "Touchdown Tony" Nathan and the Jets' player, Jeff Rutledge. Birmingham filmmakers and brothers John and Andrew Erwin recreated the historic night of decades ago, when the game was witnessed by more than 42,000 people. It took the brother-filmmakers only a few weeks to shoot their movie based on that rivalry. Given the title *Woodlawn*, the making of the film was watched by the Erwin brothers' father, Hank Erwin, who had also been the Woodlawn team's chaplain in the early 1970s. He stated to Moore, "To see that my boys are taking a story that I walked through and turning it into a motion picture of this magnitude, I never dreamed of that." Stars slated for roles in the film included Sean Astin (*Lord of the Rings*) and Osy Ikhile (*In the Heart of the Sea*).

Much of the footage of *Woodlawn* was shot at Legion Field, while some of it was filmed at Hueytown's Gilmore-Vines Stadium. Scores of extras were in the movie playing the part of cheering fans, who had to dress as they might have been in the era of the early 1970s. Perhaps the most interesting part of the filming was that the players from that epic 1974 game were invited to come watch the filming and have their pictures taken with the actors portraying them on the field.

Incidentally, Bob Carlton, who also wrote about this 1974 game for AL.com, wrote that as time has gone on "the details [about the game] have gotten fuzzier and the legends have grown larger." He wrote that no one could seem to remember the final score. What they could remember was people came in such numbers that the start of the game had to be delayed.

ALABAMA—THE BAND

The band Alabama was started in 1969 by cousins and Fort Payne, Alabama, natives Teddy Gentry and Randy Owen. Later, another cousin (Jeff Cook) joined forces. Their natural talents made them an instant hit, as they came out with one Number One country and soft rock single after another (the band's record stands at 21 such #1 singles). In 1999, they were named Country Group of the Century for songs such as "My Home's in Alabama," "The Closer You Get," and others. The group was inducted into the Country Music Hall of Fame (in Nashville, Tennessee) in 2005. In November of 2018, Randy

Owen was inducted into the Alabama Business Hall of Fame (in Birmingham). The press release said the award was given "as a result of [Owen's] business dealings in music, agriculture and humanitarianism."

An example of this band's generosity in keeping with its popularity is this: in the fall of 2018, the band raised $1.3 million in funds to help Jacksonville State University in the aftermath of a terrible tornado. They are a true "Dixieland Delight." The band now has a museum and gift shop in their hometown of Fort Payne, on 101 Glenn Boulevard SW near the intersection of State Highway 35 and US Highway 11.

DID YOU KNOW?

Demopolis was the setting for the 1949 movie, *The Fighting Kentuckian*, starring John Wayne.

Q & A

Q. What Grand Ole Opry performer was born in Hackleburg?

A. Sonny James.

Q. Singer Toni Tennille, of the duo Captain and Tennille, was born in what Alabama city?

A. Montgomery.

Q. What song, that came out in 1947, catapulted Montgomery-born Nat King Cole to national fame?

A. "The Christmas Song."

Q. Decatur-born actor Dean Jones was most famous for his roles in what two Disney movies?

A. *That Darn Cat* and *The Love Bug*.

Q. What Jazz-Age actress was the daughter of one of Alabama's most powerful political families?

A. Tallulah Bankhead.

Q. What actor, born in Birmingham, was best known for his role as friend to Hawkeye Pierce and played "Trapper" John McIntyre in the hit series, *MASH*?

A. Wayne Rogers.

Q. What movie producer filmed the Huntsville-based young adventure movie, about campers who inadvertently become part of a Space Shuttle mission?

A. *Space Camp*.

Q. What was the name of the movie about the life of Hank Williams, Sr., that was released in 1964?

A. *Your Cheatin' Heart*.

Q. What was the name of the Blues singer who wrote the song made famous by Janis Joplin, "Ball and Chain"?

A. Montgomery-born singer Willie Mae "Big Mama" Thornton.

Q. What movie, starring Tommy Lee Jones and Sally Field, was filmed in Mobile?

A. *Back Roads*.

Q. What Mobile-born trumpeter played with Duke Ellington in the early 1960s?

A. "Cootie" Williams, also known as Charles Melvin Williams.

Q. The film *Stay Hungry*, starring Jeff Bridges and Sally Field, was made in what Alabama city?

A. Birmingham.

Q. What Alabama group has played back-up on more than 500 records, ranging from disco to country, to R&B and rock and roll?

A. The Muscle Shoals Sound Rhythm Section.

Q. What number-one hit did Lionel Ritchie write for country-music crooner Kenny Rogers?

A. "Lady."

Q. Who, during the 1950s, was the most popular black female singer?

A. Tuscaloosa-born Dinah Washington.

Q. Singer Percy Sledge was born in what Alabama community?

A. Leighton.

Q. Seaboard hosts what musical event every May?

A. Bilbo Spring Bluegrass Festival.

Q. What movie, filmed in Talladega, featured Jim Nabors and Burt Reynolds?

A. *Stroker Ace*.

Q. Parts of what 1977 science fiction adventure movie, filmed in Mobile, starred Richard Dreyfuss?

A. *Close Encounters of the Third Kind*.

Q. What adventure television series did Birmingham-born Jaclyn Smith and Farrah Fawcett-Majors star in with Kate Jackson?

A. *Charlie's Angels.*

Q. Florence-born Sam Phillips is best known for being the pioneer of what kind of music?

A. Rockabilly.

Q. Where was Emmylou Harris born?

A. Birmingham.

Q. The singing duo known as Captain and Tennille (Daryl Dragon and Toni Tennille) won a Grammy Award in 1975 for what song?

A. "Love Will Keep Us Together."

Q. With which famous singer did Lionel Hampton sing between the years 1943 to 1946?

A. Dinah Washington.

Q. What country-music singer made the song "Easy Loving" famous?

A. Freddie Hart.

Q. Where in Montgomery was Nat King Cole born?

A. On St. John Street, in the Cole-Samford House.

Q. What movie was made in Birmingham in 1984, for which actress Sissy Spacek received an Academy Award nomination?

A. *The River.*

Q. Born in Tennessee but raised in Florence, Alabama, Melba Montgomery became part of a famous singing duet with what country music star in the 1960s?

A. George Jones.

A. What student left school at Auburn University in order to eventually play in Roy Orbison's band?

A. Bobby Goldsboro.

Q. What Jimmy Buffett song won "Single of the Year" in 1977, and is still played regularly today at virtually every tiki bar around the world?

A. "Margaritaville."

Q. What 1968 song about a young man tragically losing his wife brought singer Bobby Goldsboro fame?

A. "Honey."

Q. What movie about an engaged Alabama girl starred Reese Witherspoon in 2002?

A. *Sweet Home Alabama*.

Q. Percy Sledge became famous with what 1966 R&B song, which later was used as the theme song for a 1994 movie by the same name, starring Meg Ryan?

A. "When a Man Loves a Woman."

Q. Who was named "Queen of the Harlem Blues" in the mid-1950s?

A. Dinah Washington.

Q. What 1968 movie, which told the life of a young girl who was deaf, was filmed in Selma and based on a Southern Gothic novel by Carson McCuller?

A. *The Heart is a Lonely Hunter*. The novel has the same title.

Q. What was the Mobile rock group Wet Willie's name initially?

A. Fox.

Q. What movie about a mental institution had a role of a villainous nurse, that was played by Birmingham-born Louise Fletcher that garnered her an Oscar in 1976?

A. *One Few Over the Cuckoo's Nest*. Incidentally, when Fletcher accepted the award, she also signed a message of thanks to her parents—both of whom were deaf. In thanking the nominators, she quipped, "Thank you for hating me so much!"

Q. The play "God's Highway" relives the story of the Coosa River. Where is this play given?

A. Noccalula Falls Park, in Gadsden.

Q. What film, made in Opelika in 1978, starred Birmingham-born actress Gail Strickland and won Sally Field an Academy Award for Best Actress?

A. *Norma Rae*.

Q. Birmingham-born female country singer Marion Worth is best known for her song about a doll. What is the song's name?

A. "Shake Me, I Rattle."

Q. What jazz festival travels the state, with various bands performing for free at community parks throughout Alabama?

A. It's known as Jazz in the Park. According to the Alabama Travel website, jazz groups travel to cities such as Tuscaloosa, Alabaster, Irondale, Gadsden, and other cities, exposing jazz to people who might not otherwise see it being performed.

Q. What play, based on teacher Annie Sullivan's role of teaching deaf and blind student Helen Keller, was made into a movie for TV won Patty Duke an Emmy in 1980?

A. *The Miracle Worker*.

Q. What is Alabama's official state drama, performed in Tuscumbia as part of the Helen Keller Festival?

A. The answer is the same: the outdoor play, *The Miracle Worker*.

Q. Composer William Levi Dawson was born in what Alabama town in 1899?

A. Anniston.

Q. Located on the Commons area of The University of Alabama campus, Denny Chimes has how many bells?

A. 305.

Q. Just south of Birmingham, the Indian Springs School hosts a Southern Appalachian festival focused on what musical instrument?

A. The dulcimer. Its full name is the Southern Appalachian Dulcimer Association Festival.

Q. What theater in Alabama is the oldest playhouse still in use?

A. The Fort Payne Opera House. It's been in operation since 1889.

Q. What Montgomery-born musician wrote the score of "Dixie," which was played at the parade during President Jefferson Davis's inauguration?

A. Herman F. Arnold.

Q. In what town was the Alabama Shakespeare Festival originally held, before it was moved to Montgomery?

A. Anniston.

Q. A bronze statue of the mischievous character Puck from English folklore is on display in the Carolyn Blount Theatre in Montgomery. What Alabama sculptor created the statue?

A. Elizabeth MacQueen.

CHAPTER 13

FLORA, FAUNA AND NATURAL PHENOMENA

ALABAMA'S AMAZING UNDERWATER FOREST

Scientists say that approximately 60,000 years ago, there was a lovely cypress forest in what is now just off the coast of Alabama. This Ice Age forest existed when sea levels were about 400 feet lower than they are now. This cypress forest, in just 60 feet of water off the coast of Gulf Shores, was a hidden mystery to everyone, lay person and scientist alike, until in 2004 the fierce winds and forceful waves of Hurricane Ivan uncovered it.

Preserved for tens of thousands of years under mud and sediment stirred up by rising sea levels, the cypress forest is in near-pristine condition. It is the only known place in the entire world where a coastal, Ice Age forest has been preserved. Filmmaker, naturalist and writer Ben Raines wrote about this phenomenal forest and produced a documentary film. Titled *The Underwater Forest*, the film has been and continues to be shown at various venues and dates, with donations and viewers' ticket sales going toward making this site a marine sanctuary (as of press time, it is now protected by the U.S. government).

... AND MORE FROM BEN RAINES: AMAZING FACTS ABOUT ALABAMA'S DIVERSITY OF WILDLIFE

In the summer of 2018, Ben Raines wrote a post, "Alabama: Where the Wild Things Are," for al.com. He wrote "More than 77,000 miles of rivers and streams ... crisscross the state." Since many of these rivers and streams flow into the Mobile-Tensaw Delta, Alabama has a great number of what Raines referred to as "biological rarities." For example, 120 species of fish live in the Cahaba River alone. Raines wrote, "That's roughly one-sixth of all the freshwater species known in the U.S." He also wrote that there are 182 species of mussels to be found in Alabama, representing 60 percent of the total mussel species in the entire United States. Raines recently completed an amazing documentary about the Delta, called *The American Amazon*. It's well worth the viewing!

HOLY BAT CAVES!!!

In Jackson County, Alabama, many caves are home to a great variety of bats, especially gray bats. Cathedral Cavern is most likely the best known, but nearby Sauta Cave may have the bat population claim to fame. Just at dusk, you can watch more than 250,000 (yes, that's a quarter-MILLION) bats fly out for their mosquito dinners. It's quite a sight to see.

North Alabama in particular has a plethora of caves to explore. Just outside Sheffield, you will find Key Cave National Wildlife Refuge. Near where Alabama meets the Tennessee and Georgia borders, you can explore Russell Cave National Monument. Just northwest of Scottsboro, both Blowing Cave National Wildlife Refuge and the aforementioned Cathedral Caverns can both be explored within a day (and if I can do it, anyone can). Finally, Neversink Pit in Fackler (about 15 miles outside Scottsboro) is a rappeller's and caver's dream: it's a vertical cave with a more than 160-foot drop to the cave floor and is one of the most photographed sinkholes in the U.S. and, perhaps, the world. Neversink Pit was purchased by the Southeastern Cave Conservatory, Inc., so it is on private property. You would need a permit to cave there. See "Virtual Alabama" for websites.

THE MAN WHO DISCOVERED FIRE (ANTS): "THE NATURALIST" E. O. WILSON

Long before Wilson became a world-renowned biologist and Pulitzer-prize-winning author (twice), this Birmingham native had an innate curiosity about living things. As a young boy, he was the first person to discover the presence of fire ants in Alabama (near his boyhood home of Mobile), an invasive species of insect that had arrived via ship from South America.

Edward Osborne Wilson, better known as E.O. Wilson, is an esteemed biologist and naturalist who was born in Birmingham, Alabama. He initially studied biology at the University of Alabama (1949-1950) then went on to receive his doctorate at Harvard University in 1955. Today, he is the University Research Professor Emeritus at Harvard and is commonly called "a Darwin of modern day" because of his studies in the behavior of ants, for which is he is most recognized. His work brought him to write his Pulitzer Prize-winning books *On Human Nature* and *The Ants* (the latter of which he co-authored with German entomologist Bert Hölldobler), and many more (including *The Social Conquest of Earth*, *The Naturalist*, and *Creation: An Appeal to Save Life on Earth*. He was inducted into the Alabama Writers Hall of Fame (in Tuscaloosa) on September 29, 2016.

As a child, he wanted to go into ornithological fieldwork (the study of birds), but this interest was put to an end after his right eye was injured in a fishing accident. His close-up vision remained intact, however, so over time he developed a love for insects.

According to E.O. Wilson himself (from his book, *The Naturalist*), he had identified virtually every species of ant in Mobile, Alabama, and even stumbled across the very first colony of fire ants to invade the United States. The colony's mound was in a vacant lot by his house while he was living in Mobile. His interest in ants was sparked by these early discoveries and grew with time.

Wilson is most highly noted for his studies in sociobiology (the study of social behaviors among living things) in both ants and humans alike.

Besides being a part of the Alabama Writers Hall of Fame, Wilson's work is acknowledged and exhibited at the E. O Wilson Biophilia Center in Freeport, Florida. This is an environmental education center created in honor of the naturalist, carrying on the legacy he is building in attempts to help preserve as much wildlife as possible. The center holds events (everything from 5K runs to school programs) and summer camps, easily accessible by any young person interested. The center is regularly open to the public.

BIG SPRING INTERNATIONAL PARK: SOPHISTICATED HAVEN FOR NATURE-LOVERS

I remember as a teenager exploring Big Spring Park in Huntsville. It's become much more sophisticated since those days, though, and is a haven for those who love nature and the outdoors. Now known as Big Spring International Park, the place that first lured early settlers to the area (for its natural spring) entices people of all ages to enjoy its beauty. The country of Norway gave a gift of a lighthouse, which stands prominently in the park. The cherry trees in the park were a gift from Japan, which further enhances visitors' enjoyment. People use the park for musical entertainment, weddings, and other events.

WHEELER NATIONAL WILDLIFE REFUGE: A NATURAL GEM IN ALABAMA'S CROWN

Along the Tennessee River on I-65 about halfway between Huntsville and Decatur lies Wheeler National Wildlife Refuge (WNWR). This lovely gem of natural beauty sprawls across 34,500 acres (with roughly 16,000 of those over water). Although many people like to visit in the spring, my favorite time of the year to visit is in winter. It is then that migratory birds come and winter-over here.

The birds that are here in the winter are more than plentiful: the wildlife refuge has seen as many as 60,000 geese and nearly 100,000 ducks, and when the cranes are there, they make quite a cacophony! You can get a close visual on the wildlife through the use of coin-operated binoculars inside viewing houses on the grounds; most of the time, there are naturalists and biologists on hand to answer questions. Last time I was there, I was lucky enough to talk with Dr. Andrew W. Cantrell and Teresa Adams, the latter of whom serves as Supervisory Ranger.

Besides Whooping Cranes and Sandhill Cranes, the WNWR is home to nearly 300 different species of birds. The refuge is also home to more than 70 species of reptiles and 115 species of fish. Inside the main building you will find a wonderful museum with great, life-like exhibits and well-informed, friendly staff, as well as a gift shop.

ANYTHING BUT DISMAL

Dismals Canyon (formally known as "Dismals Wonder Gardens") in northern Alabama is beautiful and primeval. Privately owned, this 85-acre natural wonder is anything **but** dismal. It is thought that it got its name from ancient Scotch-Irish settlers who were reminded of a place in Scotland called "Dismals."

Dismals Canyon, which became a National Natural Landmark in the mid-1970s, is extremely biologically diverse, with fascinating rock formations, six natural bridges and two lovely waterfalls within its boundaries. One of the many things which makes Dismals Canyon unique is an amazing phosphorescent insect that lives within the canyon property (the biological name is *Orfelia fultoni*, but locals call them "Dismalites"). When I first explored Dismals Canyon in the mid-1980s, there was not much development, but now there is a campground for those who like to rough it. Dismals Canyon also has a couple of romantic cabins on the site. A country store and grill and soda fountain are some of the latest additions.

Despite these upgrades, the Dismals Canyon owners are strict about keeping this natural wonder pristine: for example, they do not allow guests to bring in firewood from outside the area, in order to protect their trees from outside diseases (they have the State Champion Hemlock in their borders). Also, other than clearing the trails, the site is much the way the Paleo-Indians might have found it in prehistoric days.

I highly recommend taking a night tour. Seeing the dismalites light up the canyon walls is worth the trip! See "Virtual Alabama" for the website or to inquire about day or night guided tours.

THE STORY OF "THE LITTLE ZOO THAT COULD"

In the fall of 2004, the zoo in Gulf Shores, Alabama, made history. The Alabama Gulf Coast Zoo was the first zoo in the U.S. to launch a full-scale evacuation of its animals, as Hurricane Ivan bore down on the coast.

The hurricane completely destroyed the little zoo, but both the employees and volunteers were undaunted. Their story of coming back from the brink of total destruction, and of the care they gave their animals during this time of displacement, soon went, as they say, viral. The story of their recovery was made into a 13-part documentary on the beloved series, *Animal Planet*. Called *The Little Zoo that Could*, the documentary showed the evacuation, Ivan's destruction of the zoo, and recovery of the animals and the zoo. People around the world were enthralled by the documentary series.

Jasper, Alabama native and my friend, Bonnie Mayhall Williams, pets a yellow acaconda, Magic, as keeper Austin Everett holds his charge. Photo by the author.

The Alabama Gulf Coast Zoo still sits in a place where they are vulnerable to storms and rising waters during hurricanes. Since Ivan, the little zoo has endured the battering of Hurricanes Dennis, Katrina, Nate and others.

A family grew concerned about the zoo's location. Clyde Weir and his daughter, Andrea Weir, donated 25 acres four miles north of the existing zoo. This land was on a higher elevation and flood-proof—an ideal location for the zoo's new home. The little zoo still had a dilemma: what to do about funds to be able to move their more-than-600 animals to this new and safer land? And how would they fund the building of a new and better zoo?

A solution to this dilemma came in the form of art, and not just any art. Someone had the bright idea to have a fundraiser and auction off art created by the zoo animals themselves. The auction was held on October 27, 2018, with many of the zoo animals (under the watchful eyes of their caretakers) mingling with the guests and posing for photos. My husband bid on a painting a baboon created. As of press time, with the funds raised from this night and other donors' influx of money, the zoo is slated to be moved in September of 2019.

IT WILL "BUG" YOU IF YOU DON'T CHECK OUT <u>THIS</u> MUSEUM

As a little kid, I remember singing the jingle to a pest control company begun in Decatur, Alabama. Formed in 1928 by John Cook, Cook's Pest Control quickly became a household name and is now the 8th largest such company in the U.S.

The Cook family wanted to give back to the community and educate the public about how "Life is Amazing" (their iconic saying). The Cook Museum of Natural Science was opened in the late 1980s and was expanded and moved to its present location in downtown Decatur in 2017. Its exhibits aren't just about bugs: in 2017 they had a phenomenal exhibit about Madagascar and previously had an amazing one about the Congo ("we can't go to Congo, but Congo can come to us," they wrote in their e-newsletter).

ALABAMA'S AMAZING BIRDING TRAILS

If you're a bird enthusiast like I am, you like to go to places where you can go bird watching and see as many species as possible. Bird watching destinations that come to mind might include exotic places such as Puerto Rico or Hawaii, but in Alabama you can have a bird's-eye view of a wide variety of bird species you might be surprised to find in the Yellowhammer State.

For example, the rare yellow cardinal, whose color is canary-yellow due to its lack of an enzyme that would otherwise turn the bird's feathers red, is seen on occasion at birdfeeders in Alabama.

According to Ansel Payne, Executive Director of the Birmingham Audubon Society, even people who call Alabama home are often surprised by the state's diverse bird population. According to the Alabama Birding Trails website, more than 430 known bird species make Alabama their home, and their range can be from the foothills of the Appalachian Mountains in the north to the coast in the south.

During the migratory months of late fall to mid-winter, you will be delighted to see orioles, indigo buntings, painted buntings, scarlet tanagers, American gold finches and bluebirds. In the summer months, scores of purple martins come and stay. Red-winged blackbirds' songs can be heard throughout the coastal plains as well as farther north.

A wide assortment of owls, from the tiny screech owl to the Great Horned Owl, live, nest, and hunt throughout the Yellowhammer State. Bald Eagles can be found nesting as far north as Florence and as far south as Point Clear. On the coast in Alabama, every January there is a group of bird lovers who come for the task of banding migratory hummingbirds (if you're in the Fort Morgan area during this time, don't miss it!).

These cranes and mallard ducks enjoy a winter's afternoon of sunshine on the water at Wheeler National Wildlife Refuge. Photo by the author.

Payne said that due to the diversity of habitats for bird and other wildlife, Alabama is the fifth most bio-diverse state in the U.S.—and ranks first in the Eastern U.S. The state of Alabama is home to the Alabama Birding Trail that consists of, according to their website, news and information about their "8 birding trails around Alabama with over 270 locations, all with excellent bird-watching opportunities." The trails range from the northern part of the state to the coastline, marshes, and estuaries.

Makes you want to "take wing" and go tour the Alabama Birding Trail. Even if you're into a "stay-cation," why not fill your birdfeeders, put more water in your birdbath and grab your binoculars and notebook? See "Virtual Alabama" for websites pertaining to Alabama's bird life.

Amazing Alabama

DID YOU KNOW?

The official bird of Alabama is the common flicker, a variety of woodpecker. Its scientific name is *Colaptes auratus Linnaeus*, but folks in Alabama know it best by the name "Yellowhammer."

OTHER OFFICIAL STATE INSECTS, PLANTS AND ANIMALS

You can read more about these plants and creatures by reading about them on *The Encyclopedia of Alabama* online, but here's a short list:

The STATE INSECT is the Monarch Butterfly; the STATE CRUSTACEAN is the Brown Shrimp; the STATE AMPHIBIAN is the endangered Red Hills Salamander; the STATE MAMMAL is the Black Bear; the STATE WILDFLOWER is the Oak Leaf Hydrangea; the STATE FLOWER is the Camellia; the STATE REPTILE is the Red-Bellied Turtle; the STATE NUT is the Pecan; the STATE FRUIT is the Blackberry; and the STATE TREE FRUIT is the Peach.

Alligators like this little six-footer can be found pretty much anywhere in Alabama where there's water. Photo by the author.

"IT'S A JUBILEE!"

A "Jubilee" is a rare natural phenomenon that occurs in only two places in the world: one is on the eastern shore of Mobile Bay and the other is in a part of the Mediterranean. Coastal Alabamians call this phenomenon a "Jubilee," and many locals will call each other in the wee hours of the morning to tell each other where this is happening and meet on the shoreline to pick up gifts from the sea.

During a Jubilee, all kinds of seafood such as crabs, flounder, stingrays, eels and shrimp rush toward the shore. This local phenomenon often has local people on a "Jubilee watch," as this only happens in the summer months. Renee Collini, Science Coordinator with Dauphin Island Sea Lab (DISL) and Mobile Bay National Estuary Program, explained in an interview why and how this works: "The bay is where fresh water and salt water come together," she began, "and the eastern shore of Mobile Bay has some high bluffs, which protect that side of the bay from wind." Donnie Barrett, Director of Fairhope Museum of History, explained a bit further: "You have to have a specific number of things happening all at the same time, or else you won't have a Jubilee." He said that the circumstances included a perfect balance of water, weather and season (Jubilees occur only in the warm months of the year).

Locals know to look for a Jubilee when they notice they are having the perfect "Jubilee balance" of an east wind, a calm bay, warm weather and in the aftermath of rain (and you'll hear some say things such as, "Things are looking Jubilee-ish."). The aforementioned balance of weather, rain and water salinity causes certain sea life's metabolism to be higher than usual, so they consume more oxygen. The rain, especially a heavy rain, will bring all kinds of other things into Mobile Bay from the watershed to the north. Five rivers flow into the northern part of Mobile Bay, adding to the freshwater-saltwater mix. The oxygen level of the eastern shore becomes lower as well, which makes the fish try to get out of the water.

The result of all these things coming together is a Jubilee. When one happens, early in the morning just before dawn, locals and visitors alike converge on the shore, picking up all kinds of seafood, still alive and virtually on the beach or in just inches of water by the shore. One Jubilee I witnessed had a couple of people loading their truck with flounder, still flopping, with the fish stacked clear to the top of the truck-bed! There are no two Jubilees the same: you might see more crabs in one Jubilee, more catfish in another, and mostly shrimp and flounder in another.

Once a Jubilee begins, you will see all kinds of people dressed in whatever they were wearing when they realized a Jubilee was going on. Some locals, still in their pajamas, will walk the beach, gigging fish and putting them in their buckets. A Jubilee only lasts for a few hours, and it's over just about as suddenly as it begins. Once the sun begins to rise, the wind changes, and the fish are gone.

A Jubilee is an angler's and seafood-lover's Christmas! Maybe you'll be lucky enough to catch a Jubilee next time you're vacationing at the Eastern Shore of Mobile Bay.

DID YOU KNOW?

The city of Daphne has as one of its nicknames "The Jubilee City."

WILLIAM BARTRAM AND HIS LEGACY

In 1775, naturalist William Bartram of Pennsylvania arrived in Alabama in what is now Russell County. His mission: to explore Georgia, Alabama and Florida to catalog all manner of flora and fauna he could find. According to the Alabama Scenic River Trail's official website, he was on assignment from King George III of England to conduct this mission.

A trained observer and artist, Bartram studied plants and wildlife as he traveled, but also made detailed notes of Native Americans that he met along the way. He published a book in 1791, called *Bartram's Travels*, which detailed his experiences. His work would go on to influence and inspire another naturalist, John James Audubon.

There is something else today you can experience that also was inspired by Bartram's work. An idea first espoused by Greg Lein of the Alabama Department of Conservation and Natural Resources, the state began to create a canoe trail through the delta. Created in the mid-2000s in conjunction with the Alabama State Lands Division and the Alabama Department of Conservation and Natural Resources, using lands secured by Alabama Forever Wild, the Bartram Canoe Trail is accessible for canoeists and kayakers to float through the second-largest river delta system in the United States.

Parts of the trail have elevated camping platforms, maintained by the Alabama State Lands Department. This waterway offers modern naturalists a way to get up close to more than 50 rare and endangered plant and animal species while paddling an area of more than 250,000 acres of cypress-tupelo swamps, bottomland ecosystems and estuarine marshland. This 200-mile-long system is one of the longest in the entire U.S.

I've canoed stretches of the Bartram Canoe Trail; I say it is something you and your family should not miss! See "Virtual Alabama" for websites.

THE BRITISH PETROLEUM OIL SPILL AND THE MIRACLE OF THE MICROBES

I remember when on April 20, 2010, the Deepwater Horizon oil rig in the Gulf of Mexico exploded, killing 11 workers and then leaking an estimated 3.19 million barrels of oil into the Gulf (the rig wasn't capped until July 15—87 days later). The capping took a while because the leak was 5,000 feet below the water's surface, and with temperatures down there just above freezing, combined with incredibly high water pressure, made it a challenge to cap it and stop more oil from leaking into the Gulf of Mexico.

That summer was for many Alabamians and others living in coastal states a sobering reminder of how extreme a disaster can be, how quickly it can happen, and how powerless humanity can be in the face of such vast destruction. But, as with all natural and man-made disasters, people came together in a massive effort to contain the oil spill and keep it from spreading further. Entire families went out in boats, putting out what they called "booms" in an effort to prevent further spread of the massive oil spill (the booms were round, cylinder-shaped floatation devices). Other people went on the water with nets and buckets, scooping up what they could. Still others found marine life befouled by oil and bathed the poor creatures if possible.

People said it would take a miracle for the oil to disappear from the Gulf of Mexico and Mobile Bay. The miracle came in the form of tiny microbes.

The microbes that came to the rescue were tiny creatures called zooplankton. Since this oil was not processed, it could be used as food for the zooplankton. Scientists used specially-made nets to take samples of the zooplankton. They studied zooplankton taken from four different sites—two in the

Gulf of Mexico and two others in Mobile Bay. They also tested other life forms which in turn ate the zooplankton to check for evidence of toxic materials that might have moved up the food chain. The studies were a cooperative effort of Dauphin Island Sea Lab scientists, who worked on a grant from the National Science Foundation for oil-spill research. Further funding was also provided by the National Oceanic and Atmospheric Administration (NOAA) and the Alabama Department of Conservation and Natural Resources, as well as British Petroleum's Gulf Research Initiative.

In 2018, eight years after the disastrous oil spill, reporter Bryan Henry wrote about the Alabama Gulf Coast and its "resounding recovery" in a column published by AL.com in May of that year. He wrote that Alabama tourism has seen a jump of 12 percent per year since the oil spill. Gulf Shores, he wrote, rebranded itself with its new slogan of "Small town, big beach." Other towns along the coastline used their money from the so-called BP Oil Settlement to improve their infrastructure, add to existing parks and campgrounds, and create new venues such as museums to attract more tourists. The BP oil spill and its aftermath were covered extensively by journalist Terese Collins, who wrote a comprehensive and interactive article for *Smithsonian Magazine* in April of 2018 (and to which I referred in writing this story).

Now, the waters and sugar-white sands of the Alabama coastline are often thick with bathers and sun-worshippers. Boaters are once again enjoying heading out and catching bounty from the sea. Campers and those in recreational vehicles are thronging to campgrounds and RV parks. And Gulf Coast tourism currently sees an average of more than 7 million visitors per year. The town of Gulf Shores opened its new hotel, The Lodge at Gulf State Park, which has been proclaimed to be

"Alabama's crown jewel." Alabama Governor Kay Ivey was ready with her scissors at the ribbon-cutting ceremony in November of 2018.

Maybe you should collect the family, grab some sunscreen and your fishing gear and head down to what some refer to as "Paradise Restored."

PELICANS OF ALABAMA

In Alabama there are two kinds of pelicans that stay year 'round; these are the white pelican and the brown pelican. There are eight different species of pelican that are scattered around the world, except for Antarctica and parts of South America. Other pelicans migrate through Alabama, and they are all somewhat different from the other species.

The white pelican is the larger of the two pelicans, weighing an average of 30 pounds when fully grown. Its wing span is around 8-9 feet. White pelicans usually fly in a "V" formation and alternately soar and flap their wings. They have a large yellow or orange-colored bill. White pelicans feed by swimming and ducking their heads to catch small fish and crustaceans. They are voracious eaters, sometimes consuming as much as 40% of their body weight when they are feeding their young. They may fly as much as 100 miles to find food.

One of the white pelicans' favorite places for easy meals has come with the influx of fish farms to Alabama. Ask any aquaculture farmer in places such as Greensboro, which is probably home to the most fish farms in the state, and they will tell you they are challenged by white pelicans trying to get some fish out of their ponds. (By the way, Alabama's aquaculture industry is now one of the biggest industries in Alabama, producing 25 different species of fish, but the most popular is catfish. It's currently a half-a-BILLION dollar industry).

Both types of pelicans feed their young through a large pouch below the mother's beak. They will come to the nest, open their beaks, and the young will take the fish out. At first, the parents will make the food more digested—more like baby food—but as the baby pelican grows, it becomes able to eat regular food such as small fish and crustaceans.

The brown pelican has a large range that extends from North America to parts of coastal South America. The brown pelican is smaller than others, weighing in at about 8 pounds, but it has a wing span of about 7 feet. The brown pelican used to be endangered but is now thriving, especially in Alabama and Florida, thanks to EPA restrictions on the use of dangerous pesticides such as DDT. The brown pelican is the one you will see at the bay that dives for its food. If you watch closely, just before the bird hits the water, it turns its head slightly. The brown pelican's skull is made in such a way that the impact will not hurt the pelican's brain, but such a landing would give anyone else a colossal headache.

Like many other birds, the pelican, especially the brown pelican, is making a comeback. Brown pelicans nest in colonies, and the most popular nesting ground is on Gailliard Island in Mobile Bay (see Chapter 2 for the interesting story on the controversy over the creation of that island).

Brown pelicans have the longest life span of the two pelicans. In the wild, they can live to be 30 years old; the longest ever recorded pelican lifespan was 54 years old, but that was in captivity. You can see and learn more about the wildlife of the coast at the Five Rivers Delta Center on the Causeway, between Mobile and Spanish Fort, Alabama. You and your family can easily spend a day exploring the Center and its environs.

LOOKING BACK WHILE PAYING IT FORWARD: DR. EUGENE ALLEN SMITH

Appointed as State Geologist in 1873, Dr. Eugene Allen Smith spent almost forty years collecting scientific specimens throughout the state of Alabama while also surveying and mapping. Completed in 1910, the building known as Smith Hall on The University of Alabama campus in Tuscaloosa houses the aforementioned Alabama Museum of Natural History. It is open for tours and is family friendly. When you go, check out the Grand Gallery Exhibition Hall which docents say has one of the most beautiful interiors in the entire state of Alabama.

Q & A

Q. Sylacauga has a naturally-occurring material that was quarried and used in the construction of the U.S. Supreme Court Building in Washington, D.C. What was it?

A. Marble.

Q. What unique archeological place in Jackson County was bought by the National Geographic Society in 1956?

A. Russell Cave. Its formal name today is Russell Cave National Monument.

T. Jensen Lacey

CHAPTER 14

FOOD AND FASCINATING CULTURAL TIDBITS

Food is an important part of living, and living well, in Alabama. In Alabama, go to any covered-dish luncheon and you'll see a smorgasbord of foods that represents the diverse culture of the state. And Alabamians have a celebration for just about every kind of food there is. The Alabama Department of Tourism has at least two publications that are all about food ("100 Dishes to Eat in Alabama before You Die" and "The Barbecue Trail in Alabama").

Food; is a part of every celebration, every event, every funeral. Alabamians celebrate food as much as they do life's (and death's) milestones.

Fellow author Rick Bragg, who became a household word with his book *All Over But the Shoutin'*, also wrote a book about his mother's culinary talents. Titled *The Best Cook in the World*, he wrote about how his mother "never measured anything" but how every dish she made turned out incredibly delicious. Many cooks in Alabama cook this way, and if you ask them for a recipe, they'll suddenly become quite vague. There's

My friend and fellow author, Rick Bragg, at one of his book events. Photo by T. Jensen Lacey.

one rather famous Alabama chef I know who, when asked for one of his recipes, will give it to you—with one vital ingredient omitted.

FAVORITE FOODS OF THE PEOPLE OF ALABAMA

Over the last couple of years, I've asked hundreds of Alabamians the question, "What is your favorite food—what foods say 'Alabama' to you?" Here is a partial list of replies:

"Shrimp—cooked just about every way (a la the movie, *Forrest Gump*)."

"Grits—especially cheese grits. You've got to have those with shrimp."

"Chicken Fried Steak."

"Okra. But it's got to be fried!"

"Fried chicken."

"Baked macaroni and cheese."

"Bacon—especially Chef Will Stitt's bacon."

"Oysters, just about any way, but I like 'em Bienville or Rockefeller style."

"West Indies Salad."

"Crab cakes with Remoulade sauce."

"Rice with tomato gravy—or ANY gravy."

"Silver Queen corn."

And then there's gumbo. Virtually every family, especially those living in the coastal parts of Alabama, has its own family recipe. Once I saw two different contestants at a seafood cook-off nearly get into a punching match—not over whose gumbo was the best but whether a "true gumbo" also contained okra.

SPEAKING OF FOOD: HERE IS A PARTIAL LIST OF SOME OF THE OLDEST RESTAURANTS IN ALABAMA

In many towns in Alabama, there are some folks who won't go to a restaurant right away—until it's stood the proverbial test of time, say, several years. Then they'll go check it out. These restaurants have remained in business for decades and some even longer. And there's a reason why they're still serving their food to locals and travelers alike: it's just good food. Here's a partial list:

THE BRIGHT STAR RESTAURANT—Established in 1907, The Bright Star is the oldest family-owned restaurant still in operation in Alabama. Located on 19th Street in Bessemer, its specialties are Greek-style steak and seafood. This place is definitely worth veering off the interstate!

TROWBRIDGE'S—As a student at The University of North Alabama in Florence, it was a real treat to be able to stop in at Trowbridge's for one of their sandwiches, ice cream sundae or their famous orange-pineapple ice cream. Located on North Court Street, Trowbridge's has been serving up good food since they first opened in 1918.

PAYNE'S SANDWICH SHOP & SODA FOUNTAIN—When it opened on Laurel Street in Scottsboro in 1869, it was initially just a pharmacy; today, it's one of the last remaining soda fountains in Alabama. Go back to your childhood and try an old-fashioned Coke Float!

BUFFALO ROCK COMPANY—This ancient beverage industry began in Birmingham in 1901 and today sells nearly one billion containers of their product annually. It's located on Oxmoor Road.

CHRIS' HOT DOGS—Located in Montgomery on Dexter Avenue (near the State Capitol), this hot dog venue has been serving up hot dogs with their signature chili sauce since 1917. Just one taste of their legendary 'dog will thrill your taste buds! It's worth a detour off the interstate.

WINTZELL'S OYSTER HOUSE—Now with several restaurant franchises to its credit, this outstanding seafood restaurant celebrated its 80th birthday in 2018. It was begun by Oliver Wintzell with just the one restaurant in Mobile and is still run by that family.

JULWIN'S RESTAURANT—The oldest restaurant in Baldwin County, Julwin's traditional "meat-and-three" is something you can always count on when you're extra-hungry. Julwin's is in the heart of downtown Fairhope.

GAMBINO'S ITALIAN GRILL—This restaurant was first started in 1975 and is considered by many Fairhope locals as THE place to go for dinner. It's often that a member of the Gambino family is the chef for the night (such as Josh) and owner Rick Gambino will come to your table and greet you.

THE OLD COOKSTOVE—An Amish delight. In July of 2018 my mom and I had just left the Jesse Owens Museum in Danville (see his story in the Sports chapter) and realized we were starving. We literally stumbled upon The Old Cookstove—it's located behind Yoder Lumber in the middle of nowhere (also in Danville). Run by local Amish folks, the restaurant was started three generations ago by some Yoders. You'll get a real sense of family here—the cashier had her baby on one hip as she checked us out—and the food is all made from scratch, including their homemade ice cream. They're only open on Friday afternoons and Saturdays, so make sure you check out this place!

PIRATE'S COVE MARINA & RESTAURANT—Located in the community of Josephine, Pirate's Cove has a flair all its own. They have been serving up good food and entertainment since they opened their doors in 1967. Many people wouldn't even think you'd had a true "this is Alabama" experience if you hadn't included a stop here on your itinerary. Pirate's Cove has been a fixture in the Josephine community; their signature hamburgers and cheeseburgers, both served with "Miss Kitty's vermouth sauce" and their bushwhackers will keep you coming back. Pirate's Cove is also very dog friendly.

WHISTLE STOP --Author Fanny Flagg probably helped make this place famous when she penned her novel *Fried Green Tomatoes at the Whistle Stop Café*. Locals in the Mobile area, though, already knew about it. Their reputation of having an outstanding Sunday brunch has been well-known since they opened their doors in 1998.

... AND HERE ARE A COUPLE OF STORIES OF SOME ODDLY-NAMED DISHES IN SOME ALABAMA RESTAURANTS

DEPRESSION BURGERS: First established in 1919 in Cullman, the Busy Bee Café served an inexpensive hamburger during the Depression era. Also known as "Poor Man Burgers," the Busy Bee filled many a poor person's stomach during those economically lean years. They still make their Depression Burgers—but the taste is so good, you'll be happy you stopped in. The Busy Bee is on 5th Street Southeast and is open six days a week.

SLUG-BURGERS—Although its origin is claimed by the town of Corinth, Mississippi, the lowly slug-burger is popular in small, family-owned diners throughout Mississippi, Tennessee and Alabama. This burger is also said to have its roots in The Great Depression, when people tried to extend ground beef patties by adding breading and other fillers before frying them. When they first came out, they were sold for a nickel, the slang word for which is a "slug." My favorite place to enjoy a slug-burger is at C. F. Penn Hamburgers in Decatur, Alabama. It's currently owned and operated by William Vandiver, who bought the grill from C. F. Penn some time back.

THE SWEET STORY BEHIND GOLDEN EAGLE SYRUP

I remember sitting at my grandparents' long, plank dining table, watching my grandmother use a fork to cream together her fresh-churned butter with Golden Eagle Syrup before spreading the sweet mixture over one of her fresh-from-the-oven homemade biscuits. She got me "hooked" on the delicate sweetness of the Alabama-made syrup, and it's a staple in my kitchen today.

The company that makes Golden Eagle Syrup was started by Victor and Lucy Patterson in 1928 in a small wooden building behind their family home in Fayette, Alabama. Today, it's still a family-run business, under the guidance of a man named Temple Bowling, with his partner John Blevins and their families. I stopped in at the headquarters, which is in downtown Fayette.

Martha Kimbrell, who has worked at Golden Eagle since 1990, was answering the phone and my questions, simultaneously and effortlessly. She said that they are open to guided tours during production days, which are usually on Tuesdays and Thursdays. You can go watch how this unique blend of syrups is made, and see that, just like back in 1928, each jar of this delicacy is hand-tightened before shipping. "Miss Martha" told me that production is up "a bit" from back in 1928—to 6,000 jars of syrup a week! See "Virtual Alabama" for their website.

PERHAPS THE WORLD'S LARGEST CINNAMON ROLL?

The bakery Mr. Coffee Bean in Dothan, Alabama, bakes what could very well be the world's record cinnamon roll. The bakery regularly makes delicious cinnamon rolls, and of a size to share: they weigh two POUNDS each!

Mr. Coffee Beans' 2-pound cinnamon roll is said to be a world record for the pastry. Photo Courtesy Mr. Coffee Beans.

LES BON TEMPS ROULEE! HERE'S WHERE THE AMERICAN MARDI GRAS STARTED!

Mardi Gras has been celebrated virtually around the world from ancient Greece and Egypt to Brazil. Usually—in those other parts of the world—it is called "Carnival," which translates to mean "farewell to meat." It began as a Catholic celebration where everyone "pigged out" on their favorite fatty meat dishes and sweets, just before the beginning of the penitential time of the Lenten season, which commemorates when Jesus fasted and prayed in the desert for 40 days and nights.

The American Mardi Gras began in what is now Mobile in 1703. Masked balls then began in 1704. As the years went by, there were also parades with secret societies making increasingly elaborate floats and participating in the street processions.

During the Civil War, Mardi Gras celebrations were suspended. Then in 1866, Joe Stillwell Cain, a Confederate veteran who had returned to the city after the Civil War had ended, decided to begin a resurgence in interest in and celebration of the Carnival holiday.

Naturally, then, as part of the Mardi Gras celebration in Mobile, there is a Joe Cain Day to honor his memory and achievement. On that day there is a pedestrian parade with some people dressed as Joe Cain himself and some women dressed as "Joe Cain's widows." Everyone pays their respects at Joe Cain's grave (in the Church Street Graveyard in Mobile's Central Business District) as part of the celebration. Now, many towns in south Alabama have their own Mardi Gras societies, parades, and masked balls.

Today, even if you're not in Alabama around Mardi Gras time, you can still experience much of what you're missing. A museum in downtown Mobile is committed to telling its visitors all about the pre-Lenten celebration. The Curator of The Mobile Carnival Museum, Cartledge Blackwell, told me that the museum houses all kinds of amazing displays, including floats, masked mannequins depicting reveling float-riders, and a wide array of gowns and suits worn by previous queens and kings of a given year's Mardi Gras. The trains that are displayed with the gowns and suits were all made in Alabama. Many of the gowns are so heavy with sequins and jewels, they look to weigh about as much as the wearer of the piece! The Mobile Carnival Museum is open most days of the week so you can experience "letting the good times roll" for yourself. See "Virtual Alabama" for website(s).

ATHENS, ALABAMA, WHERE THE LAST WEEKEND IN SEPTEMBER IS ALWAYS "FRY-DAY"

The city of Athens hosts a food celebration the last weekend in September. Called the "Grease Festival," it celebrates all things fried. The town also celebrates the Greek origin of the city's name, and asks attendees to wear a toga.

THERE'S BARBECUE, AND THEN THERE'S ALABAMA BARBECUE

When thinking about barbecue, two places come to mind for most Alabamians: Archibald's in the town of Northport and Dreamland in Tuscaloosa. Archibald's has been in the barbecue business since 1962, when it was started by grill guru George Archibald, Sr. and his wife (and sauce maker) Betty. It was later run by George Archibald, Jr., his sister Paulette Washington, and her son, Woodrow Washington III. George Jr. passed away in 2017, and Paulette retired. Archibald's is currently run by Woodrow Washington III with family members Reginald Washington and Lashawn Washington Humphreys.

Archibald's barbecue is legendary not only in Alabama but also throughout the U.S. They cook their barbecue "low and slow" over hickory wood and an open fire. Archibald's barbecues Boston butts, ribs, and more, served with slices of white bread.

Now the single barbecue establishment has grown to three, with the other two locations in nearby Tuscaloosa, and their name has been changed to Archibald and Woodrow's BBQ.

I wanted a recipe for this book, but when asked what their barbecue sauce's secret ingredient is, Woodrow Washington III smiled and said simply, "Love."

In Tuscaloosa, Dreamland Cafe has been a landmark since John "Big Daddy" Bishop, who built the original Dreamland by hand in 1958. Everything about this barbecue spot in the heart of Bear Bryant Country has the look and feel of a place that people have put their hearts into, and if you notice that, you'd be right: Legend has it that Big Daddy, a brick-mason at the time, got down on his knees one night and prayed for another way to support his family. It's been said that, that night in a dream, God told Big Daddy to build a barbecue restaurant on his property adjacent to his family home.

The ribs are as delicious as anything you've ever put in your mouth, made with Big Daddy's wife, Lilly's, secret barbecue sauce. Like Archibald's, their barbecue is served with sliced white bread. Now, Dreamland has grown and includes locations in Alabama, Florida and Georgia. The menu, too, has expanded to include smoked sausage, pulled pork, barbecued chicken, and side dishes like potato salad, spring rolls and cole slaw. They serve more than 1 million people every year and ship orders to anywhere.

The atmosphere of any Dreamland location I've visited still has the "down-home casual" feel of the original Dreamland. When you visit any location, you'll feel like you're visiting family. And that's just the way Big Daddy and Miss Lilly would have wanted it.

THIS BARBECUE PLACE OUT-SMOKED EVERY OTHER!

As good as many barbecue places in and around Alabama are, there's one place that's been barbecuing longer than any other in the Yellowhammer State. Irondale's Golden Rule Barbecue first set up their grill in 1891, and they're still smoking. Next time you're passing through Irondale, check out Golden Rule!

JIM 'n NICK'S AND THEIR AWARD-WINNING BARBECUE

Jim 'n Nick's is a chain of barbecue restaurants that was begun by father-and-son team Jim and Nick Pihakis, the latter of whom has been named six years in a row by the James Beard Foundation as a semifinalist for the country's outstanding restaurant. There are quite a few Jim 'n Nick's in Alabama and Florida, but my favorite is in Montgomery.

SUITS ALABAMA TO A "TEA"

Milo's Sweet Tea has been a staple at Alabama dinner tables for three generations. It was first created in Bessemer by Milo and Bea Carlton and has been a hit ever since. One taste and you'll "get it."

YOU'LL BE "IN A PICKLE" IF YOU DON'T TRY THESE

Wickles Pickles came from a recipe that was closely guarded for 90 years; the secret got out in the late 1990s. Since 1998, this deliciously-brined pickle has been famous all over the South. Wickles Pickles have been used in recipes created by chefs Emeril Lagasse and Rachel Ray, and restaurateur Bob Baumhower fries them in his restaurants. The home office is in Dadeville, and although they don't currently offer tours, you can purchase items on their on-line gift shop (see "Virtual Alabama").

SOME FOODIE CELEBRATIONS

Alabama is known for its plethora of good cooks and famous chefs, and the Yellowhammer State has the festivals to highlight and enjoy all kinds of dishes. In Gulf Shores in October, they hold the National Shrimp Festival (which includes a cook-off they call "Restaurant Challenge"). If you're into exotic eats, though, you want to make sure you go to Opp. Opp's Rattlesnake Rodeo is held the second weekend in April. It includes, among the usual vendors and arts and crafts, rattlesnake meat cooked in various ways. Tastes just like chicken?

ARE WE IN PARIS OR NEW ORLEANS? NEITHER—WE'RE IN MOBILE!

When you visit the deeply Southern town of Mobile, you may feel in some places as though you're in another country. In parts of Mobile, especially in the "old downtown" area, you will get a feel that this town is distinctly different from the rest of Alabama.

If you feel that way, you're feeling right: Mobile was originally founded as the capital of colonial French Louisiana. That was way back in 1702, when Jean-Baptiste Le Moyne de

Bienville founded what later became nicknamed "Moon Pie City" (among other nicknames). Note this was also years before Bienville founded La Nouvelle-Orleans, what you know today to be New Orleans (founded in 1718).

BRAGGIN' RIGHTS

Alabamians take pride in a great many things and will be quick to educate you about 'most anything they know. Here are some of "Alabama's Claims to Fame":

WORLD'S LARGEST OFFICE CHAIR—you can see this 10-ton, steel monstrosity in Anniston. The chair stands at 33 feet tall and 15 feet wide at the seat. The chair is in front of Miller's Office Furniture on 625 Noble Street. No one takes a back seat to THIS chair (couldn't help myself).

FIRE HYDRANT CAPITAL OF THE WORLD—is claimed by the city of Albertville. The city is home to the Mueller Company, a fire hydrant manufacturer. When the company came out with its millionth fire hydrant, the Chamber of Commerce placed a large chrome one made especially to commemorate the event. The shiny fire hydrant is just outside the Albertville Chamber of Commerce building. There is also a red, white and blue fire hydrant downtown to show the town's patriotic spirit.

CRAPPIE CAPITAL OF THE WORLD is claimed by the town of Cedar Bluff. *Outdoor Life Magazine* once featured Cedar Bluff's jewel, Weiss Lake, as a crappie-angler's Paradise.

LARGEST PEACH IN THE WORLD—can be found at the Clanton city exit just off I-65. It's actually a water tower, shaped and painted in the shape of a ripe peach.

Stop in at any of their many roadside produce stands for some of the best peaches (real ones) you can ever bite into.

WAVE POOL CAPITAL OF THE WORLD—Decatur claims this title. They created what they say is the first-ever wave pool in the world. The pool located at Point Mallard Park opened to visitors in 1970. This claim has been disputed by Big Surf, a Tempe, Arizona-based wave pool which says its wave pool opened in 1969.

Chilton County claims "The World's Biggest Peach," which is located at the Clanton, Alabama exit off I-65.

PEANUT CAPITAL OF THE WORLD—is claimed by the city of Dothan. The area in and around Dothan produces approximately 25% of the nation's peanut crop. They have a Peanut Festival to celebrate this "nutty" title.

WATERCRESS CAPITAL OF THE WORLD—long before Huntsville became known for being home to NASA and the U.S. Space and Rocket Center, it held this title. During the first half of the 1900s, watercress was an important commodity in Alabama, and it grew in abundance in and around Huntsville.

BASS FISHING CAPITAL OF THE WORLD—is claimed by the town of Eufaula. The man-made lake created in 1963, Lake Eufaula, is said to have such an abundance of bass that they practically guarantee anglers, regardless of experience, ability and equipment, a catch they can be proud of.

OLDEST INCORPORATED TOWN IN ALABAMA—that claim to fame is held by the town of Mooresville, incorporated in 1818. The Athens-Limestone County Tourist Association offers guided walking tours of both Mooresville and Athens (the latter of which is the county seat). Mooresville is also home to the oldest continually-operating post office in the state. Mooresville has been referred to as "Alabama's Williamsburg."

WORLD'S LONGEST YARD SALE—is held by the city of Gadsden. Held the first Thursday through Sunday in August, the yard sale trail begins at Gadsden's Noccalula Falls Park, and goes up Lookout Mountain Parkway, through Chattanooga, Tennessee, and ends in Hudson, Michigan. Begun in 1987, the yard sale has grown to be 690 miles in length! The folks at Gadsden's Chamber of Commerce advise people who want to come to make their hotel reservations well in advance, and to bring cash for the yard sale. This yard sale has evolved with the times: now they have an "app" you can download to your phone to stay informed.

THE ONLY MAIL DELIVERED BY BOAT IN THE U.S.—is in the lovely coastal community known as Magnolia Springs. Since its residents live on Magnolia River, their mail boxes are all placed at the end of their piers. Some of the mail boxes are highly decorative and whimsical.

IF YOU'RE FROM ALABAMA, YOU'RE FROM … EVERYWHERE!

There are many parts of Alabama that have been settled by people from other parts of the world. The town of Brookside was settled by Russian/Slovak immigrants, mostly miners. The early immigrants who settled Cullman were mostly German. The Greek community of Malbis, settled by a family by the name of Malbis, is famous for its Byzantine-style Greek

Orthodox Church. Many Greeks also settled in and around the coastal town of Gulf Shores.

The city of Silverhill was settled largely by Czech and Swedish immigrants, and nearby, the town of Elberta was settled by Germans (and many of their signs around town to this day are in German and English). The city of Demopolis was largely settled by French expatriates (and was first called "The Vine and Olive Colony" before being called Demopolis, which is Greek for "City of the People"). In Mobile, you can see architectural influences of French, British and Spanish settlers. Finally, many coastal cities have communities of Vietnamese immigrants.

Q. & A.

Q. What city hosts the Alabama Scottish Gathering, a festival which celebrates Alabama people with Scottish heritage?

A. Wetumpka.

Q. In what city is the Annual East Alabama Pine Tree Festival held?

A. LaFayette.

Q. What Mobile-born poet and sculptor was instrumental in reviving Joe Cain's role in re-establishing Mardi Gras in that city, right after the Civil War?

A. Julian "Judy" Lee Rayford. He is buried in Mobile's Church Street Graveyard next to Joe Cain's grave.

Q, Where is the Annual Watermelon Jubilee Arts and Crafts Festival held?

A. Greenville.

Q. What excursion riverboat has, for more than 30 years, provided entertaining cruises in Montgomery's part of the Alabama River?

A. *The General Richard Montgomery.*

Q. The town of Winfield holds what event every September in which people bring their horses and mules for a competition?

A. Mule Day.

Q. What June event in Clanton celebrates one of their numerous fruits?

A. The Chilton County Peach Festival.

Q. What green, wild-growing vegetable is celebrated by the people of Arab?

A. Arab holds its "Poke Salat Festival" every spring, usually the middle of May.

Q. What city hosts the official Alabama Renaissance Faire, held every October?

A. The city of Florence.

T. Jensen Lacey

CHAPTER 15

UNUSUAL GRAVE, GHOST AND BURIAL-SITE STORIES

WRONGLY ACCUSED: THE FACE IN THE WINDOW

The Pickens County Courthouse, located in the county seat of Carrollton, is the third courthouse to be built on its present site. The first was burned by invading Union troops in 1865; the citizens built the second courthouse on the same site in 1877-78. This courthouse, too, burned, and investigators determined that the fire had been set intentionally.

Blame fell on a well-known criminal named Henry Wells, an emancipated slave after the Civil War. It was said that he was the guilty party because he wanted any and all records of every criminal charge against him destroyed and had thus set the fire. Wells fled town, protesting his innocence to any who would hear him (although a Georgia newspaper, the *Daily Inquirer*, reported that he had "confessed to burning the Court House at Carrollton.").

He stayed away from Alabama and those in authority to arrest him for two years, during which time the people rebuilt the courthouse again. It is believed that he returned to visit his sickly grandmother. Wells had slipped into town and thought his re-entry was undetected by locals, but someone spotted him and reported this to the sheriff. The sheriff appeared at the grandmother's house and arrested Wells for arson.

Assuring Wells that he would be given a fair trial, the sheriff took him to the jail near the courthouse. Meanwhile, word spread like proverbial wildfire about Wells' arrest and jail detention. A group of angry citizens appeared outside the jail. The sheriff, wanting to keep his promise to Wells and also follow the letter of the law, sneaked Wells from the jail to the newly rebuilt courthouse.

The sheriff brought Wells to a garret at the top of the building. This garret was built with windows looking out over all four sides. From these windows, Wells could see an angry mob had formed outside the courthouse—they'd figured out where the sheriff had taken him—and were threatening to lynch him themselves.

Legend goes that Wells pressed his face against the glass of one of the windows and shouted to the angry mob, "I am innocent, and if you kill me, I will haunt you forever!" Just then, a storm sprang up, with terrible lightning and huge gusts of wind.

The sheriff thought that this would drive away the mob, but it only seemed to cement their resolve: they stormed the courthouse, dragged Wells from out of the garret and hanged him from a tree outside the courthouse. Later, one of the people who had taken part in this lynching was walking by the courthouse and, looking up at the garret, could plainly see a face in the one of the garret's windows; it seemed almost to be etched in the glass and looking down at him (The legend goes that, as Wells was shouting his vow to the mob, lightning struck the window and etched his image into the glass).

People tried to remove the image by washing the window, to no avail. When I visited the courthouse to see the image for myself, office clerk Chelsea Hamlin told me that all the other windows have been replaced several times, damaged or destroyed by storms and hail, but the pane bearing the image of a man's face has somehow remained the only one unbroken. It seems that Wells was good to his word.

Today you can see the "face in the window" for yourself. It's on the north side of the courthouse garret, on Phoenix Avenue. If you have any trouble making out the ghostly image, an arrow is beside the window pointing to it. The City of Carrollton published a pamphlet, free for the asking, telling about the story of the now-famous "Face in the Window." In addition, a historical marker is on the grounds, telling the story. This ghostly tale was further immortalized by author and storyteller Kathryn Tucker Windham in her book *13 Alabama Ghosts and Jeffrey*. Read more about her in Chapter 4.

THE STORY OF THE GHOST BEHIND A COUNTRY-WESTERN SONG

Hank Williams Sr. lies interred at Oakwood Annex Cemetery in Montgomery, but some people say he's still very much with us and haunting that graveyard.

The ghost legend began when country music singer Alan Jackson was passing through Montgomery on his way to a performance in Mobile and stopped by the cemetery to pay his respects. He claimed to have seen Williams' ghost. He wrote a song about that night and called it "Midnight in Montgomery." Oakwood Cemetery spokesman Phillip Taunton says that since Williams' burial in 1953, people have been coming by almost daily, and leave little mementos at the gravesite. If you go, keep an eye, and an ear, out for the ghostly crooner.

ALABAMA HAS ITS OWN VERSION OF "GHOST-BUSTERS"

I was amazed to discover that there are several paranormal societies in Alabama—one in Gulf Shores, one in

Mobile, one covering central Alabama and another in Huntsville. But in the tiny town of Calera (near Montevallo) is a group that goes by the name Alabama Paranormal Consultants. They mostly do their "ghost-sleuthing" on Saturdays and don't charge a fee. It will "haunt" you forever if you don't check them out! See "Virtual Alabama" for website.

NOW YOUR LOVED ONE CAN HUNT WITH YOU EVEN AFTER THEY'VE PASSED ON!

In Stockton, Alabama is a company that offers people an unusual way to, as its website says, "create a tribute to your outdoors person like no other." It began a few years back when two game wardens, who were also good friends and avid hunters, began talking about what could be done with their remains after they themselves had passed away. They shared a concern about the fact that most burial scenarios weren't ecologically friendly and also were extremely costly for grieving family members. Another concern was how they might protect their families even after their demise.

The two became partners in a company they formed known as Holy Smoke, LLC. Theirs offers grieving families a truly unique memorial. The family sends some of the cremated remains to Holy Smoke, and the company puts some of the ashes into pistol or rifle cartridges. With these specially-made bullets, family members can use them for hunting or simply display them in memory of their deceased. In addition, Holy Smoke offers a way to give tribute to a deceased family member who might have been a veteran: they offer bullets that make red, white and blue smoke when fired. For people who want to carry their loved one's ashes as a piece of jewelry, Holy Smoke can do that as well. And for those whose best hunting companion is a four-legged one, Holy Smoke offers their services for hunting dogs, too.

The ashes have no effect on the rifling, propellant or the firearm itself, and the procedure is done with reverence and care. As of press time, the film company NetFlix was planning on making a documentary about this unusual way to go hunt or even protect your family after you're gone.

Partners Thad Holmes and Clem Parnell say their services are cost-effective and leave a "virtually nonexistent" environmental footprint. See "Virtual Alabama" for their website.

GIRL WITH A PEARL NECKLACE: THE GHOSTLY LOVERS

It was on December 7, 1941, that young Pearl turned 17. That was also the day that the Japanese bombed Pearl Harbor. That month saw a record number of young men sign up for the armed forces, as a result of the unprovoked attack on this country.

At the time, Pearl and her family lived in Mobile. As many Alabamians do, the family would rent a summer home on the coast, and it was in Foley, Alabama, that Pearl met a young recruit named Joey. She most looked forward to Saturday night, for it was when Pearl and her sister could go to the USO dance at the American Legion Hall and show their support for the local military, who were stationed at various places. She always looked for Joey, and when he would come into the dance hall, he would head straight to the lemonade table to talk to Pearl.

Pearl always wore a navy blue dress to these Saturday night dances; with rationing underway, it was the dress for which she had scrimped and saved. With her carefully-crimped hair draping her face, Joey thought she had the countenance of an angel. They began their Saturday-night conversations with her saying, "Would you like some lemonade?" and him responding with, "What I'd like is a dance." Everyone in the room would admire their grace as they seemed to float over the wooden dance floor.

As the weeks passed, they took the Glen Miller song, "String of Pearls," as "their" song. Finally, with summer coming to a close, Joey received word that he would be deployed. On their last Saturday night together, Joey walked her outside the dance hall and gave her a little box. Inside the box was a beautifully matched necklace of pearls. Joey, telling her he wanted her for his "own little Pearl," asked her to be his bride; they were married a week later.

After Joey was deployed, Pearl moved to Foley to be there for his return. One day, she got the telegram every parent, wife, and family member dreaded: Joey was missing in action.

Pearl never saw Joey again. After a time, locals say she seemed to lose touch with reality and began living increasingly in the past. She would often go to the USO hall and dance as if with an unseen partner or go to the place where she had last seen her beloved—the Foley Railroad Depot. There, she would sit on a bench, wearing her blue dress and pearls, as if waiting for her hero to return.

Finally, Pearl passed away. Many of the locals say after her death, they missed seeing her waiting for her soldier at the depot, or walking the streets in her blue dress and pearls.

Then, Pearl came back; people began to report sightings of Pearl at the dance hall, which has gone through several iterations and is now The Gift Horse Restaurant and Gift Shop in downtown Foley. Others reported seeing what looked like Pearl and her Joey, dancing as though they were floating just above the wooden planks. Employees would report hearing the tune "String of Pearls" in the shop. Still other people would see her apparition sitting on the bench at the railroad depot, as if waiting for her soldier's return.

Today, the depot is restored to its original splendor and is home to the Foley Train Museum. When you visit either the Gift Horse or the Foley Train Museum, be on the lookout for a girl in a navy dress, wearing a pearl necklace!

THE PLAYHOUSE IN A CEMETERY

In Lanette, Alabama, just northeast of Auburn, is a graveyard known as Oakwood Cemetery. It contains a very unusual sight you usually wouldn't see in a place of interment. It is located over the grave of Nadine Earles. She was only four years old when she fell ill back in 1933. Just before Christmas, her father had begun to build the playhouse as a gift for his little girl. But a week before the big day, little Nadine passed away. Her parents were, of course, heartbroken, but her father was determined to finish her playhouse. He did—and placed it on top of her grave.

Just before little Nadine Earles died, her father was putting the finishing touches on her playhouse. It now stands over her gravesite. Photo courtesy of Oakwood Cemetery, Lanette, Alabama.

The people in the offices at City Hall told me that during Christmas and on other special occasions, little Nadine's playhouse is decorated. They said cemetery workers will place a Christmas wreath on the door to the playhouse and often put up a decorated tree inside.

SHE CARRIED OUT HER THREAT, ALL RIGHT!

In the town of Clayton (practically due east of Troy, near the Georgia line), there is a cemetery marker that will tell you to listen to your wife. The Clayton Town Cemetery contains the remains of a man locals say drank himself to death. Seems his wife threatened that if husband Amos Mullins continued with this bad habit and died from refusing to give it up, she'd have a tombstone made in the shape of a whiskey bottle!

He did—die from drinking—and she did—have his tombstone shaped just like a whiskey bottle. It won't be difficult to find in Clayton Cemetery: the tombstone is seven feet tall! You can see this unusual headstone at the Clayton Town Cemetery, located on North Midway Street. This headstone was once featured in *Ripley's Believe It Or Not*!

ONE OF THE OLDEST CEMETERIES IN ALABAMA?

Located along Fort Morgan Road in Gulf Shores (Baldwin County), you will find a small graveyard surrounded by live oaks awash with Spanish Moss. Shell Banks Cemetery may have the remains of some of the earliest conquistadors and settlers, as well as Civil War soldiers' remains. According to the historical marker in front of Shell Banks Baptist Church, the Spanish explorer Hernando De Soto visited Native Americans here as early as 1539.

HOME TO THE "DEATH MASK GRAVE MARKERS": MT. NEBO BAPTIST CHURCH CEMETERY

In Carlton (Clarke County), you'll find a most unusual type of grave marker. The cemetery of Mt. Nebo Baptist Church is the place where you will find graves marked, not with traditional tombstones, but with death masks.

Even more unusual is the fact that the masks were made of the deceased *before they were dead*.

An inventor born in the 1880s, Isaac Nettles created these unusual markers. He came up with a way to make mud impressions of the person's face, then transfer that cast to Plaster of Paris, then to the tombstone once the person passed away.

Mt. Nebo's cemetery contains many so-called "death masks." Photo courtesy of Mt. Nebo.

Although these masks (and thus, the cemetery) are listed on the National Register of Historic Places, some of them have suffered at the hands of vandals. The Clarke County Historical Museum Director, Kerry Reid, says that he looked into ways to repair the masks but was told by an art expert that any attempts to repair the masks would render them valueless as they are considered folk art.

The best known and most unusual of all these masks would have to be the one Nettles made of his wife and two daughters. Along with his wife's image, he also placed the masks of their two daughters (but only Mrs. Nettles is buried at Mt. Nebo—the daughters lie interred elsewhere).

Thus, the church has gated the cemetery to prevent further vandalism. If you would like to stroll the cemetery grounds and view these unusual grave markers for yourself, however, you can contact the Clarke County Historical Museum. As of press time, their telephone number was 251.275.8684.

THIS KILLER IS STILL RUN OVER, MORE THAN A HUNDRED YEARS LATER

There were not many criminals who could boast the infamous exploits to the equal of "Mountain" Tom Clark. When he arrived in Lauderdale County in 1862, he was already on the run from Confederate conscription law. He ran from the law, headed north to Tennessee, and joined with the Union Army (Second Tennessee Mounted Infantry), from which he also deserted.

Back in north Alabama, Clark joined forces with a group of bloodthirsty cutthroats called The Booger Gang. Like Clark, these other ne'er-do-wells had also deserted the Army, staying with it long enough to get supplies. Over the course of the next several months, Clark and the rest of the Booger Gang terrorized Florence and the surrounding area, shooting, beating, torturing and killing people, doing so with unbridled glee (Clark himself confessed later to killing 19 people and one 12-month-old infant). Many members of the Booger Gang were caught and executed, followed by a fair trial, but Tom Clark evaded capture—for seven long years.

When in 1872 Federal authorities caught up with Clark in Waterloo, Alabama, he was with two other wanted men. The three criminals were taken to jail in Florence, but an angry mob took them out and lynched all of them.

The ladies of Florence approached the mayor and asked that Clark's body not be laid in the consecrated ground of the cemetery. Then someone remembered a long-time boast of Tom Clark's.

"He said many times, no one would ever run over Mountain Tom Clark!" someone said, and this gave the crowd an idea.

The lynch mob took Clark's body, dug up the road (Tennessee Street), and dumped his body there. His grave is still there, near the center of Tennessee Street, where Clark is run over many times a day.

LIVING HISTORY: TAKING IN THE ANNUAL MAPLE HILL CEMETERY STROLL

In Huntsville, the Maple Hill Cemetery (listed on the National Register of Historic Places) has its annual Cemetery Stroll every October. This isn't just any such stroll: it has grown so much that it is now one of the largest living-history events in the entire United States, with approximately 75 people in period costume, taking on the personae of their historic person. The half-day stroll is free, but the Huntsville Pilgrimage Association accepts donations that go toward monument restoration.

Some of the characters portrayed are not all buried in Maple Hill Cemetery—for example, in October of 2017 there were two ladies portraying actress Tallulah Bankhead, whose mother lies interred on the grounds.

Besides the re-enactors' portrayals, there is an antique car show and music of all kinds. People who make donations to the Huntsville Pilgrimage Association become "Angels of Maple Hill."

Who says you can't live forever?

THE TOP TEN HAUNTED PLACES IN ALABAMA

According to the TV series "Creepy World," Fort Morgan is among the top ten most haunted placed in Alabama. Here is the complete list that made this infamous cut:

THE TUTWILER HOTEL (Birmingham)—Now owned by Hampton Inn and Suites, legend has it that lights in what is now the bar area come on by themselves. Also, one bartender back in the 1980s claimed that when he opened the bar one evening, there was a full, 5-course meal, complete with wine and lighted candles, waiting for him. He believed it was the ghost of Colonel Tutwiler, the original owner of the hotel. As they come on duty, they say bartenders are to respectfully greet the Colonel with a "Good evening," and all will go smoothly that night.

FORT MORGAN (Gulf Shores)—Since the Battle of Mobile Bay during the Civil War (see that chapter), this fort has been the site of strange and frightening sightings by employees and tourists alike. People say they sometimes hear screams of men, possibly ghosts of soldiers who were killed in the battle. Locals say they have seen a ghostly woman walking the grounds, appearing to be looking for someone. Although I have never seen or heard anything myself of any of this, there is a place at one of the parapets where one soldier was killed during the battle; it is said that the stains you can see on the parapet are of his blood.

ST. JAMES HOTEL (Selma)—This is one of the oldest hotels still in operation in Alabama. During the Civil War, high-ranking soldiers used the hotel to plan their battle strategies. During the Battle of Selma, nearly all of Selma was destroyed by fire; the St. James was spared the torch. After the war, it is said that the notorious James Gang stayed here while on the run from the law (see their story in Chapter 1). Guests have reported sightings of Jesse James and his girlfriend Lucinda in several of the rooms (314, 315, and 214).

BRYCE HOSPITAL (Tuscaloosa)—The former mental institution is now a popular tourist attraction for those who are intrigued by paranormal activity. The sounds of screams and footsteps have been reported by those brave enough to tour its halls.

GAINES RIDGE DINNER CLUB (Camden) - This place has the dubious distinction of being named the most haunted restaurant in Alabama. A former family antebellum home, dinner guests and employees have reported hearing screams and smelling the aroma of pipe smoke. Other guests have reported seeing the reflection of a bearded man in mirrors, although they cannot see anyone in the room itself. Yet other people have said they have seen a woman's image floating by the house's windows.

JACK COLE ROAD (Hayden) -– Near Highway 70 in Blount County is an unpaved road locals call Jack Cole Road. It is in this area that approximately 120 people have died, mostly due to a cholera epidemic years ago. A few others were murdered here. Locals say that they often see ghostly orbs floating above the road; others claim there is a half-man, half-wolf roaming the area.

HIGHWAY 5 (Lynn)—This stretch of highway in Lynn is said to be haunted by the ghost of a woman who was struck and killed by someone driving an 18-wheeler. Truckers say their windows are banged on by a ghostly image of a woman; others say she peers in at them, as if wondering if they were the ones who killed her. Today, most truckers take an alternate route.

REDMONT HOTEL (Birmingham)—this is the city's oldest hotel—and the oldest hotel in the state of Alabama still in operation. On the ninth floor, guests say they have seen the ghostly image of a woman who passed away in one of the rooms years ago. The Redmont Hotel is also said to be haunted by the original owner, Clifford Stiles, whose spirit has been seen wandering the halls. The ghost of Hank Williams, Sr., who was a guest here, is also said to haunt the halls. Guests of this hotel have reported their personal items moved around as they slept! I've been a guest at the Redmont several times and never noticed anything amiss (now, where did my brush go?).

SLOSS FURNACE (Birmingham)—In the aftermath of the Civil War, Sloss Furnace was the place where pig-iron, an intermediate product of the iron industry, was made. In the early 1900s, a man named James Slag Wormwood was supervisor of the night shift. Legend says that, under his cruel supervision, he worked his employees literally to death: approximately 50 workers died in accidents due to Wormwood forcing them to work ever-harder and cut corners to produce more. Once there was an explosion which caused half a dozen of the workers to become blind and unable to work. In the fall of 1906, angry, overworked employees caused Wormwood to fall into the furnace; he was burned alive. Shortly after, workers began hearing their former supervisor's voice shouting to get back to work. Other supervisors were once locked in a boiler-room by unseen hands. According to Birmingham Police reports, there have been more than 150 calls to them about incidents in and around Sloss Furnace.

If you have a "burning" desire to tour the furnaces, it is now open for tours.

UNIQUE IN ALL THE WORLD: THE COON DOG CEMETERY

Near Tuscumbia in the town of Cherokee, you will find a cemetery unlike any other in the entire world. Also known as the Coon Dog Memorial Graveyard, the Coon Dog Cemetery currently has nearly 200 of man's best friends interred there. The cemetery was begun by a man named Key Underwood back in 1937, when he buried his faithful coon-hunting pal, Troop. The property was a great hunting camp, where coon (raccoon to those who are confused) hunters gathered to share stories, chew tobacco and compare their coon-hunting dogs. The best dog of them all was Troop, and when he went to Coon Dog Heaven, Key Underwood knew that the hunting camp was where Troop wanted to spend eternity.

Underwood buried Troop on Labor Day of 1937. Troop was followed some years later by Underwood's other coon dog, Red. As time went on, other coon hunters buried their favorite coon dogs on the property. One of the most famous such dogs buried here is Hunter's Famous Amos, who was the Ralston Purina's Dog of the Year in 1984.

The Coon Dog Cemetery members are strict in that the dog to be interred on the property must be an authentic coon dog. As Key Underwood once quoted to a newspaper reporter, when she asked why the cemetery was only reserved for coon dogs, "You must not know much about coon hunters and their dogs, if you think we would contaminate this burial place with poodles and lap dogs." And former caretaker of the Coon Dog Graveyard, the late O'Neal Bolton, was once quoted as saying,

"We have stipulations on this thing. A dog can't run no [sic] deer, and he's got to be a full hound."

You can pay your respects to these coon dogs by setting your GPS to 4945 Coon Dog Cemetery Road, Cherokee.

HERE'S THE COON DOG EULOGY, written by William W. Ramsey, with the Introduction by Bradley W. Ramsey. Used with permission.

INTRODUCTION: A group of solemn men, dressed in black mourning coats and hip boots, wearing carbide lamps on their heads, stood beside a mound of soil and a freshly dug hole. A hunting horn sounded and the bay of hounds filled the air. Four similarly dressed men walked slowly toward the gathered crowd, a small wooden box carried between them. When the box was lowered into the ground one of the men spoke the following.

> Let not your hearts be troubled,
> for in his master's swamp are many den trees.
> If it were not so, I would have told you.
> He has gone to prepare a place for you
> and where he has gone Ole Red will go also.
> Dogs, they say, do not have souls.
> They only have hide and bones.
> But I believe there is a coon dog heaven
> and Red is gone were the good coon dogs go.
> Anybody that coon hunts has to believe in God.
> If you have known the music of coon hounds on a trail
> and heard the excitement in their voices when they strike,
> and seen their eagerness and determination when they tree,
> if you have seen their courage and bravery
> in a tough fight with an old boar coon,

Amazing Alabama

if you have heard their anguished cries and howls,
if you have seen the ugly gashes
and bleeding wounds
and witnessed their resolve to never quit,
you know there has to be a God to make an animal like that.
And a God that would make a coon dog
won't forget him when he is gone.
There is a coon dog heaven and Ole Red is there.
And every night he runs
and the den trees are there in the old swamp
and the old hunter's moon hangs low in the west
and the coons don't go up no slick barked trees
and the carbide don't run out
and there ain't no bull nettle and saw briars
and old master always knocks the coon out
and lets Ole Red grab him and give him a good shake;
and then he gets a pat on the head
and climbs back into the kennel in the back of the pick-up truck
and goes home and sleeps all day.
'Cause he knows in coon dog heaven he can hunt again
when the sun goes down and the tree frogs holler.
May the bones of Ole Red rest in peace,
through the mercy of God
and may the coon hunters light perpetually shine upon him.

AMEN

T. Jensen Lacey

CHAPTER 16

LIGHTHOUSE AND COASTAL STORIES

SHEDDING SOME LIGHT ON MOBILE BAY: THE STORY OF THE MIDDLE BAY LIGHTHOUSE

For generations of anglers, sailors and shippers, the image of Middle Bay Light, as the locals call it, means you are about halfway across the Bay of Mobile. Built "up north," the prefabricated house arrived in Mobile in 1885. Mobile Bay itself is quite shallow, and before the arrival of the lighthouse, a channel was marked by wooden stakes and barrels. When in the early 1880s a 17-foot channel was dredged so large vessels could reach the Port of Mobile, a lighthouse was deemed necessary to mark the channel.

Middle Bay Light is located at the bend in this dog-leg-shaped channel, and when it was placed here in 1885, its location (at roughly the middle of the bay) led to its nickname. People who witnessed the lighthouse being erected atop 48 fifty-foot piles must have been amazed.

The wooden hexagonal house with a pyramidal roof, sloping to a lantern room on the top of the structure was placed on top of screw-piles, which had been sunk deep into the bottom of the bay. Once it was in place, the entire structure settled 7 ½ feet, and the house was set nearly perfectly—it was only about three inches from being totally level.

This feat of engineering still stands proudly in Mobile Bay. The house has been through hurricanes, tornadoes, electrical storms and once was struck by a shrimp boat. It once was also home to a cow, when during World War I, the lighthouse keeper and his wife had a baby, and the cow was needed for its milk.

No keeper was in care of the lighthouse in the decades from the mid-1930s until the late 1960s, however, and the lighthouse fell into disrepair. In 1967, the General Services Administration granted the Coast Guard permission to demolish the lighthouse, but before this could be carried out, several groups protested. When the Mobile Bay Pilots Association pointed out that the lighthouse could be picked up by ships' radar much more easily than the small, more modern buoys, plans for the lighthouse's demolition were abandoned.

Middle Bay Lighthouse. Picture courtesy of Alabama Lighthouse Association

Shortly after the lighthouse was put on the National Register of Historic Places (in 1975), the Alabama Historical Commission (AHC) took over care of the lighthouse. With the approach of the lighthouse's centennial, the Middle Bay Light Centennial Commission, along with the volunteers of the Alabama Lighthouse Association, did fundraising and worked to restore the lighthouse to its former beauty, putting down new decking, replacing doors and windows, and giving the lighthouse a new coat of paint. In

December 1, 1985, ships from all over the world and smaller boats of all sizes amassed at the lighthouse to celebrate.

Since then, the lighthouse has undergone further repairs and improvements. In 2002, Thompson Engineering, under contract with the Alabama Historical Commission, gave the lighthouse a new slate roof, repaired damaged wood, and replaced corroded metal tie rods. The lighthouse also had its flashing red light replaced with a solar-powered one (its original Fresnel lens is currently on display at the nearby Fort Morgan Museum).

In 2009, the Alabama Lighthouse Association (ALA) proposed to move Middle Bay Light on land to nearby Battleship Park (in Mobile). When I asked Alabama Lighthouse Association member Stephen Quinlivan to "shed some light" on why this move was proposed, he told me this: "The proposal in 2009 to move the light was based on a lack of funding to maintain the light in its place. We were worried about the long-term survival of the structure." He added, "Our biggest struggle is raising funds to keep up with the rapid deterioration associated with a building standing in such an environment." Fortunately, with the combined efforts of the AHC, Seamen's Foundation and the ALA, they were able to complete a $50,000 project in the fall of 2017. The roof was repaired, the exterior painted, and all needed carpentry work done. Quinlivan added, "Many projects are still in need of funding to keep this local treasure in good shape. As you can imagine, the limited access makes repair work extremely costly."

SAND ISLAND LIGHTHOUSE: KEEPING SAILORS SAFE FOR MORE THAN A HUNDRED YEARS

At the mouth of Mobile Bay, near Dauphin Island (which locals call a 'barrier island'), lies Sand Island Lighthouse. Its shape and color are nothing extraordinary, compared to other lighthouses: it's a simple brownstone tower in the shape of a cylinder, with a balcony and a lantern.

The lighthouse you can go see today is not the original lighthouse. The first lighthouse on this spit of land was constructed in 1837. A later lighthouse which stood here (at the entrance to Fort Gaines and Fort Morgan) was destroyed during the Civil War, not by Union troops, but by Confederate soldiers. They observed Union soldiers at the lighthouse, spying on them. The Confederates opened fire and totally destroyed that lighthouse.

The current lighthouse faces another and more persistent enemy: erosion. The island's size in the mid-1800s was 400 acres; at the time, the real estate of Sand Island was big enough to support a lighthouse-keeper's dwelling. The lighthouse stands now on just a blurb of real estate.

In 2011 the state of Alabama spent six million dollars to dredge and add nearly 1.5 million yards of sand to the lighthouse's base; much of that work was undone by Hurricane Isaac in 2012. Other hurricanes since then have added to the erosion problem.

Today, you can go see the lighthouse (and fishing around it is pretty good), but no one is allowed to explore it. It's currently under the care of the Dauphin Island Foundation and the Alabama Lighthouse Association, who are conducting an ongoing Sand Island Restoration Project.

What you can see of the Sand Island Lighthouse is its original Fresnel lens; it is on display at the Fort Morgan Museum. See "Virtual Alabama" for websites.

IN ALABAMA, THE WORLD'S YOUR OYSTER

The 413-mile span of the Bay of Mobile is the fourth-largest estuary in the U.S. (an estuary is where fresh and salt waters come together). The waters of rivers and creeks feed the Bay of Mobile with nutrients upon which the tasty and economically helpful oysters thrive.

A single oyster can filter nearly 70 gallons of water each day, so they help keep Mobile Bay healthy. The oyster reefs also provide habitat for other marine wildlife.

WHEN A FISHING RECORD WAS BROKEN TWICE IN ONE DAY!

The dock at the Mobile Big Game Fishing Club (in Orange Beach, Alabama) is always an exciting place to be at any fishing competition's "weigh-in"; here, spectators watch the fishing boats come in and weigh their catches, and as the scores go up on the board, the suspense builds until the last vessel makes it to the dock, all catches are recorded, and the winners are congratulated (and take home their winnings).

These happy anglers are thrilled over catching a nice-size swordfish in the Gulf of Mexico. Photo by Eric Lacey.

In the Blue Marlin Grand Championship of July, 2013, the record that had stood for 24 years—Marcus Kennedy's 779.3-pounder in May, 1989--was shattered twice within a 90-minute period. Angler Toby Berthelot brought to the weigh-in his catch of a 789.8-pound monster marlin, the biggest marlin ever caught off the coast of Alabama. An hour and a half later, Chris Ferrera—a "newbie" to fishing tournaments—brought in a marlin weighing a little more than 845 pounds. According to Chris Discipio's article in *Outdoor Life*,

Ferrera fought the fish for more than 6 and ½ hours. The marlin was given to an Alabama food bank for the homeless.

I wonder if those folks knew they were eating a new Alabama record-breaking fish?

SO YOU WANT TO TRY YOUR HAND IN A FISHING TOURNAMENT?

For those who would like to experience the sheer exhilaration of catching a truly "big one," I suggest you check out the Mobile Big Game Fishing Club (located in Orange Beach, AL). They have more than a half-dozen fishing tournaments,

These happy anglers look tired but excited after catching their legal limit during Red Snapper season. Photo by the author.

ranging from one for ladies, one for junior anglers, and one just for smaller (outboard) fishing boats. In the entire United States, two of the biggest such fishing tournaments are put on by the

MBGFC. I recommend you try your hand in at least one, and see what fishing tales you take away from it.

HURRICANE CULTURE

The people of Alabama are well accustomed to the vagaries of Mother Nature, whether it's storm surge, hail, the occasional rare snowstorm or hurricanes. With the latter, however, since there is usually fair warning, folks in Alabama know how to prepare.

Like other coastal states, they know to get at least three days' supply of food, water and medicine together in the probability of a power outage. But they also are aware of their neighbors' needs and help each other out. I've seen neighbors who never even met each other help another neighbor remove a tree from the roof, deliver food to a neighbor without power, or even invite them into their own homes. And when other states have suffered damage from storms, the people of Alabama have hearts as big as Texas.

You can learn more about Alabama and how the state and its people have endured hurricanes by visiting the Gulf Shores Museum. Located on 19th Avenue in the coastal town of Gulf Shores, the museum offers visitors what it's like to fly through the eye of a hurricane with a "Hurricane Hunters" exhibit. The museum is in a vintage, pre-World War II beach cottage, and the docents are knowledgeable and welcoming.

JEWEL OF THE SEA: DAUPHIN ISLAND SEA LAB

On Dauphin Island you will find a fascinating place now known as Dauphin Island Sea Lab. Originally begun back in 1960 as a laboratory of the Seafood Division (a part of the Department of Conservation and Natural Resources), it provided students from the University of Alabama a place to learn about all the resources the Gulf had to offer. By 1963 efforts were underway to build a modern marine research facility, and in 1971 Dr. C. Everett Brett was named the first director. In 1972 the facility was officially named the Dauphin Island Sea Lab. In 1975, a move was made to create the "Discovery Hall," where the lab welcomed high school students to learn more about animal and plant life in the Gulf and estuaries.

In 1980, summer exploratory sessions were offered at Spring Hill College (in Mobile), and in 1998, the Estuarium opened to the public. This facility explores such marine habitats as not only the Gulf of Mexico but also Mobile Bay, the Tensaw Delta, and the barrier islands. The years 2010-2017 saw further expansion, with the addition of research vessels (one of which is named after the famous naturalist E. O. Wilson—see Chapter 13 for more on him), the opening of the Marine Mammal Research Center, and a new exhibit hall, complete with a 500-gallon tank. The Marina Mammal Research Center educates explorers of all ages to learn more about local marine life.

Dauphin Island Sea Lab and the Estuarium are now considered key stops for travelers and tourists along the Alabama coast. They are located near the

The Gulf Shores Museum is near the beautiful, sugar white sands of the beaches nearby. Photo courtesy of Gulf Shores Department of Tourism

Mobile Bay ferry and Historic Fort Gaines (see the Civil War chapter for a story on the fort). You and your family can easily spend a day at this fascinating place in Alabama.

T. Jensen Lacey

CHAPTER 17

GHOST TOWNS OF ALABAMA

BLAKELEY: ONE-TIME RIVAL TO MOBILE

Just a few miles north of Spanish Fort lies the area known as Blakeley, which in its heyday was a rival to the city of Mobile. It was founded by a Connecticut man named Josiah Blakely, who arrived in Alabama in 1806. By 1813, the town of Blakeley had been surveyed, with streets laid out. In 1814, the town was incorporated. In 1818, the businessmen of the town sent a petition to the United States Congress to become recognized as an official "Port of Entry and Delivery." The town continued to grow, at one time rivaling Mobile in size. Then, disaster in the form of three yellow fever epidemics struck the town (in 1822, 1826 and 1828). By the time the Civil War began, Blakeley was a ghost town; most of its inhabitants, ironically, had moved to the town's former rival—Mobile.

Blakeley was the site of a fort during the Civil War—see more on that in Chapter 8—and it is now a state park, with camping, guided eco-tours by boat, and hiking trails. See Virtual Alabama at the back of this book for their website.

BELLEFONTE

Once a vibrant town, Bellefonte in Jackson County is now only a ghost town. Originally named Riley's on Mud Creek, Bellefonte (locals pronounce it "bell-font") was established a few days after Jackson County was created in 1819. Two of the settlers who purchased property there renamed it Bellefonte after the nearby spring which was the town's water supply. The town became Jackson's first permanent justice center, and the townspeople built a two-story courthouse. Bellefonte remained the seat of Jackson County from 1821 until 1859.

In 1820, a stage coach line began to include Bellefonte in its route from Knoxville, Tennessee to Huntsville, Alabama. One settler (Daniel McNair Martin) built and operated an inn on the courthouse square. By 1844, the population had swelled to approximately 400 people. The town had two stores, two blacksmith shops, a wagon-repair shop, a saddle-making shop, a jail, and a school called Bellefonte Academy. As time went by, the town added two churches, two schools, 12 stores, more than fifty homes and more than 400 people. Robert T. Scott (founder of Scottsboro, Alabama) started an inn he called "Belle Tavern." Another inn, known as the Mansion Hotel, was added to the growing number of structures in the town. A man by the name of Major Robert A. Eaton began to publish a newspaper, *The North Alabama Star*.

A resident of Bellefonte, Nelson Kyle, who was born there in 1862, wrote of what the town was like in its heyday. He wrote of Bellefonte as "a handsome little village before the war," with a bustling courthouse square and "a large flowing spring located at the northeast border of town." He also added that the town had "a fine bar" and mentioned that many prominent settlers and lawyers practiced law in Bellefonte, including among them his grandfather, Nelson Robinson.

Hindsight, they say, is always 20/20, and in 1849 the citizens of Bellefonte made a decision that much contributed to the city's downfall. Some of the people wanted a rail line running through their town, but most of the people rejected this proposal. Thus, the rail line was set outside of town. Robert

Scott donated the land on which the rail line's depot was built, and it was called Scott's Mill (later renamed Scottsboro).

With the rail line not coming into town, Bellefonte began to shrink. In 1859, the post office closed. With the coming of the Civil War, raiding Union soldiers burned down the courthouse. After this, the county seat was moved to Scottsboro. By 1883, Bellefonte's once-thriving population was down to a mere 100. By the 1920s, the town of Bellefonte was abandoned.

Today, all you can see to tell that people used to live in this area two miles southeast of Hollywood, Alabama, are the remains of one of the chimneys of an inn, the cemetery, and scattered bricks. In the cemetery, you can see the headstone of a deceased child of Daniel Martin, etched with the date 1826, the earliest date in the Bellefonte cemetery.

It's a bit eerie to stand in this place, within sight of the Bellefonte Nuclear Generating Station, and hear only the birds and the wind.

THE GHOST COUNTY (or, Your Tax Dollars at Work)

In December 7, 1821, the Alabama Legislature created Decatur County out of parts of Jackson County and Madison County. Named after Commodore Stephen Decatur of U.S. Navy fame, Decatur County's seat was established in the town known as "Woodville." Surveyors were appointed to survey and map out the new county. This took the survey workers approximately two years to complete.

When they were finished with the survey, they discovered disturbing news: Their findings revealed that, as set out by the Alabama Constitution, this new county did not contain the required number of square miles to be a county!

So, on December 28, 1825, the Alabama Legislature corrected this "oops," abolishing Decatur County and returning the territories to the original counties. Oh—and in case you're wondering what happened to Woodville, it was on the part of the land that reverted back to Jackson County.

ST. STEPHENS: FIRST CAPITAL OF THE ALABAMA TERRITORY

Located approximately 100 river-miles north of Mobile, Alabama, this area had been initially under French, then British and later Spanish authority. Only the Spanish actually occupied the area, establishing a fort in the late 1800s they named "Fort San Esteban." The Spanish finally gave up control of the area when a final, definitive survey granted that it was, by the Treaty of San Lorenzo, part of the U.S.

American troops arrived at the fort once the Spanish relinquished it in 1799, and under the command of Lt. John McLary, they raised the American flag and renamed the fort Fort St. Stephens. As more settlers arrived in the area, the "fort" was dropped from the name and it became simply St. Stephens. An Indian agent by the name of Joseph Chambers arrived in 1803 and opened the Choctaw Trading House. When Chambers moved, his position was taken over by a man named George S. Gaines, who became a close friend to the eminent Choctaw chief, Pushmataha. The area grew, with a federal courthouse built on the property, and a federal judge by the name of Ephraim Kirby arrived.

Upon his arrival in 1803, Kirby wrote to President Thomas Jefferson about the people of St. Stephens: "The present inhabitations," he wrote, "with few exceptions, are illiterate, wild and savage, with depraved morals." He also wrote of the local officials as being "without dignity, respect, probity, influence or authority, leading local justice in an imbecile and corrupt state." Ironically, the author of these judgmental lines died the next year—of liver disease.

Jefferson appointed his former vice president, Harry Toulmin, to replace Kirby (Toulmin would later become involved with many historic events, including the arrest of Aaron Burr). Toulmin was also destined to become a major negotiator in the Alabama Territory out of the Mississippi Territory and penned the first law book of Alabama.

St. Stephens continued to grow and prosper, with wide streets and the opening of the first official school in Alabama, Washington Academy (later changed to St. Stephens Academy). By the time Alabama became its own official territory, they had a newspaper and everyone assumed it would be the capital of the new territory.

Alabama continued to make advances toward becoming a state. The first meeting of the General Assembly was in St. Stephens, and the next one, in Huntsville. It was at this second meeting that the legislature would write and approve the state constitution.

After St. Stephens and Huntsville were the capitals, the third one was Cahaba (see the following story about that). After it was moved from Cahaba, Tuscaloosa was the next capital. Finally, Montgomery was named permanent capital, in 1846.

By the 1820s, the population of St. Stephens began to shrink, with most of its population moving downriver to Mobile. By the mid-1860s, St. Stephens was totally desolated.

Today, you can tour what is now known as St. Stephens Historical Park. You may be able to see where excavations are taking place, walk the peaceful grounds and see a few remnants to show you that this was once a thriving community. On occasion, the Museum of Natural History (based in Tuscaloosa) hosts archeological digs there, as they did in 2018.

CAHAWBA—TWICE A GHOST TOWN

Before it became known as Cahawba, this area near Selma in southeast Alabama was a thriving village, home to a large number of prehistoric Indians. For reasons still unknown to archeologists, researchers and historians today, the village was abandoned.

By 1820, it was settled by a handful of white and African-American settlers and, until 1826, served as the capital of Alabama. Like the Indian settlers of old, these citizens agreed that Cahawba was a perfect place for human habitation. The earth was fertile, the climate mild, and Cahawba's geographical location between two rivers (the Alabama and the Cahaba) offered an abundance of fish, mussels, and transportation opportunities. Travelers could reach the Gulf of Mexico by the Alabama River and thereby travel the world by water if they wished.

The town was thriving, with a new brick building for the capital. But being near so much water has its proverbial downside: In 1825, the town flooded and part of the new capital building collapsed. In January, 1826, the state legislature voted to move the capital to Tuscaloosa.

Cahawba began to go into decline after this, but even as a ghost-town, today it continues to attract visitors, researchers, historians and archeologists. Now known as "Old Cahawba," the site has been made into an Archeological Park and is run under the auspices of the Alabama Historical Commission. Visitors can go to the Visitors' Center, tour St. Luke's Episcopal Church on the grounds, hear a talk by one of the resident archeologists, hike the many trails, tour the cemetery, or rent a canoe to paddle the Cahaba River.

DID YOU KNOW?

The marble flooring in Selma's Tally-Ho Restaurant came from the state of Alabama's first capital building at Old Cahawba. Take a close look at the floor at the Tally-Ho when you're in Selma.

T. Jensen Lacey

BIBLIOGRAPHY

Alabama Department of Archives and History. "State Spirit of Alabama: Official Symbols and Emblems of Alabama." Retrieved 10-5-18. www.Archives.State.Al.Us. www.AL.com.

Atkins, Leah, PhD., and Dr. Harvey H. Jackson III. <u>Alabama: The History, Geography, Economics and Civics of an American State</u>. Montgomery, AL: Crystal Clear Press, Inc., 2005.

<u>www.Biography.com/MartinLutherKing,Jr</u>. Accessed March 12, 2018.

Bragg, Rick. <u>Best Cook in the World: Tales from My Momma's Table</u>. New York: Alfred A. Knopf, 2018.

Bridges, Edwin C. <u>Alabama: The Making of an American State</u>. Tuscaloosa: The University of Alabama Press, 2016.

Causey, Donna R. <u>Alabama Footprints</u>. 2017: Alabama Pioneers Publishing (no city).

Cochran, Hamilton. <u>Blockade Runners of the Confederacy</u>. Tuscaloosa: The University of Alabama Press, 1898, repub. 2005.

Elric, Wil and Kelly Kazek. <u>Covered Bridges of Alabama</u>. Charleston, SC: The History Press, 2018.

Gailliard, Frye. <u>Go South to Freedom</u>. Montgomery: NewSouth Books, 2016.

Gaines, W. Craig. <u>Encyclopedia of Civil War Shipwrecks</u>. Baton Rouge: LSU Press, 2008.

Ghigna, Charles. <u>Alabama: My Home Sweet Home!</u> Montgomery: Whitman Publishing/Alabama Bicentennial Commission, 2018.

Hammond, Ralph. <u>Antebellum Mansions of Alabama</u>. New York: Architectural Book Publishers, 1951.

Kazek, Kelly & Wil Erick. <u>Alabama Scoundrels: Outlaws, Pirates, Bandits & Bushwhackers</u>. The History Press, Charleston, S.C., 2014.

Lacey, T. Jensen. <u>Amazing North Carolina</u>. Fairhope, Alabama. Moon Howler Publishing, LLC. 2019.

Manning, Sidney E. <u>www.history.army.mil/html/moh/worldwari.html. Accessed 3-8-2018</u>.

Marshall, Benny, et al. <u>All-Time Greatest Alabama Sports Stories</u>. Tuscaloosa: Fire Ant Books, 2003.

Murray, Laura, PhD. <u>Amazing Alabama: A Coloring Book Journey through Our 67 Counties</u>. Montgomery, AL: New South Books, 2017.

Musgrove. Anita. <u>Alabama Back Road Restaurant Recipes</u>. Kosciusko, MS, 2014.

O'Brien, Cormac. <u>Secret Lives of the Civil War</u>. Philadelphia: Quirk Books, 2007.

Schleifstein, Mark. "Researchers find more evidence that microbes ate BP oil in Gulf." *New Orleans Times-Picayune*. November 8, 2010. Accessed August 6, 2018 on <u>www.NOLA.com</u>.

Sledge, John S. Southern Bound: A Gulf Coast Journalist on Books, Writers, and Literary Pilgrimages of the Heart. Columbia, SC: The University of South Carolina Press, 2013.

Sledge, John S. These Rugged Days: Alabama in the Civil War. Tuscaloosa: The University of Alabama Press, 2018.

Tarabella, Leslie Anne. The Majorettes are Back in Town! And Other Things to Love about the South. New Orleans: River Road Press, 2017.

Taylor, Kendall. The Gatsby Affair: Scott, Zelda, and the Betrayal that Shaped an American Classic. Lanham, Maryland: Rowman & Littlefield, 2018.

Taylor, General Richard Taylor. Destruction and Reconstruction: Personal Experiences of the Civil War. New York: De Capo Press, 1995.

Tunks, Karyn W. The USS *Alabama*: Hooray for the Mighty A! New Orleans: River Road Press, 2015.

Tunks, Karyn W. Jubilee! Gretna, Louisiana: Pelican Publishing Company, 2012.

VIRTUAL ALABAMA

In conducting research for this book, I looked at each of the websites listed below; you may consider this part of my bibliography.

Disclaimer: The internet is constantly in a state of flux and both Author and Publisher encourage you to use a search engine in the event you encounter any difficulties in getting to any of these websites. All websites were checked for currency and correctness at the time of publication.

GENERAL ALABAMA WEBSITES

Alabama Department of Archives and History (ADAH): www.Archives.State.AL.US

Alabama Department of Tourism: www.Tourism.Alabama.Gov or www.SweetHomeAlabama.org

Alabama Women's Hall of Fame: www.awhf.org

Museum of Alabama (under auspices of ADAH): www.Museum.Alabama.gov

Alabama Historical Commission: www.AHC.Alabama.gov

General Alabama News and Commentary: www.Al.com

Yellowhammer News: www.YellowHammerNews.com

Diane Causeway's excellent websites on anything relating to Alabama history and culture: www.daysgoneby.me and www.AlabamaPioneers.com

Kelly Kazek's "Weird News" of all things Alabama: www.KellyKazek.com (you can also read her columns on www.AL.com)

CHAPTER NOTES

CHAPTER 1: TRULY BIZARRE EVENTS AND NOTORIOUS ALABAMIANS

Alabama Bigfoot Society: www.AlabamaBigfootSociety.com

Clyde Mays Website: https://www.mayswhiskey.com/

Each County Historical Museum also has exhibits relating to their most notorious people. Use Google!

CHAPTER 2: POLITICS, TRANSPORTATION, MILITARY TALES

Huntsville Depot, Early Works Museum and Alabama's Constitution Village: www.EarlyWorks.com

Alabama Veterans Museum & Archives: www.AlabamaVeteransMuseum.com

Heart of Dixie Railroad Museum: www.HODRRM.org

USS Battleship Memorial Park: www.USSAlabama.com

Southern Museum of Flight: www.SouthernMuseumofFlight.org

The *Harriett II* Riverboat: www.funinmontgomery.com/parks-items/harriott-ii-riverboat

LaGrange College & Military Institute: www.LaGrangeHistoricSite.com

U.S. Space and Rocket Center (Huntsville): www.RocketCity.com

Marshall Space Flight Center Website: https://www.nasa.gov/centers/marshall/home/index.html

U.S. Space and Rocket Center Website:
https://www.rocketcenter.com/

Marion Military Institute Website: https://marionmilitary.edu/

Fort Conde Website: https://www.colonialmobile.com/

The American Village Website:
http://www.americanvillage.org/site/PageServer

Karl C. Harrison Museum o f George Washington:
http://www.washingtonmuseum.com/

Constitution Village, Huntsville Website:
http://www.earlyworks.com/

Magnolia Hotel Website: www.thehotelmagnolia.com
GulfQuest Maritime Museum: www.gulfquest.org

Tuskegee Airmen National Historic Site:
https://www.nps.gov/tuai/index.htm

USS *Alabama* Website: https://www.ussalabama.com/

Alabama Historical Commission Website (for planning tours to the capitol):
https://ahc.alabama.gov/AlabamaStateCapitolPlanYourVisit.aspx

Alabama Veteran's Museum:
www.alabamaveteransmuseum.com/

CHAPTER 3: PREHISTORIC ALABAMA

Martin Petroglyphs: www.tvaa.net/exhibitions/permanent-exhibit.html

Wetumpka Impact Crater: www.WetumpkaImpactCraterCommission.org

Russell Cave National Monument: https://www.nps.gov/articles/russellcave.htm

Russell Cave National Monument: https://www.nps.gov/ruca/index.htm

Moundville Archeological Park: https://moundville.ua.edu

Fort Toulouse-Fort Jackson: www.AHC.Alabama.gov and https://fttoulousejackson.org

Tennessee Valley Museum of Art: www.tvaa.net/

Alabama Historical Commission's Page on the Bottle Creek Indian Mounds: https://ahc.alabama.gov/properties/bottlecreek/bottlecreek.aspx

McWane Science Center: https://www.mcwane.org/

Alabama Paleontological Society: www.alabamapaleo.org/Alabama_Paleontological_Society.html

Arab Historic Village: http://www.arabcity.org/index.php/living_in_arab/historic_village

History Museum of Mobile:
http://www.historymuseumofmobile.com/

Wetumpka Impact Crater Commission:
www.wetumpkaimpactcratercommission.org/

Alabama Museum of Natural History: https://almnh.ua.edu/

Moundville Archeological Park website:
https://moundville.ua.edu/

CHAPTER 4: FAMOUS ALABAMIANS IN EDUCATION, ART, SCIENCE, AND LITERATURE

Helen Keller: www.HelenKellerFestival.com/site and www.HelenKellerBirthplace.org

Weeden House Museum and Gardens:
www.WeedenHouseMuseum.com

Gee's Bend Quilting Collective: www.QuiltsOfGeesBend.com

Alabama Women's Hall of Fame: www.awhf.org/

Alabama Writer's Hall Of Fame:
https://www.writersforum.org/hall-of-fame/about.html

Montgomery Visitor Center: https://visitingmontgomery.com/

F. Scott and Zelda Fitzgerald Museum:
https://www.thefitzgeraldmuseum.org/

Kathryn Tucker Windham Museum-Encyclopedia of Alabama:
http://www.encyclopediaofalabama.org/article/m-7524

Alabama Newspaper Hall of Honor: https://www.alabamapress.org/contests-awards/hall-of-honor/

Holmes Medical Museum: https://cityoffoley.org/holmes-medical-museum/

George Washington Carver Museum in Tuskegee: https://www.nps.gov/tuin/index.htm

Booker T Washington Home: https://www.nps.gov/tuin/planyourvisit/things2do.htm

Monroeville's Old Courthouse Museum: https://www.monroecountymuseum.org/

Gorgas House: https://gorgashouse.ua.edu/

CHAPTER 5: FROM AGRICULTURE TO ARCHITECTURE

Alabama Department of Agriculture: www.Agi.Alabama.gov

Alabama State Agricultural Museum: Landmark Park: https://www.landmarkparkdothan.com/

The Pea River Historical & Genealogical Society: https://www.peariver.org/

MOOseum Website: https://www.bamabeef.org/p.aspx?pID=about/273&

Alabama State Capitol Building: https://visitingmontgomery.com/play/alabama-state-capitol-building

Quinlan Castle: https://www.bhamwiki.com/w/Quinlan_Castle

Guntersville Museum & Cultural Center: https://www.guntersvillemuseum.org/

Sturdivant Hall: https://en.wikipedia.org/wiki/Sturdivant_Hall

Fort Morgan: www.fort-morgan.org/

Mobile Convention Center: https://www.mobileconventions.com/

McWane Science Center: https://www.mcwane.org/

Montgomery Mall: https://en.wikipedia.org/wiki/Montgomery_Mall_(Alabama)

Colbert County Courthouse: http://www.colbertcounty.org/

Alabama Theatre: https://alabamatheatre.com/

The Saenger Theatre: https://www.mobilesaenger.com/

Hargis Hall: http://www.lib.auburn.edu/arch/buildings/hargis_hall.htm

Gorgas Hall: https://www.lib.ua.edu/libraries/gorgas/

Rosenbaum House: http://wrightinalabama.com/

Victory Teaching Farm Website: https://www.victoryteachingfarm.org

Alabama Historical Commission's Page on Gaineswood: https://ahc.alabama.gov/properties/gaineswood/gaineswood.aspx

Alabama Historical Commission's Page on Pond Spring: https://ahc.alabama.gov/properties/pondspring/pondspring.aspx

Belle Mont: https://ahc.alabama.gov/properties/bellemont/bellemont.aspx

Fendall Hall: https://fendallhall.weebly.com/

Magnolia Grove: https://ahc.alabama.gov/properties/magnoliagrove/magnoliagrove.aspxVictory

Gaineswood Plantation Museum: www.Gaineswoodmuseum.org

Auburn University: www.Auburn.edu

Pioneer Museum of Alabama: https://www.pioneer-museum.org

Baldwin County Heritage Museum: https://m.facebook.com/BCHeritagem/

Burritt on the Mountain: www.BurrittontheMountain.com

CHAPTER 6: NATIVE AMERICAN, COWBOY, AND RODEO TALES

Poarch Band of Creek Indians (includes museum): www.pci-nsn.gov and also www.PoarchNeighbors.com

University of South Alabama's Native American Studies Program: https://www.southalabama.edu/colleges/artsandsci/nativeamerican/

Rodeos USA: www.RodeosUSA.com/rodeo/Alabama

Professionl Cowboy Association: www.PCARodeo.com

Moundville Archeological Park: www.MoundvilleAlabama.com

Orange Beach Indian and Sea Museum: www.orangebeachal.gov/facilities/indian-sea-museum/about

Mount Vernon: www.MtVernonAl.com/History.html

Tuscaloosa Children's Hands-On Museum: www.chomonline.org/
https://rodeosusa.com/rodeo/alabama/

Tallapoosee Historical Museum: www.dadeville.com/directory

Fort Mims Historic Site: http://www.fortmims.org/

Florence Indian Mound and Museum: http://www.visitflorenceal.com/things_to_do/florence-indian-mound-and-museum/

Horseshoe Bend National Military Park: https://www.nps.gov/hobe/index.htm

Noccalula Falls Park: www.noccalulafallspark.com/

CHAPTER 7: RELIGION AND UTOPIAN COMMUNITIES

City of Fairhope: www.cofirhope.com

Demopolis's Marengo County Museum: www.theclio.com/web/entry?id=21026

Bayou La Batre/Coden's Blessing of the Fleet: www.FleetBlessing.org

Website for "Brother" Bryan Mission: www.BrotherBryanMission.com

Ave Maria Grotto: www.AveMariaGrotto.com

First Baptist Church of Montgomery: www.FirstBaptistChurchMontgomery.com

First Baptist Church Montgomery: http://www.firstbaptistchurchmontgomery.com/

St. Bernard Abbey: https://stbernardabbey.com/

Cathedral Basilica of the Immaculate Conception: http://www.mobilecathedral.org/cms/

Marengo County History and Archive Museum: http://www.marengomuseum.com/

Central Church at Flora-Bama: https://www.centralonline.tv/flora-bama/

Flora-Bama: https://www.florabama.com

Malbis Memorial Church-Encyclopedia of Alabama: http://www.encyclopediaofalabama.org/article/m-7106

St. Athanasios Greek Orthodox Church: http://www.stathanasios.al.goarch.org/

Huntsville's First Presbyterian Church Website: http://www.fpchsv.org/

City of Mooresville Tours: https://www.mooresvilleal.com/guided-group-tours/

Fairhope Museum: https://www.fairhopeal.gov/departments/museum

CHAPTER 8: SPORTS, RECREATION, AND AMUSEMENT STORIES

Alabama Sports Hall of Fame: www.ashof.org

International Sports Hall of Fame (Chicago): www.SportsHOF.org

International Motorsports Hall of Fame (Talladega): www.motorsportshalloffame.com

Hank Aaron Childhood Home and Museum: www.Mobile.org/listings/Hank-Aaron-Childhood-Home-and-Museum.org

OWA Amusement Park: www.VisitOWA.com

Barber Motorsports Park: www.BarberMuseum.org

Little River Canyon National Preserve: http://nps.gov/liri/index.htm

National Speleological Society: www.Caves.org

Bird Dog Monument & Mural: http://www.unionspringsalabama.com/birddogmonument.html

Alabama Whitetail Deer Records: http://www.alabamawhitetailrecords.com/

Rickwood Field: https://rickwood.com

Paul W. Bryant Museum: http://bryantmuseum.com/

Jesse Owens Museum: http://jesseowensmuseum.org/wordpress1/

Alabama Sports Hall of Fame: http://ashof.org/
Barber Vintage Motorsports Museum: https://www.barbermuseum.org/

Cathedral Caverns State Park: https://www.alapark.com/cathedral-caverns-state-park

Robert Trent Jones Golf Trail: https://www.rtjgolf.com/

CHAPTER 9: THE CIVIL WAR AND ALABAMA

First White House of the Confederacy: www.FirstWhiteHouse.org

Streight's Raid (The Lightning Mule Brigade): www.CullmanCountyMuseum.com

Tallassee's "Battles for the Armory": http://TallasseeArmoryGuards.com

Hunley Website: https://www.hunley.org/

Gulfquest Maritime Museum: www.gulfquest.org/

Wheeler NWR: https://www.fws.gov/wheeler/

Ft. Morgan Website: www.fort-morgan.org/

Tannehill Ironworks Park Website: www.tannehill.org/

Tallassee Armory Website: http://tallasseearmoryguards.org/

Old Cahawba Archaeological Park: https://cahawba.com/

The Admiral Hotel (formerly The Admiral Semmes): https://www.theadmiralhotel.com/

Crooked Creek Civil War Museum: (No official Website, but here's this) https://alabama.travel/places-to-go/crooked-creek-civil-war-museum

Limestone County Chamber of Commerce: https://www.tourathens.com/

Confederate Memorial Park (Marbury, Alabama) website: https://ahc.alabama.gov/properties/confederate/confederate.aspx

Double Springs Town Website: http://www.townofdoublesprings.com/

Blakely State Park: https://www.blakeleypark.com/

Arlington Antebellum Home & Gardens: http://www.arlingtonantebellumhomeandgardens.com/

CHAPTER 10: FROM CIVIL WRONGS TO CIVIL RIGHTS

Scottsboro Boys Museum and Cultural Center: www.Scottsboro-Multicultural.com

Scottsboro Boys' Story: www.ScottsboroBoysMuseum.org

Birmingham Civil Rights Institute: www.BCRI.org

Amazing Alabama

First Baptist Church of Montgomery: www.FirstBaptistChurchMontgomery.com

Freedom Rides Museum (Montgomery): www.FreedomRidesMuseum.org

Rosa Parks Museum & Children's Annex: www.Troy.edu/rosaparks/museum

Anniston Civil Rights Trail: toureastalabama.com/attraction/civil-rights-heritage-trail/

Tuskegee History Center: www.TuskegeeCenter.org

Tuskegee Institute National Historic Site: www.nps.gov/tuin

Selma-to-Montgomery March: www.SelmaAlabama.com

Selma's Interpretative Center: www.nps.gov/semo

Dexter Avenue King Memorial Baptist Church and Dexter Parsonage Museum (both in Montgomery): www.DexterKingMemorial.org

Sixteenth Street Baptist Church: www.16thStreetBaptist.org

Tuskegee University Campus: www.nps.gov/tuin

Monroeville Courthouse: www.MonroeCountyMuseum.org

Kelly Ingram Park: https://www.nps.gov/nr/travel/civilrights/al10.htm

Montgomery First Baptist Church: http://www.firstbaptistchurchmontgomery.com/

Bethel Baptist Church: https://whc.unesco.org/en/tentativelists/5241/

Museum of Mobile: www.historymuseumofmobile.com/

The Legacy Museum: https://museumandmemorial.eji.org/

Murphy-Collins House/Murphy African-American Museum: https://www.historictuscaloosa.org/properties/murphy-collins-house-murphy-african-american-museum/

CHAPTER 11: WHEELERS AND DEALERS (BUSINESS & ENTREPRENEURS)

The Gee's Bend Quilt Mural Trail: www.ruralswalabama.org/attractions/the-gees-bend-quilt-mural-trail

The Gee's Bend Quilt Collective Site: http://www.quiltsofgeesbend.com/

Quilts of Gee's Bend Website: http://www.quiltsofgeesbend.com/

John Emerald Distilling Company: www.JohnEmeraldDistilling.com

Conecuh Sausage: www.ConecuhSausage.com

Alabama Gold Camp: www.alabamagoldcamp.com

Vulcan Park & Museum: www.VisitVulcan.com

Harrison Brothers Hardware: http://harrisonbrothershardware.com/

First Bank of Alabama: https://www.firstbankal.com/

Battle House Renaissance Hotel and Spa: https://www.marriott.com/hotels/travel/mobbr-the-battle-house-renaissance-mobile-hotel-and-spa/?scid=bb1a189a-fec3-4d19-a255-54ba596febe2

Alabama Power Website: https://www.alabamapower.com/our-company.html

Unclaimed Baggage Website: https://www.unclaimedbaggage.com/

Cahaba Brewing Company: http://www.cahababrewing.com/

(Clay City) Tom Jones Pottery: https://www.tomjonespottery.com/

The Poarch Band of Creek Indians: Wind Creek Casino Atmore: https://windcreekatmore.com/

>Wind Creek Casino Wetumpka: https://windcreekwetumpka.com/
>Wind Creek Casino Montgomery: https://windcreekmontgomery.com/

The Prattaugan Museum: http://www.autaugahistory.org/prattaugan-museum.html

See Coast Website: www.seecoast.com

Constitution Village: http://www.earlyworks.com/

Red Diamond Tea: https://reddiamond.com/

Golden Flake: https://www.utzsnacks.com/pages/golden-flake

Milner-Rushing Drugs: https://www.mrdrugs.com/

Bromberg & Company: https://brombergs.com/

CHAPTER 12: FILM, MUSIC AND DRAMA OF ALABAMA

"Come Home It's Suppertime" Folklike Play (We Piddle Around Theatre): www.Piddle.org/ComeHome.htm

FAME Recording Studios: www.FAME2.com

Jazz in the Park (travelling Jazz festival): www.MagicCitySmoothJazz.com

The Commodores: www.CommodoresLive.com

Hank Williams Museum: WWW.HankMuseum.com

(Nat King Cole) Southern Museum of Music: www.Southernmuseumofmusic.com

George Lindsey/UNA Film Festival: www.LindseyFilmFest.com

Alabama Music Hall of Fame: www.AlaMHOF.org

Alabama Film Office: www.AlabamaFilm.org

Alabama (the band): www.TheAlabamaBand.com

Alabama Shakes: wwww.AlabamaShakes.com

Excelsior Band: www.excelsiorband1883.com

W.C. Handy Birthplace, Museum & Library: https://www.visitflorenceal.com/things_to_do/w-c-handy-birthplace-museum-library/

Sun Records Website: https://www.sunrecords.com/

Sam Phillips Music Celebration: http://www.samphillipsmusic.net/

Steiner Shipyard: www.steinershipyard.com/

CHAPTER 13: FLORA, FAUNA, AND NATURAL PHENOMENA

Bartram Canoe Trails: www.AlabamaScenicRiverTrail.com and www.AlabamaCanoeTrails.com/Bartram and www.BartramCanoeTrail.com

Dismals Canyon: www.DismalsCanyon.com

Cook Museum of Natural Science: www.CookMuseum.org

Alabama Birding Trails: www.AlabamaBirdingTrails.com

Anniston Museum of Natural History: www.AnnistonMuseum.org

Cathedral Caverns State Park: https://www.alapark.com/cathedral-caverns-state-park

Key Cave NWR: https://www.fws.gov/refuge/key_cave/

Sauta Cave NWR: https://www.fws.gov/sautacave/ **(NOTE: formerly known as "Blowing Wind Cave")**

Russell Cave National Monument: https://www.nps.gov/ruca/index.htm

Neversink Pit: http://www.scci.org/preserves/neversink/

E.O. Wilson Biophilia Center: www.eowilsoncenter.org/

Gulf Shores Zoo: www.alabamagulfcoastzoo.org/

5 Rivers Delta Center: https://www.outdooralabama.com/activities/5-rivers-alabama-delta-resource-center

Wheeler National Wildlife Refuge: http://www.fws.gov/refuge/wheeler/

CHAPTER 14: FOOD AND FASCINATING CULTURAL TIDBITS

Archibald and Woodrow's BBQ: www.archibaldbbq.com

Dreamland Café: www.dreamlandbbq.com

Carnival Museum of Mobile: https://www.mobilecarnivalmuseum.com

Vulcan Park & Museum: www.visitvulcan.com

Woods Quad Sculpture Garden: https://art.ua.edu/category/woods-quad-sculpture-garden/

The Bright Star: https://thebrightstar.com/

Trowbridge's: https://www.facebook.com/Trowbridges-in-downtown-Florence-Alabama-104867216212710/

Payne's Sandwich Shop: https://www.facebook.com/pages/Paynes-Sandwich-Soda-Fountain/1385080728397213

Buffalo Rock Company: https://www.buffalorock.com/

Chris' Hot Dogs: http://chrishotdogs.com/

Wintzell's Oyster House: www.wintzellsoysterhouse.com/

Julwin's: https://www.facebook.com/Julwins/

The Old Cookstove: www.oldcookstove.com/wp/

Pirate's Cove: www.piratescoveriffraff.com

Whistle Stop: (now called Irondale Café)
www.irondalecafe.com/
Depression Burgers-Busy Bee Cafe:
https://www.facebook.com/theoriginalbusybee/

Slug Burgers--C.F. Penn Hamburgers:
http://www.facebook.com/pages/C-F-Penn-Hamburgers/189401257741637

Golden Eagle Syrup: https://www.goldeneaglesyrup.com/

Wickles Pickles: www.WicklesPickles.com

Mobile Carnival Museum:
https://www.mobilecarnivalmuseum.com/

Golden Rule BBQ: www.goldenrulebbq.com/

Largest Office Chair-Miller's Office Furniture:
https://www.millersofficefurniture.com/

Fire Hydrant-Albertville Chamber of Commerce:
www.albertvillechamberofcommerce.com/

Crappie Capital-Weiss Lake: www.lakeweiss.info/

Wave Pool-Point Mallard Park: www.pointmallardpark.com/

Peanut Capital-Dothan Peanut Festival: www.nationalpeanutfestival.com/

Bass Fishing Capital: www.lakeeufaula.info/

Oldest Incorporated Town--Limestone County Chamber of Commerce: https://www.tourathens.com/

World's Longest Yardsale: www.127yardsale.com/

CHAPTER 15: UNUSUAL GRAVE, GHOST, AND BURIAL-SITE STORIES

Clarke County Historical Museum/death masks: www.ClarkeMuseum.com

Holy Smoke, LLC: www.MyHolySmoke.com

Pickens County Courthouse Window Website: http://www.courthousewindow.com

Alabama Paranormal Consultants: www.AlabamaParanormalConsultants.com

Gift Horse Restaurant: www.thegifthorserestaurantandantiques.com/

Foley Train Museum: http://www.foleyrailroadmuseum.com/

Event Site-Maple Hill Cemetery Stroll: https://www.huntsville.org/events/fall-annual-events/maple-hill-cemetery-stroll/

Tutwiler Hotel: https://hamptoninn3.hilton.com/en/hotels/alabama/hampto

n-inn-and-suites-birmingham-downtown-tutwiler-BHMDNHX/index.html?SEO_id=GMB-HP-BHMDNHX

Fort Morgan: www.fort-morgan.org/

St. James Hotel: (no official website-may be closed for reno)
https://alabama.travel/places-to-go/st-james-hotel

Bryce Hospital:
http://www.mh.alabama.gov/MHSA/BryceHospital.aspx

Gaines Ridge Dinner Club:
http://www.wilcoxwebworks.com/gr/

Redmont Hotel: www.redmontbirmingham.com/

Sloss Furnaces: https://www.slossfurnaces.com/

Coon Dog Cemetery Website:
http://www.coondogcemetery.com/index.html

CHAPTER 16: LIGHTHOUSE AND COASTAL STORIES

Alabama Lighthouse Association:
www.AlabamaLighthouses.com

Friends of the Lighthouses: http://lighthousefriends.com

Mobile Big Game Fishing Club: www.mbgfc.org

Alabama Historical Commission Page:
https://ahc.alabama.gov/properties/middlebay/middlebay.aspx

Sand Island LH Preservation Group's Page:
http://www.sandislandlighthouse.com/

Gulf Shores Museum: www.gulfshoresal.gov/356/Museum

Dauphin Island Sea Lab Website: https://www.disl.org/

Blakely State Park: https://www.blakeleypark.com/

The Lodge at Gulf State Park:
https://lodgeatgulfstatepark.com

CHAPTER 17: GHOST TOWNS OF ALABAMA

St. Stephens Historical Park:
www.oldststephens.net/museum-and-old-courthouse.html

Alabama Museum of Natural History: https://almnh.ua.edu/

Old Cahawba Archaeological Park: https://cahawba.com/

Tally-Ho Restaurant: www.tallyhoselma.com/

About the Author

An award-winning author, novelist and freelance journalist, Lacey's work has been published for more than 50 years. Her published works thus far include six Native American history books, two young adult novels, a murder mystery, a children's bilingual picture book, four books in he Amazing series and more. She has been a frequent contributor to the New York Times Bestselling anthologies, CHICKEN SOUP FOR THE SOUL. Lacey's website is www.TJensenLacey.com and her email address is TJensenLacey@yahoo.com. Lacey is available for book signings, writers' workshops and speaking engagements.

T. Jensen Lacey

Amazing Alabama Index

A
Aaron, Henry "Hank", 234
Africatown, 239
"Agritourisim", 118
Alabama Business Hall of Fame, 275
Alabama, The Band, 274
Alabama Frontier Days, 76
Alabama Historical Commission, 73
Alabama Jazz Hall of Fame (AJHOF), 270
Alabama Lighthouse Association (ALA), 341
Alabama Music Hall of Fame (AMHOF), 270
Alabama Paranormal Consultants, 324
Alabama Power, 246
Alabama, USS (Battleship), 51
Alabama Veterans Museum and Archives, 65
Alabama Women's Hall of Fame, 123
Alabamians from Everywhere, 317
Alabama's Amazing Architecture, 123
Alabama's Claims to Fame, 315
Alabama's Constitutional "Claim to Fame", 25
Alabama's Got its Own T-REX, 73
Alabama's Own Arlington, 215
Alabama's Own Superwoman, 35
Allen, Eugene: State Geologist, 301
American Village of Montevallo, 32 ?
America's Earliest Highway, In Alabama, 43
Amistad Ship and Murals, 239

A Native American Alphabet, 92
Anderson, Mary, 27
Andrews, Andy, 107
Annual Blessing of the Fleet, 146
Another Family of Soldiers, 64
Arbacoochee Gold District, 255
Archibald's Barbecue, 311
Archives War of 1901, 61
Arlington Antebellum Home and Gardens, 215

B
Baccaroon: The Last "Black" Cargo, 239
"Bagwell Bridgade," 64
Baldwin County Heritage Museum, 118
Band: Alabama Shakes, 271
Banks-Woodlawn Game: The Biggest High School Football Game Ever Played in Alabama, 179
Barbara, George: Vintage Motorsports Museum, 176
Bartram, William, 295
Bartram Canoe Trail, 296
Bass Fishing Capital of the World, 316
Bat Caves in Alabama, 284
Battle House Renaissance Hotel, 245
Battle of Horseshoe Bend, 133
Battle of New Orleans: Roots in Alabama, 23
Battles of Spanish Fort and Fort Blakely, 213
Bellefonte, 349
Bennett, Lorretta Pettway, 245
Bentley, Governor Robert, 240
Bethel Baptist Church, 235
Bibb Country Iron, 216

Bicentennial Beers, 248
Big Foot Society, Alabama, 4
Big Spring International Park, 286
Birding Trails, 291
Black Heritage Council, Alabama's, 232
Black, Hugo: Helped form United States Law, 24
Blakeley: One-Time Rival to Mobile, 349
Blockade and Its Runners, 196
Boll Weevil Statue, 119
Booger Gang, 330
Bottle Creek Indian Mounds Story, 72
Bragg, Rick, 303
Brazile, Robert: "Doctor Doom" 177
Bright Star Restaurant, 305
British Petroleum Oil Spill, 297
Bromberg & Company, 258
Brother Bryan: Walking the Talk, 150
Brown, Frank Loton, 249
Brown, Joe David, 87
Bryant, Paul "Bear," 169
Bryce Hospital, 333
Buffalo Rock Company, 305
Burritt on the Mountain, 118
Burrow, Rueben Houston: Mothered by a Witch, 10
Butterworth, William E., 81

C
Cahawba and its Civil War Ghost, 210, 354
Cain, Geoff and Geraldine, 252
Camp Sheridan, 39
Capote, Truman, 101

Carver, George Washington, 93
Catfish Capital of Alabama, 121
Cedar Creek Furnace, 216
CEO's in Alabama, 253
Chief Tuskaloosa: Battle of Maubila, 131
Chris' Hot Dogs, 306
Churches You Won't Want to Miss, 154
Civil Rights Memorial, 234
Civil War: Engagement at Little Bear Creek, 202
Civil War: Fort Morgan, 194
Civil War Gold, 205
Civil War Museum, New, 208
Civil War Trail, 206
Civil Wrongs to Civil Rights, 225
Clay City Products, 249
Clay, Clement Comer, 26
Clayton Town Cemetery, 328
Clotilda, 237
Cole, Nat "King," 261
"Come Home it's Suppertime" Play, 265
Commodore Museum, 260
Conecuh Sausage, 246
Confederacy's "First White House," 190
Confederate Rest Cemetery, 214
Constitution Village of Huntsville, 37
Cook Museum of Natural Science, 290
Cook's Pest Control, 290
Coon Dog Cemetery, 335
Corbin, Myrtle: Four-Legged Woman, 5
Cox, Courtney, 272
Crappie Capital of the World, 315

Crooked Creek Civil War Museum, 209
Cumming, Kate, 208

D
Dauphin Island Sea Lab, 345
Death Mask Grave Markers, 329
Demopolis, Setting for John Wayne, 275
Dep. of Archives and History, Montgomery, 237
Dinosaurs of Alabama, 74
Depression Burgers, 307
Dismals Canyon, 288
Diversity of Wildlife, Alabama, 284
Don't Monkey Around: Story about Miss Baker, 109
Drafting a Constitution for a Draught, 26
Dreamland Barbecue, 311
Dye, Coach Pat, 165

E
EarlyWorks Family of Museums, 40
Economic Moses of the South, 123
Edmund Pettus Bridge, 233
Estuarium, 346
Excelsior Band, 259

F
Fairhope Alabama Castle, 125
"Fair Hope" of Our Success, The, 143
Father Goose of Alabama, 105
"Father of the Blues," W. C. Handy, 262
Favorite Foods in Alabama, 304
Fendall Hall, 122

Film Industry in Alabama, 266
Fire Hydrant Capital of the World, 315
First Bank in Alabama, 245
First Baptist Church of Montgomery, 147
First Native American Alphabet, 92
First Nursing Academy, Alabama, 93
First Open-Heart Surgery, 90
First Railroad: Trails to Rails, 54
First Steam Locomotive, 54
First White House of the Confederacy, 191
Fishing Record Broken Twice in a Day, 343
Fitzgerald, F. Scott and Zelda, 85
Flagg, Lily: The Jersey Cow, 254
Flora-Bama Bar and Church, 151
Florence Alabama Music Enterprises (FAME), 271
Forkland, Home to What the Hay?, 59
Formichella, Joe, 106
Forrest Gump: A Cultural Icon, 104
Forrest, Nathan Bedford, 209
Fort Conde, 32
Fort Morgan, 332
Fort Toulouse: A Wetumpka Experience, 76
Founding the Vision: Before the Constitution, 40
Freedom Riders, 230
"Free State of Winston County," 211
French Experiment, 149
French "Pelican Girls," 46

G
Gaines Ridge Dinner Club, 333
Gaineswood Plantation Home, 128, 133

Gaillard Island Creation, 59
Gambino's Italian Grill, 306
Gaston, Barney, 62
Gee's Bend, 243
Geronimo in Alabama, 167
Ghigna, Charles, 105
Ghost Behind a Country-Western Song, 323
Ghosts: Top Ten Most Haunted Places in Alabama, 332
Ghost Towns of Alabama, 349
Girl with a Pearl Necklace: The Ghostly Lovers, 325
Gold, Eli: Voice of Crimson Tide Football, 167
Gold Rush of Alabama, 255
Golden Eagle Syrup, 308
Golden Flake Company, 257
Golf Trail: Robert Trent Jones, 181
Gorgas, Dr. William C., 107
Graves, Governor David Bibb, 42
Governmental Renaissance Man, 50
Grand Canyon of Alabama, 159
"Grease Festival," 311
Great Gatsby Affair, The, 85
Greece in Alabama, 128
Greek Orthodox Church in Malbis, 154
Greek Revival House, 126
Griffin, W.E.B., 81
Groom, Winston, 104
Gulf Coast Zoo, Alabama, 289
Guess (Gist), George, 91

H

Hall, Rick, 271
Handy, William Christopher, 262
Hank Williams Museum, 261
Hank Williams Sr. Boyhood Home
and Museum, 261
Harrison Brothers Hardware, 245
Hawkins, Benjamin and The Creek Indians, 138
Heart of Dixie Railroad Museum, 54
Hermit of Montrose, 145
Herndon, Thomas Heard: Alabama Governor, 197
Highway 5, 334
Hill, Dr. Luther Leonidas, 90
Hobson City, 234
Holmes Medical Museum, 90
Holy Smoke, LLC, 324
Holyfield, Evander, 180
Hopkins, Juliet Opie, 208
Hooper, Johnson J., 47
Horseshoe Bend, Battle of, 133
Horton Jr., Judge James E. Monument, 249
How Schoolchildren Brought a Battleship
to Alabama, 51
Hudson, Suzanne, 106
Hunley, Horace Lawson, 191
Hunley Submarine, 191
Huntsville's First Presbyterian Church, 155
Hurston, Zora Neale, 238

I

Insect, State Agricultural, 120

Inventers in Alabama, 253
Iron Bowl, The 78th, 181
Irondale's Golden Rule Barbecue, 313
Isbell National Bank, 245
Ivey, Kay: From Farm Girl to Governor, 21

J
Jack Cole Road, 333
Jackson, Andrew: The Jackson Oak, 26
Jackson, Harvey H., 248
James Gang, The, 16
Jim n' Nicks Barbecue, 313
Joe Cain Day, 310
Joe Wheeler Plantation, 129
John Emerald Distilling Company, 248
Jordan, Ralph "Shug," 181
Jubilee, 294
Julwin's Restaurant, 306

K
Karl C. Harrison Museum: George Washington, 32
Keller, Helen, 22, 90
King, Dr. David, 73
King, Horace: Slave Turned Legislator, 56
Kolb, Sr. Reuben F., 121

L
Landmark Park, 118
Largest Peach in the World, 315
Lee, Harper: To Kill a Mockingbird, 106
Legacy Museum and National Memorial

For Peace and Justice, 237
Legend Behind Noccalula Falls, 140
Lewis, Carl, 175
Little Cahaba Iron Works, 216
Little River Canyon, 159
Lindsey, George "Goober," 266
Louis, Joe: "The Brown Bomber," 182

M
Magnolia Grove, 127
Man Who Discovered Fire Ants, 285
Manning, Sydney E., 63
Mansion in Eufaula, 122
Maple Hill Cemetery Stroll, 331
Mardi Gras in Alabama, 310
Marion County Natural Bridge, 79
Marion Military Institute, 31
Marshall Space Flight Center, 27
Martyrs of Civil Rights Movement, 233
Mathis, Elizabeth Brandon, 123
May, Clyde, 7
McCoy, "Wild" Bill, 14
Meadow Gold Dairies, 254
Mentone's Memorial Chapel, 155
Middle Bay Lighthouse, 339
Milner-Rushing Drugs, 257
Milo's Sweet Tea, 313
Miss Baker: One of First Animals launched Into Space, 109
Mobile Big Game Fishing Club, 343
Mobile Carnival Museum, 311

Monroeville Writer's Trail, 103
Montgomery Motor Corps, 39
MOOseum, Hoof it Through, 122
Moree Quarter, 234
Moretti, Guiseppe, 256
Morgan County Archives, Civil War, 206
Mosher, Dean, 115
Most Prolific Novelist, Alabama, 85
Mound Island, 72
Moundville Archeological Park, 77
Mt. Nebo Baptist Church Cemetery, 329
Murphy-Collins House, 241
Muscle Shoals Sound Studio, 264
Museum of Alabama, 37
Museum of Mobile, 23
Museum of Natural History, Alabama, 301

N
New Deal in Alabama, 29
No Bull: Alabama's Big into Rodeos, 132
Noccalula Falls Park, 140

O
Oakwood Cemetery playhouse, 327
Old Cookstove, 306
Official State Agricultural Museum, 118
Official State Agricultural Insect, 120
Official State Quilt, 245
Official State Whiskey, 7
Old Courthouse Museum, Monroeville, 103
Old Town Rivalry, 50

Oldest Booming Businesses, Alabama, 245
Oldest Catholic Parish in Alabama, 149
Oldest Companies, Alabama, 257
Oldest Incorporated Town in Alabama, 317
Oldest Railroad Depot, Alabama, 26
Oldest Restaurant in Alabama, 305
Oldest Utility Company, 246
One Brilliant Military Tactician: Tricking the Enemy, 209
Only U.S Mail Delivered by Boat, 317
Opp's Rattlesnake Rodeo, 114
Orange Beach Indian and Sea Museum, 133
Osceola, Seminole Leader, 140
Outlaw, Harriet: Storyteller Extraordinaire, 122
Owens, Doyle & Byran, 247
Owens, Jesse, 171

P

Paige, Leroy Robert "Satchel," 182
Paleo Era, 71
Park at OWA, The, 179
Parks, Rosa, 228
Payne's Sandwich Shop & Soda Fountain, 305
Peanut Capital of the World, 316
Pelicans of Alabama, 299
Pershing, General's "Immortal Ten,"63
Petroglyphs in Alabama, 71
Phenomena Known as "Alabama Fever" and the influence of "King Cotton," 45
Phillips, Sam C., 268
Pickens County Courthouse: Face in the

Window, 321
Pioneer Museum of Alabama, 118
Pirate's Cove Marina & Restaurant, 307
Places Where Early Settlers Lived, 118
Planting the Seeds: Agricultural Success, 121
Poarch Band of Creek Indians, 250
Poet of Tolstoy Park, 145
Pond Spring, 129
Pratt Gin Company, 251
Prattaugan Museum, 252
Prohibition Era in Alabama, 7

Q

R
Railroad Bill, 14
Raines, Ben, 283
Record Breaking Cinnamon Roll, 309
Red Diamond Tea Company, 257
Redmont Hotel, 334
Revolutionary War in Alabama, 31
Rice, Condoleezza, 163
Richie, Lionel, 259
Richards, Judy: Award Winning Novelist, 107
Rickwood Field, 169
Robert Trent Jones Golf Trail, 181
Rodeo Queen of Alabama, 132
Royal Cup Coffee Company, 258
Run Over: "Mountain" Tom Clark," 330
Rutledge, Jeff, 273

S

Saban, Nick, 160
Saint Bernard Abbey, 153
Sanders, Joseph, 197
Sand Island Lighthouse, 341
Sansom, Emma, Civil War Heroine, 207
Scottsboro Boys Museum and Cultural Center, 240
"Second in Flight," 30
See Coast Manufacturing, Inc., 252
Semmes, Raphael: Wolf of the Deep, 203
Sequoyah, 91
Shell Banks Cemetery, 328
Shores, Janie Ledlow, 22
Shuttlesworth, Reverend Fred, 235
Sims, "Bloody" Bob: Prophet Turned Murderer, 8
Single Tax Colony, 143
16th Street Baptist Church Bombing, 236
Skyline Farms Colony, 147
Slater, Morris, 14
Slave Trade in Alabama, 236
"Sleeping Preacher" of North Alabama, 155
Sloss Furnace, 324
Slug Burgers, 308
Snook, John: Snook Militia, 38
Space Race, Alabama's Role in, 27
Spelunkers: Alabama Could be called "The Cave State," 178
Spencer, Octavia, 272
St. Athanasios Greek Orthodox Church, 154

St. James Hotel, 333
St. Stephens: First Capital of the Alabama Territory, 352
St. Stephens Historical Park, 353
Stars Fell on Alabama, 3
Stars Fell in Oak Grove, 4
State Agricultural Museum, 177
State Fossil, 77
State Insects, Plants and Animals, 293, 120
Steiner Shipyard, 273
Stonehenge and Jurassic Park, Alabama's Own, 74
Stuart, Henry, 145
Sun Records, 269
"Sweet Home Alabama" Song, 265

T
Tallassee Armory, 199
Tannehill Ironworks Historical State Park, 198
Tide's Official Fight Song's History, 163
Time-Travelling in Arab, 126
"The Strip," 165
"Touchdown Tony," 273
Toulmin, Theophilus Lindsey, 50
Town Names, Now and Then, 55
Trail of Tears, 139
Trowbridge's Restaurant, 305
Tuscumbia Railway, 54
Tuskegee Airmen, 47
Tutwiler, Julia Strudwick, 22, 86
Tutwiler Hotel, 332

T. Jensen Lacey

U

Unclaimed Baggage Center, Scottboro, 247
Underwater Forest, Alabama, 283
Union Springs: "Bird Dog Field Trial Capital of the World," 164
University of Alabama Saved From the Torch, 215
U.S. Space and Rocket Center, 28
USS Alabama, 51

V

Veteran's Day Created by Alabamian, 28
Victory Teaching Farm, 127
Vulcan Statue: God of the Forge, 256

W

Walker, Alice, 239
Wallace, George, 33
Wallace, Lurleen, 34
Walls of Jericho, 160
Washington, Booker Taliaferro, 96
War of 1901, Archives, 61
Watercress Capital of the World, 316
Wave Pool Capital of the World, 316
W.C. Handy Museum, 264
Weeks, Raymond, 28
Wetumpka, Impact Crater 74
Wheeler National Wildlife Refuge, 287
Wheeler, Joe, 193
Where Agriculture Meets Tourism, 118
Whiskey Bottle Tombstone, 328
Whistle Stop Cafe, 307

Whitetail Records Museum, 168
Whitfield, Nathan: Gaineswood Plantation, 128
Wickle's Pickles, 314
Wilder, Deontay, 180
Wilson, E.O., 285
Windham, Kathryn Tucker, 88
Windshield Wipers Invented by a Woman, 27
Wintzell's Oyster House, 306
Women in the Conflict, 201
Woods, John O' Melveny: All About Pirates, 106
WoodLawn: The Movie, 272
Woodruff, Hale, 239
Woodville: A Ghost County, 351
World Wars I & II: Women in Uniform, 38
World War II Hero, 62
World's Largest Cast Iron Statue, 256
World's Largest Jukebox, 265
World's Largest Office Chair, 315
World's Largest Oyster, 343
World's Largest Yard Sale, 317
Wright Brothers Park, 30

X

Y
Yeoman Farmers, The Plantation Elite, and Alabama's First Political Battle, 41

Z
Zoettel, Brother Joe: Famous Religious Shrines, 153

Made in the USA
Middletown, DE
04 February 2025